The Emperor Jahangir

The Emperor Jahangir

Power and Kingship in Mughal India

Lisa Balabanlilar

I.B. TAURIS
LONDON • NEW YORK • OXFORD • NEW DELHI • SYDNEY

I.B. TAURIS
Bloomsbury Publishing Plc
50 Bedford Square, London, WC1B 3DP, UK
1385 Broadway, New York, NY 10018, USA
29 Earlsfort Terrace, Dublin 2, Ireland

BLOOMSBURY, I.B. TAURIS and the I.B. Tauris logo are
trademarks of Bloomsbury Publishing Plc

First published in Great Britain 2020

This paperback edition published 2021

Copyright © Lisa Balabanlilar 2020, 2021

Lisa Balabanlilar has asserted her right under the Copyright, Designs
and Patents Act, 1988, to be identified as Author of this work.

Cover design by Charlotte James
Cover image: *Shanh Jahangir* © The Protected Art Archive / Alamy Stock Photo

All rights reserved. No part of this publication may be reproduced or
transmitted in any form or by any means, electronic or mechanical,
including photocopying, recording, or any information storage or retrieval
system, without prior permission in writing from the publishers.

Bloomsbury Publishing Plc does not have any control over, or
responsibility for, any third-party websites referred to or in this book.
All internet addresses given in this book were correct at the time of
going to press. The author and publisher regret any inconvenience
caused if addresses have changed or sites have ceased to exist,
but can accept no responsibility for any such changes.

A catalogue record for this book is available from the British Library.

A catalog record for this book is available from the Library of Congress

ISBN:	HB:	978-1-8386-0042-6
	PB:	978-0-7556-4055-3
	ePDF:	978-1-8386-0045-7
	eBook:	978-1-8386-0044-0

Typeset by Integra Software Services Pvt. Ltd.

To find out more about our authors and books visit www.bloomsbury.com
and sign up for our newsletters.

Now that Mr. Beni Prasad has in a manner exhausted the subject of Jahangir, it does not seem likely or necessary that there should be another book about the emperor. We can say that the world has now learnt all that it need know about him. He was a poor creature, and owes his celebrity only to his position.

H. Beveridge[1]

Life stories are fictions, but they are fictions that matter in clarifying the conceptions and the valued activities of the cultures at hand.

B. Metcalf[2]

Contents

Acknowledgements	x
Introduction	1
Historical sources and the story of Jahangir	2
The *Vaqa'i* and the *Jahangirnama*	5
About this book	12

Part One   *Salim Mirza, 1569–1605*

1	The prince	17
	The Timurid-Mughal dynasty	17
	Birth of a prince	19
	Childhood	21
2	The rebel	27
	Insurrection	27
	Salim Padshah	30
	Resolution	35

Part Two   The Emperor Jahangir, 1605–8

3	The new king	41
	Consolidating kingship	41
	Legitimate rule	43
	His father's footsteps	44
	Religious policies	46
	The twelve decrees and the chain of justice	48
4	Filial rebellion	53
	Khusraw's revolt	53
	The aftermath of princely revolt	56
	Babur's Kabul	57

Part Three Agra, 1608–13

5 Relationships at the royal court — 65
- The nobility — 65
- Gifting — 67
- Viewings and interactions — 74
- The wine of loyalty — 75
- Punishment and clemency — 78

6 Divine kingship and the imperial cult — 83
- The Majalis — 83
- Images of the divine — 89

7 International diplomacy and war — 97
- Europe — 97
- The Ottomans, Uzbeks and Safavids — 103
- The Deccan and Malik Ambar — 111

8 Love and marriage — 117
- Marriage and the Mughal prince — 117
- Salim in love — 122

Part Four Elegant nomad, 1613–21

9 The peripatetic court — 127
- Ajmer and the campaign against Mewar — 127
- The walking commonwealth — 130
- The fruits of empire — 136

10 The itinerant king — 139
- From garden to garden — 139
- Touring and hunting — 141
- Gujarat and the sea — 147
- An Enlightenment king of the east — 149
- Pilgrimage, shrines and holy men — 154

Part Five Kingship in crisis, 1619–27

11 Golden days — 165
- Kangra — 165
- Sikri, Agra and the road north — 166

	Poetry at the Mughal court	170
	Nur Jahan, Padshah Begim	173
12	Rising crises	181
	Threats to power and kingship	181
	A secretary's tale of filial revolt	186
	Muhammad Hadi	190
	The rebellion of Mahabat Khan	193
	The death of the king	196
Conclusion		199
	Remembering Jahangir	199
	Native son	202
Notes		205
Bibliography		240
Index		254

Acknowledgements

I would like to thank the crew at I.B. Tauris-Bloomsbury for once again proving to be the most thoughtful and supportive of editorial teams. I also want to express my gratitude to their outside readers whose sage and constructive advice gave me heart and made this a much better book. And finally, warmest thanks to my extraordinary students and colleagues – in particular our department chair, Carl Caldwell – in the history department at Rice University.

This book is for Sara Perihan and in memory of Mufit Balabanlilar.

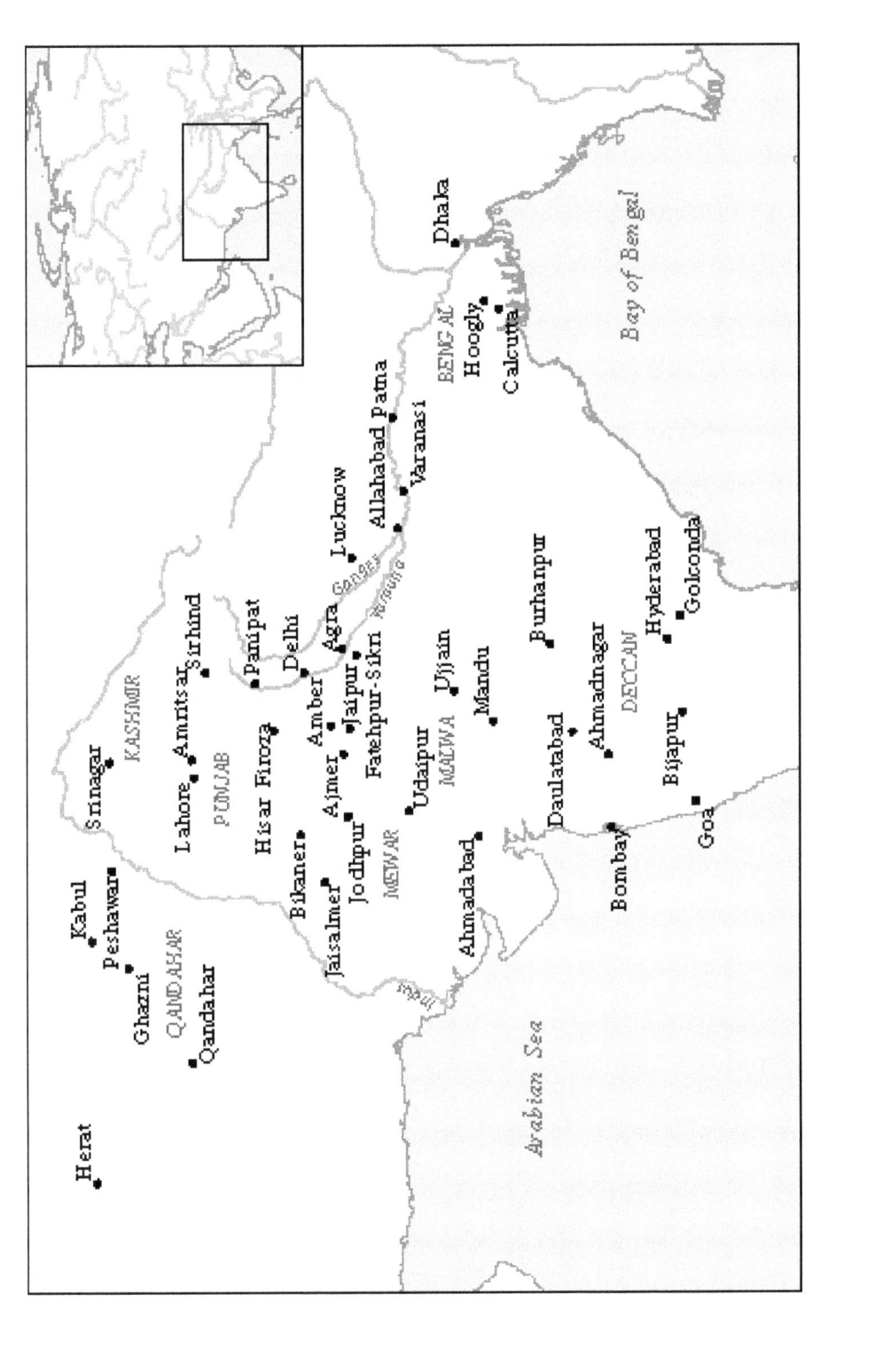

Introduction

Until very recently, the Timurid-Mughal emperors of India were routinely dismissed by scholars as too peripheral to be representative of early modern Islamic world ruling systems and imperial culture. In the last several years, however, studies of the Mughals' own prolific writings, and those of their political and economic rivals, have affirmed that the Mughal dynasty was firmly positioned in the early modern mainstream and served as a partner and a model for rulers across the Islamic world. Rather than continue to treat the Mughals as outliers, there is growing recognition that their understandings of culture and kingship can offer dramatic testimony to not only regional but global trends and adaptations.

Yet even as the dynasty finds its place in the historical narrative of Islamic and South Asian kingship, the reign of the emperor Salim Muhammad Nuruddin Jahangir (1569–1627; r. 1605–27), fourth of the six so-called 'Great Mughals', continues to be disregarded, even disdained.[1] There are many reasons for this, among the most obvious being that Jahangir had the misfortune to reign between two of the most successful scions of the dynasty. His father, the emperor Akbar, had been able at a very young age to seize control of what was a tenuous and fragile patrimony and expand it into one of the world's largest and wealthiest empires. Following Jahangir's death, his son and successor, Shah Jahan, would also overshadow his father's memory, proving to be among the dynasty's gifted military leaders, his legacy assured by his architectural manifesto, the Taj Mahal.

It is true that Jahangir's historical reputation as little more than a weak placeholder cannot be blamed entirely on the conditions or timing of his inheritance. In a dynasty known for its expansionist kings and empire builders, notably Chingis Khan and Tamerlane, Babur and Akbar, Jahangir's own military adventures were few, resulting in no dramatic gain of territory. Furthermore, as he readily admitted, Jahangir was known to be a heavy drinker and drug user who publicly agonized over his own health and sobriety. His reputation was further marred by violent rebellion against his father. Even the ability and influence of his powerful wife, Nur Jahan, would be used by historians and chroniclers to diminish the prestige of her husband – her strength cited as evidence of his ineffectual indolence. The emperor's biographer, Beni Prasad, represented the conventional understanding when he wrote that Jahangir had 'suffered from weakness of will and resolution, from a lamentable propensity to surrender himself to the mercies of superior talent'.[2] Yet just as the previously marginalized Mughal dynasty is becoming more generally recognized as a powerful and influential model of court culture and kingship, scholars must re-engage the question of Jahangir, whose reign demands a more thorough intellectual inquiry.

There are many ways in which his tenure can be counted a success. In a rare break from his father's policies and approach, Jahangir retained a minimalist military profile and demonstrated no ambition for extensive territorial acquisition. All the same, not only was there no significant loss of imperial lands during his reign but he managed to successfully conquer the territories of local kingdoms whose submission had long stymied his father. In addition, Jahangir's adept handling of the imperial elites and his attentive diplomacy established a period of political and cultural equilibrium. Apart from a brief failed insurrection by a disgruntled courtier in 1626, the only real threats to his throne or his empire would be the two princely revolts which bookended his reign. Both were successfully put down. In the twenty-two years of relative peace and stability represented by his rule, Jahangir's greatest personal legacy was two-fold. His lifelong and passionate patronage of the arts resulted in an innovative golden age of Mughal painting, and his composition of a regnal memoir explored and reinforced the sophisticated and globally influential complex of ideas and values, social and political models that represented Mughal rule. Both of these creative productions identify him as a powerful advocate for the cultural understandings and values of his ancestors but also of his ruled territories in South Asia, all of which he deliberately reinforced and passed on to the generations that followed.

Historical sources and the story of Jahangir

In the year of his accession to the throne of the Mughal Empire of India, Jahangir began to record the events of his reign.[3] For seventeen years, Jahangir wrote in the form of a chronological diary, beginning each year with the Persian festival of Nowruz. Although many contemporary scholars refer to the complete manuscript as the *Tuzuk-i Jahangiri*, The Regulations of Jahangir, the emperor himself called the memoir *Iqbalnama*, The Auspicious Story, or simply, and most often, *Jahangirnama*, The Story of Jahangir. His entries were not composed daily, yet the events of his reign seem to have been recorded soon after they occurred. While Jahangir included dense descriptions of the regulations and routines of his royal court, the manuscript was far more personal than a simple record. The *Jahangirnama* offers detailed and intimate ruminations on kingship and justice, the emperor's struggles with alcohol, his passion for the hunt and for his family, his intellectual curiosity and the depth of his concern for establishing the legitimacy of his rule. It is a comprehensive and at times stirring account of the emperor's life, but more importantly it supplies a rich context for his reign.

In 1622, five years before his death, he would turn over the task to his *munshi* (secretary) Mu'tamid Khan, yet even then, although in failing health, Jahangir continued personally editing the pages until work on the memoir completely and suddenly stopped in 1624. Almost a century later, Muhammad Hadi, who was probably a courtier of the emperor Muhammad Shah (1653–1707, a great-grandson of Jahangir), claiming to have become 'enamored by the science of history and the craft of biography' and basing his writings on other manuscripts in the Mughal imperial library, wrote an additional few chapters, offering a brief description of Jahangir's youth and of the events leading up to his death.

Apart from Mu'tamid Khan and Muhammad Hadi's attributed additions, and a single entry in the emperor's eleventh regnal year when his granddaughter's death left him so grief-stricken that he asked his father-in-law to briefly write for him, Jahangir's authorship of the work is not in doubt. Other writers of the period acknowledged the presence of the emperor's memoirs, and on a few occasions Jahangir presented his work to his sons and noblemen, describing the memoir as advice literature for those who would inherit his throne. In his thirteenth year on the throne, he gave a bound copy, representing twelve years of rule, to his son Khurram, the future Emperor Shah Jahan (1592–1666, r. 1628–59), writing on the back of the manuscript that he hoped the contents would be acceptable to the God and receive praise from its readers. He later sent copies to rival kings, which he suggested could serve as manuals for ruling.

Historical writing had been a regular feature at the royal courts of Jahangir's ancestors in West and South Asia. The founder of their dynasty, Timur (Tamerlane), had been deeply involved in the production of his royal court chronicles and they would prove both popular and influential.[4] Timur's descendants continued to produce court chronicles, treating their dynastic histories as a model for rule and an assertion of their own inherited dynastic political charisma. Five generations later, Jahangir's great-grandfather, Zahiruddin Muhammad Babur, wrote what is often described as the first autobiography of the pre-modern Islamic world, and certainly the most important and influential of the imperial histories of the Timurid-Mughals.[5] He named it the *Vaqa'i-i Baburi* (although it is commonly referred to as the *Baburnama*). Likely influenced by his uncle, with whom he spent some years, Babur's maternal nephew, Mirza Muhammad Haydar Dughlat (1499 or 1500–51), composed the *Tarikh-i Rashidi* of which one half was a history of the Mongols and the other half a personal account.[6] The emperor Akbar so valued Babur's *Vaqa'i* that he had it translated into Persian by his polymath stepson and courtier Abdur Rahim, so that its audience could be broadened. His court painters illustrated it on at least four separate occasions. Akbar would later request memoirs from all those who had memories of his father or grandfather. As his aunt, Babur's daughter Gulbadan Begim explained, 'An order was issued, "Write down whatever you know of the doings of *Firdaus makani* and *Jannat ashyani* [Babur and Humayun]." In obedience to the royal order, I set down whatever there is that I have heard and remember.'[7] Also at Akbar's command, Humayun's ewer-bearer, Mihtar Jauhar, who had spent twenty years at the emperor's side, including the period of his exile in Safavid Iran, composed the *Tazkirat al-vaqa'i*, and Bayezid Bayat wrote the *Tarikh-i Humayun*, covering the years 1542–91.[8]

Professional historians and courtiers also continued to chronicle the reigns of the Mughal kings. Babur's eldest son and successor, Humayun (1508–56/ r. 1530–40, 1555–56), retained the famed historian Ghiyasuddin Khwandamir at his court, officially inviting him to compose a history of his rule, the *Humayunnama*, although the result is more panegyric than memoir.[9] In the next generation, Akbar's close friend and advisor Abu'l Fazl composed multiple volumes on the life of the emperor, as well as a detailed compendium on the ideological underpinnings of his empire, known as the *Akbarnama* and the *A'in-i Akbar* respectively.[10] In addition, Akbar commissioned dynastic histories such as the *Chingisnama* (History of Chingis Khan), the *Timurnama* (History of Timur) and the *Tarikh-i Alfi* (History of a Thousand Years), which asserted the dynasty's Mongol and Timurid ancestry, claiming to have 'inaugurated a new millennium' with the foundation of the South Asian Timurid (Mughal) Empire. Finally, for Jahangir's own period, in addition to his own memoir, two important accounts are the *Iqbalnama*, by the emperor's secretary Mu'tamad Khan, and the *Maasir-i Jahangiri* by Khwaja Kamgar Husaini.[11]

The Mughal dynastic memoirs were highly prized and influential, representing the voice of the ancestral founding fathers. The expectation that autobiography brings the reader closer to truth has been shattered in the modern period but to these early modern state-builders, having access to highly personal, even intimate, texts that sprang directly from the foundational sources of dynastic power surely added to the *frisson* of intergenerational connection. That the manuscripts were read by every generation in the royal family is clear from the commentary and autographs in the margins of those volumes housed in the imperial library. These powerful and authoritative texts would form the base of a canonical dynastic narrative with which the Mughals justified their ambition and success, carefully positioning their ruling legitimacy in the political charisma of their Timurid ancestry and the sovereignty of Islamic kingship. Within the royal family, and in the close circle of the nobility, the unified and comprehensive story created by their imperial predecessors affirmed across the generations the history, the values and the meaning of the Mughal heritage.

The *Vaqa'i* and the *Jahangirnama*

Biographical writing in the medieval Perso-Islamic world has been described as having a 'timeless pattern' with no real interest in chronology but instead imagined and organized around events or moods, eliding individual personalities and erasing the idiosyncratic in favour of identification with ideal types.[12] Meaning and importance were assigned to a life, a battle, a spiritual revelation, a pilgrimage, a death, as it met and fulfilled or illustrated an expected moral and symbolic outcome, within traditional conventions. That the ideal was drawn with familiar codes and markers is of course still the norm on some level – Foucault wrote that history bequeaths the range of options we draw upon to conceive of ourselves. We can see these tropes as representing that range: a particularly inelastic and narrow one, perhaps, by modern standards but which offered shape and consistency to the world of the medieval observer for whom it was intended.

The Timurid princely courts and their successors, on the other hand, are noted for their demonstrated willingness to broaden this classical structure to include expressions of individualism through evocations or depictions of idiosyncratic personalities in the place of bare impersonal stereotypes.[13] An example is that of the evolution of the traditional *tadhkira*, the classical Persian professional biographies of renowned poets and literati, which have been shown in the Timurid period to have begun exploring contemporary lives, rather than historical types, the authors even including themselves in their encyclopaedias and writing what are described as truly autobiographical sketches.¹⁴ In the same period, elements of the individual and the naturalistic began to slip into the visual arts. Late Timurid artists began signing their work, which illustrated increasingly secular subject matter. Timurid portraiture had begun to demonstrate a new 'tension between individualizing and stereotyping conventions [which traditionally had relied] on a canonical language of power, whose subtly differentiated visual elements had to be decoded in order to interpret their iconography'.¹⁵ With so much evidence of artists, literary figures, and politicians of the Timurid Mughal world engaged in examining the individual self, scholars must reject the notion that these many 'distinctly personal voices' were entirely atypical for their time.¹⁶

Babur's memoir is tangible evidence of the Timurid intellectual exploration of the individual. The *Vaqa'i* did not reject the traditional tropes and classical models of medieval biography but made critical additions to them, as Babur successfully located the exemplary and the heroic in his own contemporary personality. Not every facet of Babur's life and literary career are equally well-known, but at least it is possible to see his literary life as both stereotypical and idiosyncratic, and as both formulaic and inimitable.¹⁷ He was a typical royal poet in many respects, in his regard for classic exemplars, his emulation of traditional genres, and his desire for literary fame and cultural legitimacy. He was also a unique royal poet in his relative freedom from the stylistic constraints of court culture and his frank willingness to use traditional genres to express his feelings. Babur's use of his own name as the *takhallus*, for which poets generally chose pen names, may be one measure of the degree to which he was prepared openly to reveal his emotions in verse. Using his own name was an egoistic act, reflective of the compelling, self-assured personality that he revealed in the *Baburnama*. He favourably compared himself to the greatest Timurid ruler of the day, Sultan Husain Baiqara of Herat, and felt confident enough of his literary skills to claim superiority for his essay on prosody to that of the great Ali Shir Nava'i, whose work on metrics Babur dismissed as 'full of mistakes'.¹⁸

In the absence of literary models, why would he have come to write a memoir? Babur may have been driven by the obstacles he faced in the traditional succession practices of the Timurid dynasty, which allowed every male member of the royal family to be considered a viable contender for rule. While their shared Chinggisid-Timurid genealogical charisma supported the case for a common dynastic legitimacy, it did nothing for the ambitions of a specific individual. Written in the very moment of the dynasty's transition from Mawarannahr, the autobiographical *Vaqa'i* made a claim to leadership of the Timurids that went far beyond the power of Babur's royal bloodlines. The greater dynasty was vitally important to Babur – after all, his powerful lineage was the foundation for his political claims – but in composing a personal memoir he actively differentiated himself from those other ambitious princes with whom he shared his elite lineage. Presenting himself as complex, creative and idiosyncratic, Babur made an argument for power that was highly specific and personal. Augmenting and elaborating traditional tropes and classical models of medieval biography, Babur so distinguished his singular self that even modern readers claim to come away from his memoir with a sense of personal recognition.[19]

While it is true that he did not engage in a great deal of self-examination, Babur's memoir is at times startlingly frank, as he composed poetry in a youthful flirtation with a boy in the bazaar, described his own tears at the loss of an important battle and narrated with barely suppressed hilarity a drunken return to his tent after a particularly wild party. Babur claimed to be writing advice literature, using his own personal history as a model for their sons and rival princes, but his writings – even in describing his weaknesses, failures and misjudgements – built a case for his own personal leadership over the Timurid community. Struggling to seize control in an anarchic and uncertain landscape, Babur emerges in his own pages as drunken, sarcastic, embarrassed, sometimes cruel, but always redeemed, at least in his own telling, by his personal attributes: political charisma, ambition, bravery, immense reserves of loyalty, a degree of poetic talent and a very human pathos.

In the spirit of his writings, this poet-warrior and founder of empire would come to be celebrated precisely for his personal particularities rather than any adherence to conventional standards of heroic leadership. Among his followers and their descendants Babur's *Vaqa'i* not only heightened recognition of the individual personality but also reinforced the value of self-representation. While they would never entirely forego the traditional tropes and models of the greater Islamic world, the Mughals would continue to construct their presentations of kingship from across the variety of sources available to them, including pre-Islamic Persian, Turco-Mongol and increasingly South Asian.

Seventy-five years after Babur's death, the newly and as yet insecurely enthroned Jahangir seized on the device of personal memoir as a part of his larger effort to re-invent himself and justify his ascension. Rejecting his father's model of encouraging a devotee to create the record of his reign, Jahangir chose to follow the precedent of the Mughal founding father, Babur. Notably he even emulated the tone of Babur's *Vaqa'i*, which is not only written in clear and unadorned language but is famously direct and personal, even intimate.

In both cases, the occasional revelations of startlingly personal detail were very likely to have been made deliberately. From their inception, the *Vaqa'i* and the *Jahangirnama* were created as public documents. Both authors remained fully aware of their readers and their personal exposure was self-serving, deliberate and tightly managed. In Babur's case, this is indicated by his use of Chaghatay Turkish rather than court Persian, allowing him to speak directly to a Central Asian constituency made up of the Timurid and Chaghatayyid elite who represented the followers and supporters of Babur's imperial ambition.[20] That a copy of Babur's memoirs was sent back to his base in Kabul as early as 1529, where nearly one hundred years later Jahangir would read it in the original Turkish, confirms that Babur had a very particular audience in mind as he wrote.[21]

Jahangir would be no less deliberate, publicly sharing early versions of his own memoir. In 1618, Jahangir had copies of his Nama bound, intending to distribute it to his intimate companions and even send to foreign countries as a manual for rule. The first bound copy was given to his third son and successor, Khurram, in late August. By mid-September, two more copies had been produced, which Jahangir gifted to his father-in-law I'timaduddawla and brother-in-law Asaf Khan. A fourth copy was sent to his second son, Parvez, from the emperor's temporary camp at Fatehpur Sikri, in January. While these earliest manuscripts chronicled Jahangir's first twelve years as emperor, the writing continued until 1624.

He was deliberate in pairing his work with that of Babur, while expressing self-conscious pride in his innovative illustration of the memoir. As a devoted patron of the arts, Jahangir had as early as 1612, if not before, begun ordering paintings to accompany his text. Early in 1618, before the first copy was bound, his favourite painter, Abu'l Hasan, who he had honoured with the title of *Nadir al-Zaman*, the Pinnacle of the Age, had painted a picture of Jahangir's accession to serve as the frontispiece of the *Jahangirnama*. Although Jahangir had modelled the writings of his imperial memoir on those of his great-grandfather, he relished an opportunity to surpass Babur by adding illustrations to his own work. He wrote: 'Although *Firdaws-Makani* ["He who is in the place of paradise," i.e., Babur] wrote in his memoir about the shapes of some animals, he does not seem to have ordered artists to depict them...I both wrote about them and ordered the artists to draw them for the *Jahangirnama*.'[22]

Unfortunately, there is no extant *Jahangirnama* with a complete set of illustrations, and it is not at all clear that an illustrated manuscript was ever in fact completed. Certainly the earlier versions of the memoir, including the copies gifted to his sons in 1618, likely did not include any of the miniatures that were intended for it. Even the Abu'l Hasan frontispiece had been commissioned only a few months earlier, and it would eventually be discovered in a separate album of paintings from the Mughal imperial atelier. Other individual pages of illustration, seemingly intended for the *Jahangirnama*, have appeared in various collections, showing no evidence of having ever having been bound into a manuscript.[23] Many are so damaged that their production date and artist are in doubt. Yet within the text of the *Jahangirnama* itself, the emperor explicitly described several commissions of miniatures, sketches, nature studies and portraits, and there is no doubt that many extant imperial miniatures were originally produced to illustrate his memoir. A North American turkey and an African zebra, brought to Jahangir from the port at Goa, were ordered painted by Jahangir's master painter, Mansur, specifically as an illustration for the *Jahangirnama*, 'so that the astonishment one has at hearing of them would increase by seeing them'. Affirming the inherently political nature of the manuscript, individual folios that were likely intended for the pages of the *Nama* include a painting of the submission of Rana Singh of Mewar, which retains marks that indicate it was intended to illustrate an album. That it was meant to corroborate his written text comes as no surprise – the conquest of Mewar had been one of Akbar's rare military failures, and Jahangir would proudly memorialize it in multiple formats: memoir, painting and even in rare Mughal sculpture.

Jahangir intended his illustrated memoir to fit neatly within the larger dynastic project of narrative and remembrance, even as he continually returned to themes of kingship and affirmations of his own personal political legitimacy. In his discourses on inheritance and power, he continually reinforced his identification with and loyalty to Akbar, nostalgically referenced his ancestry and dynastic legacy, elaborated his performance of Persio-Islamic kingship and asserted the inherently sacred quality of kings – making use of a dynastic literary tradition to confirm the legitimacy of his own individual inheritance, sanctioned, as Jahangir would claim, by both the dynastic and the divine.

Intensely loyal to his dynasty and its values, Jahangir used the device of memoir to affirm his position as a conduit of the powerful ideas of his ancestors, offering detailed and explicit descriptions of Timurid-Mughal courtly traditions; understandings of kingship, law, religion, succession and inheritance; and ideas of beauty, poetry, gardens and architecture. His memoir also details the workings of the seventeenth-century royal court of India, including rich descriptions of the monarch's relationship with his diverse nobility as well as the steady stream of merchants, adventurers, ambassadors and rivals who arrived before his throne. We are given an intimate glimpse into family life, spiritual practice and even detailed views of the pre-modern South Asian landscape. Yet for all its public character, his memoir also details Jahangir's struggles with alcoholism and drug use, with his father's complex legacy, his own rebellious sons and disloyal courtiers, his evolving defence of his own kingship and his passionate curiosity regarding the natural world. In other words, we can read the *Jahangirnama* as a conscious and deliberate self-portrayal that is in some ways more revealing than the author likely intended.

For these reasons, the *Jahangirnama*, acknowledged as the most important historical source for the period, is at the core of this study.[24] While it was initially inspired by the newly enthroned emperor's need to explain and justify his contested inheritance and to declare his close association to his father's ruling ethos, it would become much more than that, as Jahangir used the memoir as a commentary on both his close relationships at the royal court – personal, local and international – and his constant close attention to the lands and peoples of his ruled territories. Such a self-serving document calls for a high degree of scepticism on the part of the reader. The emperor's descriptions of specific events and actions are generally confirmed by other sources from the period, but in attempting to reveal his motives and beliefs we proceed with caution, acknowledging that the *Jahangirnama* is an extended effort at self-promotion.

Several other valuable chronicles recount the events of Jahangir's reign. They come from a diverse company – Jesuit priests, English merchants, intimates of the king – representing the eclectic nature of the Mughal royal court in the early seventeenth century. Their descriptions and interpretations of events broaden our perspective, even as they corroborate, in many ways, the emperor's own narrative of the events of his reign. There are three important Mughal court chronicles identified with Jahangir's reign: the *Iqbalnama* of Mu'tamid Khan, the *Maasir-i-Jahangiri* of Khwaja Kamgar Huseini and the more recently published *Majalis-i Jahangiri* by Abdus Sattar.[25] The first two authors used the *Jahangirnama* as their own primary source of information, and so offer little that is original or independent. They were completed several years after Jahangir's death and under the rule of his son and successor, Shah Jahan. It is hard to imagine that their editorial comments and additions were not powerfully influenced by the prevailing ruler and his effort to control the narrative of his own rebellion, succession and enthronement.

This point is best illustrated by the writings of Mu'tamid Khan who, in addition to his *Iqbalnama*, wrote several chapters of the *Jahangirnama* at the behest and under the close guidance of Jahangir. Differences in tone between the two manuscripts are obvious. For example, when collaborating with Jahangir, Mu'tamid Khan openly and explicitly described Shah Jahan's rebellion, even using Jahangir's pejorative name of *Bidawlat* (Wretched One) for the prince. In his own authored chronicle, however, produced after Jahangir's death, Mu'tamid Khan shifted his position, to place much of the blame for the princely rebellion at the feet of the queen, Nur Jahan, who in the last years of her husband's reign had become Shah Jahan's enemy. Mu'tamid Khan notably refers to the rebel prince and his supporters in sympathetic terms throughout the *Iqbalnama*. For these reasons, then, while both courtiers' chronicles have been used for this study, they do not take precedence except in those periods in which Jahangir's memoir is silent, in particular in the last few years of his reign. Finally, an important Mughal chronicle of the period has come to the notice of Western scholars more recently: the *Majalis-i-Jahangiri*, of Abdus Sattar. Sattar's focus is on the evening assemblies of Jahangir's court and he offers enormous insight where none had existed previously. His chronicle covers only a three-year period in the early period of Jahangir's reign, unfortunately, although is used here extensively where appropriate.

Other major sources for the reign of Jahangir were produced by outsiders, the Jesuit missions who remained for long periods at the Mughal court and European merchants who arrived in increasing numbers throughout the period. These records are of limited value and are used with extreme caution. A serious reading of any European sources of the period reveals not only the self-serving nature of their records, but also the confusion and inaccuracy of their analysis and explanations. In particular, favourite topics of the Western visitors that are most egregiously misunderstood include the harem and the political activities of Mughal women, the emperor and religious identity, as well as the meaning of the exchange of gifts and honours at the imperial durbar. Modern scholars have pointed out that the real value in these European commentaries can be found by turning them on themselves, revealing the culture, politics, religion and values of their own European courts. On the other hand, the observations of these outsiders can in some cases offer a glimpse of the visual display of Mughal rule in early modern India. Where the Mughals and their courtiers may not have found it necessary or interesting to describe the court progress or the crowded throne room or the streets of Mughal cities, foreign visitors were fascinated by the visual feast and wrote rich and important commentary. It is as observers, then, that the foreign visitors to the Mughal court have been useful for this study, but the gossip they shared between themselves and their pronouncements on features of the royal court and society that they themselves did not witness are not given a credible hearing here.

About this book

This biography tells two stories. The first is the story of Jahangir, describing the narrative of his life but also examining his values, expectations and relationships; his sense of the world around him and his place within it. The second story is a broader exploration of the cultural traditions and trends that drove the emperor's decisions and fuelled the events of his reign. In that spirit, this study is built on a structural compromise, retaining when possible a chronological approach but digressing into historically grounded thematic discussion surrounding issues that Jahangir grappled with throughout his reign: relationships both global and local, claims of divine kingship, the royal court progress, the arts, marriage and the power of elite women, in particular that of his favourite wife, Nur Jahan. Finally, an important goal of this book has been not only to place Jahangir in a very particular historical moment, but also to physically locate him in a highly specific geographic space. The landscape and people of South Asia were a vital part of his identity and his power, and deserve a central place in his narrative. As his own record makes abundantly clear, Jahangir had a deeply passionate and emotional connection to his ruled territories.

Using the Mughal emperor's memoir, the *Jahangirnama*, as a framework upon which historical developments are revealed and institutions, events and large-scale developments given context, this study adheres as closely as possible to the interests and itinerary of the emperor himself. If my work seems to have been driven by Jahangir's own passions and concerns – kingship, power and responsibility, loyalty, beauty, love and friendship, the natural world and the always changing and deeply fascinating landscape of South Asia – that is for the most part because, as a cultural historian, I find these topics to be just as compelling as he did.

A note about transliteration systems and sources

Words from Persian, Arabic and Turkish have been rendered using a simplified transliteration system without diacritical marks, in the interests of keeping the text uncluttered, and generally following the conventions of the International Journal of Middle East Studies (IJMES). Transliterated words from secondary works and translations of primary sources are cited without modification, except that diacritical marks are dropped. Secondary sources may offer a variety of accepted spellings and I have remained true to these variants when directly quoting. The sources on which I rely most heavily and consistently I have used in the original languages, in widely accepted editions such as the 1980 Tehran edition of *Jahangirnama* and Ejii Mano's seminal critical edition of the *Baburnama*. Most of the important primary sources of the period were written in court Persian and translations are my own unless stated. This being said, I had the good fortune to work with Wheeler Thackston on Persian palaeography at the Harvard Ottoman Institute on Cunda Island many years ago, and know well his enormous skill and intellectual generosity. It is a vain scholar who would attempt to better the work of Wheeler Bey. When Jahangir waxes most poetical, I defer to Thackston's translation.

Part One

Salim Mirza, 1569–1605

1

The prince

The Timurid-Mughal dynasty

Although the fourth of the Mughal emperors, Jahangir was the first to have been born into a stable empire, with wealth and security. In contrast, the struggle to gain and hold their northern Indian territories had consumed the lives of each of his predecessors. The founding father of the dynasty in India, Jahangir's great-grandfather, Zahiruddin Muhammad Babur (1483–1530), born in Ferghana, a descendant of Chingis Khan (r. 1206–27) on his mother's side and of Timur (Tamerlane; 1336–1405, r. 1370–1405) on his father's, was a restless and ambitious prince. In the years of waning Timurid power in Central Asia, Babur devoted his life to the conquest of Timur's former capital at Samarqand, first attempting to defeat his ambitious uncles and cousins, then to defend it from the invading Uzbek tribal confederation led by Shibani Khan. He would later describe his trials, confirming the threat from both outsiders and immediate relatives, listing Chaghatayyid and Timurid, as well as his Uzbek enemies, as foes against whom Babur was forced to struggle for eleven years.[1]

Three times Babur entered Samarqand in triumphant procession, determined to rule as a new Timur, yet on each occasion he proved unable to hold the city. In the end, the Uzbeks were able to drive the Timurids entirely out of their ancestral homeland. Forced into exile, a resentful but still ambitious Babur gathered the surviving Timurid elites around him in Kabul. Raiding south, he managed to defeat the ruling Lodi sultans at the First Battle of Panipat in 1526. From his base in Agra, Babur spent the next four years leading armies across northern India, establishing Timurid rule, crushing resistance and putting down rebellion, building gardens and composing his memoir, the *Vaqa'i*, or *Baburnama*. He died in 1530.

His eldest son, Humayun, inherited the throne, initially without controversy. Born in Kabul, Humayun had been not only witness but a full participant in his father's struggle for empire. Beginning with the assignment of his first appanage at the age of thirteen, Humayun had governed provinces and led armies, but for all his experience and talent, on becoming king Humayun seems to have repeatedly undermined his own military and political efforts. Scholars have offered various theories to explain his failures, but Humayun himself seems to have supplied a part of the answer. His sister, Gulbadan Begim, described an incident in which the women of his household criticized his lack of participation in family gatherings. A clearly irritated Humayun responded: 'I am an opium addict (*man afyun*), do not be angry with me.'[2] Humayun's personal failings were seized upon by his ambitious brothers, who eventually wrested control over the Afghan portions of their patrimony and declared themselves independent sovereigns. His real nemesis, however, was Sher Khan (later, Shah) of the Sur clan, who led a successful Afghan resurgence, driving the Mughal armies out of Bengal, Bihar and finally the entirety of Hindustan. Humayun had ruled in South Asia for only ten years. Defeated in battle, humiliated by his brothers, Humayun was forced to flee the subcontinent, taking refuge at the royal court of the Safavid shah, Tahmasp, in 1540.

For the next fifteen years, Humayun struggled to regain his kingdom. With the help of borrowed Safavid troops, he seized a foothold in Qandahar and eventually was able to defeat his brothers in Afghanistan, in a campaign rife with missteps and failures. The weakening of Sur power to his south drew him back into India, where he was able to recapture Babur's kingdom by 1555. His triumph was short-lived, however, and he died of an accidental fall in 1556.

Humayun's son Akbar was able to inherit the throne almost without rivals, for his uncles had at last been disposed of and his half-brother, Mirza Muhammad Hakim, was as yet too young to contest the succession. The new ruler was only thirteen however, and his control over the vast territories that his father had only unified a year previously was tenuous. With his father's general, Bairam Khan, serving as his advisor and mentor, the teenaged Akbar launched a career that would be defined by military success and imperial expansion. In early battles against the Afghan Sur armies and the powerful general Hemu, the victorious young king affirmed his possession of Agra and Delhi, and further added the whole of the Punjab to his kingdom. By the age of eighteen, he was ruler in fact as well as name, having rid himself of most childhood advisors. In the nearly fifty years of his reign, Akbar maintained an aggressively expansionist political culture, his conquests unifying the northern half of the subcontinent with the ancestral territories of Afghanistan, Khurasan and Qandahar. The conquest of the Deccan proved beyond his skill, and this failure continued to challenge his successors to complete the subjugation of the entire subcontinent.

Birth of a prince

Akbar's political alliances were not predicated solely upon marriage, but matrimonial diplomacy did fuel imperial expansion and unity. His first Rajput wife was probably Hira Kunwar Sahiba Harkha Bai (1542–1622; m. 1562), the daughter of Kacchwaha Raja Bihari Mal of Amber, later given the imperial title of Maryamuzzamani, the Mary of the Time, and mother of his eldest son, Salim (later Jahangir). The circumstances of his birth were legendary, even in his own lifetime and amongst his contemporaries, described by Akbar's amanuensis, Abu'l Fazl, and retold by others.

Jahangir began his own regnal memoir with this legend and of course it bore repeating, for a birth foretold and overseen by the most respected of holy men imbued both Akbar and Jahangir with a near sacred status and strengthened their claims to the throne. As Abu'l Fazl recounted, by his mid-twenties Akbar had begun to feel concern that he had not yet fathered a son. Those children born to him had died in infancy, a misfortune that he surely felt deeply, while the absence of an heir began to fuel gossip.[3] Increasingly desperate for sons, Akbar announced to members of his circle that he had determined to find the most auspicious geographic location in which to pray for a child; he settled on the shrine of the Chishti Shaykh of Sikri (Fatehpur).

It was more of a deliberate and strategic choice than this legend suggests, for throughout the 1560s, Akbar had become closely tied to the Chishti Order of Sufis. His alliance with the order had been initiated by what Abu'l Fazl described as a chance encounter while on a hunting trip at Sikri, about 40 kilometres south of the capital city of Agra. There the emperor came across a band of Chishti worshippers who sang 'enchanting ditties about the virtues and glories of the Great Khwaja Moinuddin', the founder of the Chishti Order in India.[4] The emperor cannot have been unaware of the order's presence, nor of its wide popularity in northern Hindustan. Among Babur's first acts after seizing the city of Delhi had been to show respect for a famed leader of the order, Nizamuddin Auliya, by circumambulating his tomb in the centre of the city. Akbar, 'a seeker after truth... [who] sought for union with travelers on the road of holiness and showed a desire for enlightenment' was deeply impressed by their piety and pursued a continued relationship with the order.

Akbar had already become deeply committed to a massive re-imagining of his imperial ideology. To that time, the Timurid-Mughal dynasty had been closely tied to the Naqshbandi Order of Sufis. Known for their 'particular sobriety' and direct engagement in political events, members of the order had accrued enormous power and wealth in Timurid Central Asia. Naqshbandi shaykhs accompanied Babur on his conquest of Hindustan, forming a spiritual aristocracy at the Mughal royal court, even marrying princesses of the Mughal dynasty.[5] Confronted with Akbar's increasingly idiosyncratic religious experiments, Naqshbandi leaders took it upon themselves to advice, correct and even rebuke the king himself.[6] It is no wonder, then, that Akbar seized the opportunity to marginalize the powerful order and pursue a relationship with the locally popular and highly esteemed – and significantly less entitled – Chishti Order of Sufis. Acting on the propitious encounter at Sikri, he began a very public series of pilgrimages to Chishti centres: the shrine of Khwaja Moinuddin in Ajmer, the shrine of Khwaja Nizamuddin Auliya in Delhi and the Sikri *dargah* (hospice) of the celebrated Chishti Shaykh Salim, where the king prayed for sons. The Mughal chronicles claim that Shaykh Salim prophesied the birth of not just one royal son, but three.

When his wife became pregnant, Akbar had her and her attendants taken to the household of Shaykh Salim, where she remained until she gave birth, in 1569. In the extravagant prose of Abu'l Fazl, 'The blessings of his proximity [that of Shaykh Salim] were manifested in the appearance of the desired object.' As had been foretold, the child was a son. 'Royal messengers conveyed the happy tidings to Agra [where Akbar was awaiting news of the birth]. Delight suffused the brain of the age.'[7] A greatly relieved Akbar declared a general amnesty across the kingdom, and even those convicted of serious crimes were given their freedom. Court poets composed panegyric verses to honour the birth, some of which were 'not devoid of excellence', and were lavishly rewarded by the magnanimous king.[8] The emperor celebrated with a royal cheetah hunt, and eventually fulfilled his earlier vow to walk from Agra to Ajmer, in a pilgrimage to the tomb of Khwaja Moinuddin Chishti, in gratitude for the birth.[9] At the direction of the Chishti Shaykh Salim, the child was named for him, but as the Emperor Jahangir, he would fondly recall that, 'either drunk or sober', Akbar only called him *Shaykhu Baba*, 'dear little shaykh'.[10] It is notable that Akbar gave Salim's mother the title of Maryamuzzamani, the Mary of the Age, in a direct reference to the Virgin Mary and deliberately implying a correlation between her first son, Salim, and Jesus.[11]

As had been predicted by Shaykh Salim, Akbar fathered two more sons, Murad, born in 1570, and Danyal, only two years later. Both were born at Shaykh

Salim's Sikri *dargah*, their proud father again making the pilgrimage to Ajmer, although on these occasions he seems to have ridden, rather than repeating his earlier barefoot pilgrimage, proceeding 'in enjoyment of various pleasures, and especially that of the chase'.[12] Dynastic continuity had been protected and assured with the birth of three princes, and the auspicious birthplace of his sons would serve as a symbol of dynastic power and an affirmation of Akbar's divine authority, eventually determining the location of the emperor's new imperial city, Fatehpur [Fathpur/Place of Victory] Sikri, from 1571 to 1585.

Childhood

About Salim's childhood little is known. He was raised at Sikri, where women of the Chishti shaykh's family were appointed his wet nurses, creating a relationship that would be familial in its intimacy, adding 'a material and bodily attachment to the spiritual ties' the emperor had already established with the Chishti Sufi Order.[13] As he grew older, the grandsons of Shaykh Salim would be his playmates and companions. Although it had long been the custom of the Timurid-Mughals to assign the princes to the provinces, to act as arms of the state and to learn the art of governance and command, Akbar's sons were the first generation to have been kept at home. Akbar's biographer and amanuensis, Abu'l Fazl, strongly suggested that they would learn more from their father than from any outside source.[14] Yet custom demanded that the princes benefit from the 'companionship and conversation' of teachers, and Salim began his formal education at the age of four years, four months and four days, as was customary for Timurid-Mughal princes. The occasion was marked by a great feast and a ceremony in which the prince had a Quran placed in his lap and was then lifted above the crowd of noblemen onto the shoulders of his teacher, Maulana Mir Kalan Haravi. Abu'l Fazl wrote,

> There was a great feast and the holy spirit of that pupil of the eye of sovereignty [Salim]... began outward instruction... [and] was increased in brilliancy by the oil of instruction... After that he began with the letters of the alphabet, which are the foundation of learning and the center of things visible, and so was guided to the highness of wisdom.[15]

The princes were highly literate and broadly educated. Abu'l Fazl would write that 'every boy ought to read books on morals, arithmetic, the notation particular to arithmetic, agriculture, mensuration (surveying), geometry, astronomy, physiognomy, household matters, the rules of government, medicine, logic, tabi'i (natural or physical sciences), riyazi (quantitative sciences, such as math, music, astronomy and mechanics) and illahi (theological sciences) and all history'.[16] The scholarly achievements of princes were matched by their intense physical training in horsemanship and use of arms, much of which was learned during the royal hunt and by early participation in military campaigns.

Perhaps the most important preparation for Akbar's sons was the careful establishment of each prince's independent base of power. The succession system of the Mughals was based on the traditional Turco-Mongol system of collective sovereignty, allowing every male member of the ruling house to establish a claim to the throne. In explicit acknowledgement of the potential for generational succession war, from the time of their early childhoods Mughal princes were carefully linked with influential individuals at court: powerful factions and members of the imperial military and administrative elite. Their royal fathers directed the process, carefully positioning their sons to achieve critical alliances, although at times a prince would poach from his father's household and vice versa. Salim later wrote of individuals he had 'chosen and requested' from his father's service, promoting them within his personal household.

One of the most influential relationships for a prince was with his *ateke*, chosen by the emperor from among the imperial elite to serve the prince as guardian, advisor, mentor and paternal representative. It was hoped that an *ateke* would retain a core loyalty to the father, although that would prove not always to be the case. Imperial appointments of this sort confirmed the very close ties of loyalty and patronage that already bound elite families to the Mughals. In 1573, when Akbar led an army to Gujarat, he appointed the Sufi Shaykh Salim's second son Shaykh Ahmad, as his son's *ateke*.[17] In 1577, Prince Salim was paired with Qutbuddin Khan, the brother of Akbar's own childhood *ateke*, Shamsuddin Khan, whose wife had been one of Akbar's wet-nurses (*anaga*), a relationship that made her son, Mirza Aziz, a milk brother (*koka*) of the emperor and an important notable of the imperial court. Qutbuddin celebrated his prestigious new assignment with a lavish feast.

In 1582, when Qutbuddin was sent on campaign, he was replaced by another member of Akbar's intimate inner circle and one of the most powerful men in the empire, Abdur Rahim, entitled *Khan-i Khanan* Lord of Lords, the son of Bairam Khan, the Persian general who had guided Akbar in the early years of his kingship. Abdur Rahim had been raised under Akbar's attention and care – the emperor, his step-father, called him *farzand* (son). He served as chief minister and intelligence gatherer for the king, and was a famed polymath and scholar.[18] As Salim's *ateke* he was tasked with nurturing the prince's burgeoning military and diplomatic skills, but would additionally prove to be an influential model for learning and courtly manners (*adab*) as well as generous and involved patronage of the arts.[19]

Princely relationships were deliberately forged not only through the assignment of noble supporters and mentors, but in the careful arrangement of marriage partners. While still a member of his father's household, Salim was married several times and sometimes within very short span of time.[20] His marriages to the daughters of noble loyalists and political allies were carefully chosen for very much the same reason that other princely relationships were established: to reinforce dynastic relationships and to build a strong community of personal and dynastic alliances for the individual prince.[21] Salim's first wife was his maternal cousin, daughter of the powerful and influential Raja Bhagwan Das (d. 1614) of Amber. Only two years after their marriage she gave birth to the prince's first child, a daughter named Sultan an-Nisa (1586–1646). The following year she would again give birth, this time to a son, Khusraw (1587–1622). In 1589, Salim would have a second son, Parvez, and in the following year, a daughter, Bahar Banu Begim, by Karamsi, the daughter of Raja Keshu Das Rathor. In 1586, Jahangir married Jagat Gosain Manmati (d. 1619), the daughter of Raja Udai Singh 'Mota Raja', son of Raja Mal Deo of Marwar. Later becoming known as Bilqis Makani, she would be the mother of his third son, Khurram, born in 1592. Salim's youngest son, Shahryar, would be born in 1605 to an unnamed woman. Salim's marital alliances would include the daughters of the rajas of Amber, Bikaner, Khandesh, Jaisalmer and Marwar, as well as rulers in Little Tibet, Kashmir as well as affiliated dynastic relations and noble families. Each marriage was an opportunity to create layers of protection and support, both dynastic and personal.[22]

In arranging marriages and carefully assigning trusted advisors and mentors, the emperor created for all and each of his sons a set of powerful relationships that could smooth the path to adulthood, and potentially, to kingship. To that end, training in governance and war not only prepared princes to rule, it also allowed them opportunity to demonstrate their potential for sovereignty and attract support and loyalty. Akbar's sons were employed as extensions of the emperor himself but, in a break from earlier Timurid-Mughal patterns, Jahangir and his brothers were not assigned provincial governorships at a young age. They remained at the imperial centre, presumably to learn by example and be trained in the skills of kingship by their father. 'The wise sovereign kept his children under his own care and did not appoint any guardian to them, and was constantly educating them in the most excellent manner of which there are few instances in ancient times', wrote Abu'l Fazl. 'Constantly acquiring various outward and inward excellencies in the society of His Majesty and in the Shahinshah's entourage.... by the blessing of His Majesty's holy spirit and of his exalted attentions he [Salim] learnt the rules of justice and the cherishing of subjects and the principles of settling disputes.'[23]

From an early age the princes were given impressive ranks and titles, positioning them well above their father's noblemen. Salim was ranked the highest, a very public affirmation that he was the heir presumptive. The imperial assignments of the young princes were extravagant, but in fact they were largely ceremonial and honorific, as in 1576 when Akbar, observing in his son 'obedience, good disposition, prudence and endurance' gave seven-year-old Salim authority over the entire Mughal army along with the rank of commander of 10,000. His brother Murad was assigned the rank of 7,000 and Danyal, 6,000.[24] Although even as young children the princes were occasionally assigned a task away from the royal court, to serve as representatives of the emperor, they were expected to return immediately after, to pay homage to their father.[25] In 1581, Salim was sent to Ajmer to meet the Mughal women returning from their hajj and to escort them home, where his father gave over to him the responsibility for arranging marriage and birthday feasts. The assignment publicly displayed Salim's position as heir apparent, however dull a task it was for an ambitious royal son.

Salim was eventually assigned a military role in Akbar's expansionist imperial armies, although he remained under the tight control of his *ateke* and his father's local commanders. When in 1580 Akbar planned a military expedition in the Punjab, the eleven-year-old Salim successfully begged to be included, while his brother Danyal remained at court as the representative of imperial authority. At twelve, Salim participated in his father's Kabul campaign against the rebellious Muhammad Hakim, Akbar's half-brother. In 1594 Jahangir, leading an army of 12,000 troops, defeated the rebellious Vir Singh Deo of Bundela, and captured the city of Orchha, where he ordered a citadel built to commemorate the Mughal victory. He went on to command the victorious imperial forces against Lakshmi Narayan of Koch Bihar, who was convinced to join the Mughal nobility and would, as Nazir of his ancestral territories, establish a Mughal garrison at Atharokotha. By 1585, as a newly married prince, Salim had been promoted to a rank of 12,000, his brothers commanding 9,000 and 7,000, respectively. Such high rank implied high income and mandated the support of a large numbers of troops, but for the Mughal princes even this brought no true independence. Their titles were symbolic, they continued to be supported with stipends from their father and the costs of their private troops were covered by the state.

Although their independence and power were tightly controlled, life in the royal household was neither proscribed nor narrow for Akbar's sons. It was an era marked by accelerating global political and economic interactions. In the years of Salim's childhood, the royal household of the Mughals was an eclectic community that included not only Timurid Central Asian Turks and Mongols but also large numbers of Persian emigres, local caste and tribal leaders, foreign diplomats and of course the Rajput allies and relations of the ruling family, as well as the first arrivals of European merchants and missionaries. There was a constant flow of visitors through the royal court, arriving at the bidding of the king to pay homage, settle disputes, offer what was often fabulous tribute of celebrated treasure, arrange military campaigns and hunts and raucously celebrate successes. Promotion, power and wealth were controlled at the emperor's pleasure, but Akbar was notably generous and egalitarian, his reputation attracting a steady influx of adventurers and artists, intellectuals, poets and painters, engineers, scholars and scientists from across the world, all seeking employment and the patronage of a beneficent king. They came to the newly constructed city of Fatehpur Sikri, meticulously designed by the victorious monarch to demonstrate the fusion of his Timurid inheritance with the cultural (in this case, architectural) idioms of South Asia. Diplomats and other visitors arrived with trains of tribute-bearing horses, camels and elephants. Artists and poets brought panegyric works to the king and religious scholars came to advise and confer.

The princes were often present and not only interacted with those who came to the royal court, but formed personal relationships with them. Among these were the Jesuit Missions to the Mughal throne, which first arrived in Sikri in 1580, led by Father Ridolpho Aquaviva. Father Jerome Xavier (grand-nephew of Francis Xavier), who came to the Mughal court in 1595, described regular interactions with Prince Salim, who, he claimed, demonstrated 'great affection' for the Jesuit mission, serving as their patron at court, arranging permission for the construction of a church and carrying their concerns directly to the emperor.[26]

For the brief time that it was the imperial capital, Fatehpur Sikri encapsulated the artistic and intellectual aspirations of the dynasty.[27] At the centre were those courtiers who would later become known as the Nine Jewels, the *Navaratnas*, Akbar's most reliable and loyal allies. This intimate fraternity, its membership somewhat fluid, included Akbar's close friend and biographer Abu'l Fazl, whose massively detailed exposition presented Akbar as a sacred king and provided the ideological framework for his rule; Abu'l Fazl's brother Faizi, the emperor's poet laureate and boon companion; Raja Man Singh, Akbar's nephew by marriage, the ruler of Amber and his trusted friend, military commander and governor; Miyan Tansen, renowned musician, whose performances were said to tame wild beasts and spontaneously cause candles to light, and, less benevolently, wildfires to combust; Raja Todor Mal, Brahmin warrior and innovative finance minister; Abdur Rahim Khankhanan, the son of Akbar's early mentor Bairam Khan (and who as a noted linguist would translate the memoir of the founding father, the *Baburnama*, into Persian for Akbar); Fakir Aziao-Din, religious philosopher; Mullah Do Piaza,[28] friend and advisor; and Maheshdas Brahmbhatt, diplomat, poet and noted wit, who earned the title Birbal, or 'Great Mind', from Akbar. Intellectuals and artists, warriors and philosophers, they filled the royal court and inspired Akbar's famed political and social reforms. Altogether, it was a dynamic and spirited milieu: successful in war, urbane and sophisticated, engaged by the exchange of ideas, innovation, scientific and spiritual experimentation, and owning a heightened aesthetic grounded in generous patronage of the arts and architecture.

2

The rebel

Insurrection

As the princes grew to adulthood, they began to demonstrate a growing impatience with their positions. They were highly trained and ambitious, and increasingly resentful of the limitations of their roles as servitors of their father's state. Certainly, the emperor Akbar cannot have been an easy or comfortable father. The evidence is that he was very exacting; at the very least his powerful personality may have been overwhelming.[1] The Jesuit Father Monserrate suggested that the relationship between father and sons may have been abusive and controlling, writing: 'The king's nature was such that, although he loved his children very dearly, he used to give them orders rather roughly whenever he wanted anything done; and he sometimes punished them with blows as well as harsh words'.[2] Perhaps Monserrate exaggerated or misunderstood what he had witnessed, but at the very least, for all the glories of the Akbari court, by 1590 there were serious tensions in the Mughal household.

For the increasingly ambitious princes, there could have been little hope of change in the near future. While it was true that their father had already been on the throne for decades, Akbar was still a young man – he had been crowned at the age of thirteen and was noted for his physical strength – and all were aware of the possibility that he might remain on the throne for decades more. Adding to the tension, the brothers were unable to unite as allies, driven apart as they were by the rivalry demanded by Mughal traditions of open succession and the constant competition for liegemen and allies, for promotion and prestige. The eldest sons grew combative and restless, surrounded by their personal households, members of which were increasingly critical of their father, the ruling monarch, and suspicious of the rival brothers. Eventually, the princes were physically separated, stationed in military or governing roles far from each other. Salim, as the recognized favourite, remained with his father at the imperial centre until 1599, while Murad was sent to the provinces in 1591 and the youngest prince, Danyal, assigned to Allahabad in 1597.

Akbar's sons drank heavily. In his memoir, Salim would describe the beginning of his addiction with his first drink of alcohol at the age of eighteen. While participating in Akbar's campaign against the Yousufzai Afghans in the Attock fortress on the Nilab river, the prince had spent a day hunting to the point of exhaustion. Among the company was Ustad Shah-Quli, the former chief of gunners for his uncle, Mirza Muhammad Hakim, who suggested that a glass of wine would help the prince recover.[3] Salim sent his water bearer to the camp doctor, who passed along a small bottle of sweet wine. He drank it and 'liked the feeling it gave me'.[4] Before long, he was consuming such large quantities of alcohol that concerns were expressed about his health. By 1590, Salim had become known at court for excessive drinking.

His brothers were also known topers. Like Salim, they may have begun drinking while still in residence at their father's court; as they grew older and were stationed further afield, their behaviour grew steadily more obstreperous, fuelled by the enormous quantities of alcohol they were consuming. As a young prince, Murad, one year younger than Salim, had been tutored by the Jesuits residing at his father's court. They claimed to see great promise in him, commending his 'good disposition' and his 'great natural genius'.[5] In adulthood, however, he quickly fell to pieces. Murad was assigned to Malwa in 1591, at the age of twenty-one, then to Gujarat and the Deccan. He drank heavily, maintaining a constant level of disobedience that never quite exploded into open rebellion. Murad fought over tactics and strategy with his father's generals who had been sent to lead the Mughal war effort in the region, while eluding his father's efforts at control. In 1598, a concerned and frustrated Akbar finally sent Abu'l Fazl to recall the prince to court. Murad managed to remain a step ahead of his father's agent, but would die of alcohol poisoning within a year, at the age of twenty-eight.

Meanwhile, the relationship between Akbar and Salim was increasingly strained. Their competition had become public, as when Salim petitioned to have Saiyid Muhammad Etabi, a poet known for dangerous political satire, released from prison and then helped him escape Akbar's sentence of exile.[6] A faction of noblemen formed around Salim, although in many ways their support for the prince was driven by competition with Akbar's favourites. Abdur Rahim Khankhanan continued to support the prince to whom he had served as *ateke* – his own poet, the famed Khwaja Muhammad Shirazi, known as Urfi, resentful at having been marginalized by Akbar's favourites, Abu'l Fazl and his brother, the poet Faizi, wrote glowing poetic praise of the 'age of prince Salim', 'the ornament of the empire', and described him as just, benevolent and comparable to the Emperor Akbar.[7] Akbar openly criticized the Khankhanan's support for Salim, as the prince grew increasingly oppositional and unreliable.

So greatly was the prince mistrusted by Akbar's closest allies that when the emperor became gravely ill in 1591, there were some at court who suggested that Salim had joined in a conspiracy to murder his father. All the same, apart from his continued participation in Mughal military campaigning, Salim remained at court until 1599, although increasingly at odds with Akbar. Murad's death in 1598 left the Deccani armies without princely leadership, however resentful and rebellious his had been, but an effort to send Salim as a replacement was met with intransigence. Abu'l Fazl complained that 'he [Salim] at the time … was guided by evil-minded persons and did not come to court'.[8] Prince Danyal was sent in his stead, and rewarded with a red imperial tent, an honour generally reserved for the emperor himself. Akbar then determined that Salim should lead an attack on the Rana of Mewar, and attempted to encourage him by hunting towards Malwa along with Salim's sons Khusraw, Khurram and Parvez, among other family members. Salim instead begged to be assigned to Ajmer, and Akbar finally acquiesced.

Salim, then already twenty-nine years old, dispatched his armies as ordered, but he himself lingered in Ajmer, discontented and self-indulgent. Abu'l Fazl wrote that already 'from drunkenness and bad companionship, (he) did not distinguish between his own good and evil'.[9] This was later confirmed by the prince himself, who would write that members of his own household had begun to openly encourage him towards rebellion and conspiracy. His hesitation to openly rebel may have been due in part to the presence of General Raja Man Singh, who had been assigned by Akbar to accompany Salim, to guide and restrain him as necessary. Man Singh, one of Akbar's closest allies and the ateke of Salim's eldest son, Khusraw, was not particularly sympathetic to the prince he had been sent to assist but the force of his personality was enough to keep Salim from open revolt. When the raja was suddenly called away to put down an uprising in Bengal, Salim seized the opportunity to recall his forces and begin a predatory march towards the imperial capital city of Agra.

Confronted with the arrival of a large army led by a rebellious scion of the dynasty, the commander of the city, Qulich Khan, behaved with marvellous tact. Emerging from Agra with great ceremony, he formally welcomed the prince, offering him gifts and honours – all the while respectfully preventing Salim's forces from entering and seizing control of the capital. The prince wavered and his indecision gave his grandmother time to intervene. When Salim learned that the venerable dowager was emerging from the city to confront him, he hastily fled the scene. Evading her brief pursuit, he travelled eastward by riverboat. Eventually the rebel prince and his troops reached Allahabad, at the confluence of the rivers Ganges and Yamuna, where Salim took the fortress, seizing both the territory and the rich treasury of Bihar, and established himself as ruler.

Salim Padshah

Much as his aggression would seem to suggest otherwise, the goal of Salim's advance was not to overthrow his father and seize the Mughal throne. At the end of the sixteenth century, having ruled since 1556, Akbar was deeply entrenched, and the armies at his command were vast in number and experienced. Salim had been present at the emperor's victory, years earlier, over Muhammad Hakim, who had created a rebellious counter-court in Kabul. Not only was it an authoritative demonstration of Akbar's power but also an affirmation that amongst the nobility there was strong support for a unified empire with its leadership inherited through an orderly lineal succession. Salim, after more than a decade of working in and with his father's armies, was surely aware that his own chances against the imperial forces were not promising.

It is much more likely that Salim's primary interest was in the creation of an independent appanage within the greater Mughal Empire, an arrangement based roughly on the model of his Timurid ancestors, which would offer him autonomy and authority. Perhaps recognizing the limitations of Salim's ambitions, Akbar responded to his son's flagrant disrespect with caution and patience, in no hurry to check Salim efforts at independent rule. Salim had long been publicly acknowledged as the heir to the throne and although he was proving to be defiant and unruly, Murad's death had narrowed the emperor's options. In addition, in the absence of appanage assignments which had supplied a formal governing experience provided for previous Timurid-Mughal generations, Salim's efforts might be seen to offer a similar function. Salim's later biographer, Muhammad Hadi, would argue that Akbar was not entirely displeased by the insurrections of his eldest son, for 'through this act His Highness's [Salim's] bravery and manliness were noticed'.[10]

Instead of rousing his armies and confronting his son on the battlefield, the king sent a childhood friend of the prince, Muhammad Sharif Khan, to plead with Salim to repent.[11] Soon after his arrival, however, Muhammad Sharif was convinced to join Salim's conspiracy and became the rebellious prince's chief minister at the counter-court in Allahabad, awarded the honour of drums and a yak tail standard, promotion and the valuable governorship of Bihar. In disgust, Akbar was compelled to quit his Deccani military campaign and return to the north to deal with his ambitious son's flagrant rebellion. The emperor continued to avoid direct confrontation, however, instead heading directly to Agra where he awaited the prince's next move.

Salim responded provocatively. In 1601, while claiming only to be interested in paying respect to his father, he led an army of thirty thousand towards Agra, the soldiers marauding as they marched. Akbar responded with an ultimatum, demanding that his son either dismiss his troops and come in person to Agra, or lead his rebel army back to Allahabad. Salim, demonstrating yet again his disinterest in direct military confrontation, and his only intermittent enthusiasm for rebellion, immediately sent an emissary to offer his allegiance to his father while he himself turned east.

Akbar rewarded the prince's decision to retreat, while at the same time encouraging his greater distance from the capital, by formally investing Salim with the governorship of Orissa and Bengal. Salim made no effort to remove to his new territories, far from the centre of empire. Instead he remained in Allahabad where, acting as a sovereign, he gave his supporters titles and honours, and created jagirs of the surrounding territories for his liegemen. Within a year, he had proclaimed his independence, taking the title *sultan*, and a year later adding the even more extravagant title *padshah*. In public affirmation of his claims to sovereign status, Salim ordered coins minted, inscribed in the name of 'Sultan Salim Padshah Ghazi', and ordered the *khutba*, the midday Friday sermon in the congregational mosque, read in his name.[12] Thereby proclaiming his open revolt, Salim would rule Allahabad as a semi-independent king until 1604.

In his years as sovereign in Allahabad, Salim converted his already large and complex princely household into an alternative royal court, establishing critical alliances and patronage networks and gaining governing experience. Those of his noblemen who disapproved of the prince's rebellion fled to Akbar, but there were many who remained to ally themselves with the rebel and administer Salim's independent state. In any case, those who left were easily replaced, for there were many many others who were drawn to Salim's offers of generous promotions and assignment of income producing *jagirs*. The network of alliances that had been carefully established since his birth continued in large part to support the prince in rebellion. Among his circle in Allahabad were his foster brother Shaikh Khubu (Qutbuddin Khan) and Shaikh Kabir (later Shija'at Khan) of the Chishti Shaykh

Salim's family. They, along with other members of the sufi family, would go on to receive high rank after the prince's accession.[13] Others who had long been allied with the prince included disenfranchised former supporters of his rebellious uncle, Muhammad Hakim, as well as members of the household of his deceased brother Prince Murad, including Abu'l Hasan Mashhadi, who had been Murad's treasurer and personal secretary and now applied his administrative skills to the counter-court in Allahabad.[14] Salim's court became a refuge for the disaffected and dissatisfied, a magnet for underutilized and disgruntled administrators and warriors who for a variety of reasons felt unwelcome at Akbar's royal court.

Actively campaigning to develop the largest possible base of popular support, Salim reached out to local elites in Allahabad, Awadh and Bihar, where Bundelas and Indian Muslims who had been left out of Akbar's administrative circles were now offered positions in Salim's princely state, additionally benefitting the prince by tying him closely to regional networks.[15] Local elites, and by extension those in their social and political circles, were drawn to the rebel prince who offered not only patronage and generous land grants, but even adjudication and support when appealed to as a 'just prince'.[16] Those who benefitted from the prince's largesse were not only the wealthy and powerful; Salim's generosity was as granular as the assignment of a small land grant to an anonymous local widow. In many cases, these new allegiances became permanent, as local elites served as high-ranking officials, and ultimately become integrated into the imperial service, thus extending Mughal influence and power into the region and transforming the demographics of the Mughal nobility.

Salim modelled his Allahabad milieu after the patronage-driven royal courts of his predecessors and their noblemen, and supported a large number of poets, intellectuals and artists. Father Jerome Xavier of the Jesuit mission wrote of Salim's expressed interest in European painting as early as the 1590s, and described him encouraging court artists to copy their technique. A decade before his rebellion, Salim had brought Aqa Reza Herati, a recent immigrant, into his court atelier, where he produced a series of visual panegyrics – portraits of the prince that emphasized his energy and youth. Choosing to remain with Salim after the prince's rebellion, he became the director of Salim's painting workshops in Allahabad, which rapidly grew to include such artists as Bishan Das, Abu'l Hasan, Mirza Ghulam, Nadira Banu and others. Salim's fascination with the visual arts was lifelong, continuing throughout his reign as emperor, during which time his atelier would revolutionize Mughal painting.

Salim's drinking did not abate in the Allahabad years, and with his descent into alcoholism came further misbehaviours and misjudgements. Among the worst of the reported incidents of the Allahabad period, and what certainly was the cruellest blow to his father, was his assassination of Akbar's close friend and confidante, Abu'l Fazl, in 1602. The relationship between the prince and Abu'l Fazl had been deteriorating for years. Salim was aware that Abu'l Fazl disapproved of him and was, not unreasonably, concerned that Abu'l Fazl was actively undermining his reputation at his father's court. Their mutual dislike had been on public display, as Abu'l Fazl acknowledged, writing of the temporary disgrace he had brought on himself by not coming out, as propriety demanded, to formally greet the prince on his arrival at Akbar's court. The tone of Abu'l Fazl's narration is notable, placing blame for the reaction squarely on the prince and his allies. Having had a spiritual epiphany that demanded his time and attention, Abu'l Fazl claimed to be 'unable to perform fully the outward service of attending upon the Prince. Royal and awkward explanations were not successful. From not fully considering the matter, he (the prince) became somewhat angry and base and envious people had their opportunity... Many untrue reports were (sold) as truth'.[17] Akbar seems to have banned Abu'l Fazl from the court for some days over the incident. Shortly afterwards, Abu'l Fazl was sent to the Deccan to take charge of Akbar's armies when the emperor was called north to deal with Salim's rebellion, but in the summer of 1602, Akbar requested that Abu'l Fazl return to his side in the north.

When news of Abu'l Fazl's planned return reached Salim in Allahabad, he turned for help to Bir Singh Deo of the Bundela Rajputs (1592–1627), who had been among those who flocked to the prince's counter court. The son of the ruler of Orccha, in present-day Madhya Pradesh, Bir Singh's brother had been chosen as heir to the throne, a bitter pill which he blamed on Akbar's influence. As Salim's accomplice, he gathered a military force and ambushed Abu'l Fazl's caravan on its return from the Deccan. Contemporary narratives insist that Abu'l Fazl knew of the imminent attack and refused all attempts to dissuade him from advancing. Bir Singh easily defeated Abu'l Fazl's small guard. Killing and beheading him, he sent Abu'l Fazl's head, as evidence of the murder, to Salim. Salim would later write that although it caused his father distress it was a necessary death, and the only path to reconciliation with his father lay with the removal of his enemy.[18] Bir Singh Deo was lavishly rewarded by Salim and would remain a close ally of the prince, although he was reduced to spending the next few years avoiding the vengeance of a deeply aggrieved Akbar.

Akbar's sorrow was monumental. Not only had his close friend been murdered but with that loss Akbar had suffered the deaths of nearly all of his closest companions. Few remained of the Nine Jewels: Abu'l Fazl's brother, the poet Faizi, had died in 1595, only two years after the death of their beloved father, Shaykh Mubarak; the musician Tansen had died in 1586/89; Akbar's witty advisor Birbal in 1586; and finance secretary Todor Mal in 1589. In addition, of Akbar's three sons, Salim was in rebellion; Murad was dead; and the youngest of the brothers, Danyal, had become a notorious drunk, in failing health (he would die in 1604). When, in 1603, a few months after Abu'l Fazl's murder, Sultan Salima Begim, Akbar's wife and the widow of the great Bairam Khan, offered to effect a reconciliation with his eldest son, Akbar accepted her proposal.

She immediately set out for Allahabad. Salim, on hearing of her advance, came out to meet her and escorted her into his city. Perhaps he was shaken by his own actions and drained by the tension of his revolt, for she was able to convince him to return with her to Agra. As he neared his father's capital, his grandmother, Maryam Makani, met Salim and led him with his entourage into Agra, an act which 'soothed the prince's terrified soul'.[19] When he came in humility before the throne, Sultan Salima Begim and Maryam Makani, at his request, dramatically and symbolically threw the prince at the feet of his father, who raised him from the floor and embraced the prodigal, placing his own turban on Salim's head.[20]

Having publicly welcomed Salim back to court, however, Akbar demanded that he return to imperial service and ordered his son to rejoin the previously abandoned military campaign against Mewar. Salim stalled and found excuses for delay. His efforts to avoid the assignment were motivated by far more complicated realities than simple personal indolence and debauchery. The distance between Mewar and Agra was great enough to be alarming to the prince, for should anything happen to Akbar, who though only in his sixties was obviously weakening under the weight of so many responsibilities, disappointments and betrayals, Salim would have faced the difficulty of returning to the capital before a rival seized the throne. In addition, after years of independence, however ineptly managed, to return to a subordinate role as his father's adjunct surely chafed the prince. In November of 1603, after dawdling for some weeks, Salim gave up entirely on his pretence of a campaign, and made his way back for a third time to his independent refuge in Allahabad, where he began again to drink intemperately.

It was in this period that Salim committed another notorious atrocity. A eunuch at his court had formed a relationship with a courtier of the prince, and together the two men fled Allahabad.[21] An outraged Salim immediately sent troops after them. They were easily apprehended and brought back to face the prince, along with a third man who was accused of being a co-conspirator. The prince viciously passed judgement, demanding that one of them be beaten, another castrated and the last flayed in front of him. The appalling verdict was carried out, and news of it flew to Akbar's court. The emperor was deeply affected, sending a strongly worded criticism to his son that not only emphasized his horror at the severity of the punishment, but his own inability to witness such a dreadful act as flaying – even were it to be performed, he claimed, on a dead goat. Akbar's reaction was one of obvious disgust and loathing, and perhaps even Salim was appalled by his own depravity. Such a scene was never repeated; in all the years of his kingship, there would be no incident equal in callousness to the murder of Abu'l Fazl or in sheer cruelty to the torture of the eunuch and his companions.

Resolution

With one son deceased, another dying and his grandsons still young and inexperienced, Akbar may have felt he had little choice but to finally bring to a resolution Salim's stumbling efforts at independent rule. In August, the emperor and his army began to move on Allahabad. Shortly after setting out, however, the emperor's boat ran aground on a sand bank, stranding him on the Yamuna River. Although he was released from the sand by the next morning, the day opened with torrential rains that again prevented his army from moving towards Allahabad. While the emperor waited impatiently for an opportunity to rejoin his campaign, word arrived from Agra to warn him that his mother was dying. He packed his camp at once, turning back to the city where his mother, Hamida Banu Begim, Maryam Makani, died within a few hours of his arrival.[22] It was yet another agonizing blow to the king, who had relied heavily on his mother's support and astute advice. As a sign of his love and respect, he shaved his head and took a turn in carrying her bier. She was buried with her husband Humayun, in the tomb she had helped design and construct for him in Delhi.

The death of his beloved grandmother gave Salim an opportunity to resolve the conflict with his father without the public humiliation that military defeat or surrender would have surely brought. The prince let it be known that he planned to return to Agra, to join his family in mourning, arriving with a cluster of courtiers on 9 November 1604. Akbar swallowed his wrath and accepted Salim's return to court. As soon as the public formalities were completed, however, he had Salim seized and imprisoned – not for the murder of Abu'l Fazl, nor the prince's rebellious acts, but in order to force his son, whose consumption of alcohol remained alarming, to stop drinking. After ten days of confinement in the family quarters in the company of a royal physician, the prince was released. His lands and rank reinstated, Salim would remain in Agra and his relations with his father, though strained, resumed.

No other retribution was forthcoming, in part because the emperor 'was hopeless about Prince Danyal'.[23] The emperor's youngest son had been assigned to the unending Deccani campaign, where his excessive drinking continued to undermine his health; Akbar had received reports that the prince was weak and ill, hiccupping constantly. Just as had been the case with Murad, Akbar's efforts to recall Danyal were ignored and avoided by the prince, who sent gifts and claimed he'd quit drinking for six months, but made excuses to avoid his father's summons. The emperor's close ally, and Danyal's father-in-law, Abdur Rahim Khankhanan was sent to join the prince in the Deccan, but even his attempts to intervene were insufficient. When no other remedy proved successful, Abdur Rahim finally isolated Danyal, in an effort to detoxify him. Among the prince's personal attendants, however, was one who broke the ban, smuggling alcohol to Danyal, reputedly hidden in the barrel of his gun. The gunpowder-infused drink proved fatal for the prince and he died in April of 1604, at the age of thirty-two.

While Akbar's acceptance of Salim's return was surely fuelled by the loss of his other sons, Salim's decision to give up independent rule in Allahabad in exchange for life at his father's court may have been further encouraged by the growing influence of another, increasingly serious, competitor for Akbar's throne: Salim's eldest son, Khusraw. Khusraw had been born in Lahore in 1587 of a Kachhwaha princess, the daughter of Raja Bhagwant Das. Although still in his teens he had, for the last few years, become the willing centre of a conspiracy to promote an alternative succession. Salim had certainly given many at court cause to doubt his ability to successfully rule in Akbar's place, and his eldest son, known to be a favourite of the emperor, had come to be considered by many as a superior choice. Among Khusraw's staunchest allies was his father-in-law, Mirza Aziz Koka Khan Azam, milk-brother of the emperor and among the highest of the elite, although reputed to have a contentious and combative personality. In addition, the young prince's former *ateke*, the great Rajput general Raja Man Singh, had joined Khan Azam's plot to put Khusraw on the throne, though seemingly inspired by love for Akbar and the empire rather than the self-interest demonstrated by his co-conspirator. With such powerful supporters, the plot gained attention and adherents. Tragically, in May of 1604, Khusraw's mother committed suicide by ingesting a lethal amount of opium. Her husband, Prince Salim, would later make the self-serving argument that she had always been emotionally unstable and that her son's perfidious rivalry against him had finally driven her to despair. He claimed to be distraught at her death. Akbar sent a very sympathetic note of condolence to Salim, at his counter-court in Allahabad.

Khusraw's effort to position himself as legitimate successor to Akbar had of course created sharp tensions with his father. There can be no doubt that Salim's awareness of this powerful faction of detractors at the imperial centre played a role in his decision to seek a rapprochement with Akbar, yet with his return to Agra the rivals were both domiciled in the emperor's household and the atmosphere of distrust must have been nearly unbearable. The increasing tension between father and son was publicly demonstrated at an elephant fight on the palace grounds, during which Akbar arranged to have Salim and Khusraw pit their elephants against each other. The contest was seen by many of the observers, and perhaps the emperor himself, as a proxy battle for their competing claims of legitimacy. With so much at stake, when Salim's elephant began to overpower his foe, supporters of the rivals leapt into the fight to assist their champions and the event disintegrated into an unruly and embarrassing brawl.

That evening Akbar fell into a fever, and over the next few weeks his condition worsened. The issue of succession, and the rivalry between his only surviving son and his eldest grandson, had suddenly become immediate and momentous. Fearing conspiracy, neither Khusraw nor Salim felt safe visiting the dying Akbar. Yet while Khusraw's adherents openly agitated for his candidacy, there were many who were determined to retain a direct lateral succession from father to son. With support growing among the empire's most powerful noblemen, Salim promised forgiveness to those who had opposed him, a vow that eventually brought even Khan Azam to his side. An increasingly confident Salim made his way at last to Akbar's bedside, where his father formally invested him with the robes of office, shortly before his death, on 27 October 1605. Salim took the throne of the Mughal Empire at the (solar) age of thirty-six, on 3 November 1605, assuming for himself the regnal name of Jahangir, He who Seizes the World.

Part Two

The Emperor Jahangir, 1605–8

3

The new king

Consolidating kingship

Kingship in the pre-modern world was patrimonial, the royal household serving as the hub of power from which access to wealth and promotion was measured and meted out by the hand of the king. The support of the imperial elites was not granted unreservedly, however. In an era and within a milieu in which loyalty was famously unreliable, relationships between the ruler and his nobility remained competitive, requiring regular mutual reinforcement. In the wake of his contested succession, Jahangir's most immediate dilemma was the general unease among imperial elites regarding his inheritance.

The new ruler's reputation had been deeply undermined by his years of rebellion against Akbar, as well as by the public knowledge of his alcoholism and rumours of the atrocities he had committed as an independent ruler in Allahabad. Although he had foiled the efforts of his son and the powerful noblemen who had supported Khusraw's claims, Jahangir expressed resentment that influential members of his royal court had recently been actively fomenting a counter-succession. He bitterly commented that this was a time 'when the pillars of state and mighty *amirs* were shaky and each had some melancholia in his mind and they wanted to bring about something which would result in nothing but the wreckage of the state'. Because of the precarious nature of inheritance, Jahangir's next few years would be dominated by his efforts to assert his authority and establish absolute control over the nobility, including the members of the contentious extended royal family.

The new emperor immediately addressed the anxiety at court, confirming the positions of his father's palace servants while broadcasting a general pardon for the elites of the empire, including those who had worked against his ascension to the throne. Assuring them that there would be no investigation into the mistakes and failures of which they must now be ashamed, Jahangir proffered generous gifts, robes of honour and promotions to many.[1] The emperor specifically reaffirmed his close personal ties to the powerful individuals at the court whose loyalties had been in doubt, including those, like Khan Azam and Raja Man Singh, who had openly supported Khusraw's claims.[2]

Jahangir also lavishly rewarded long-time supporters and allies, including his childhood friend Muhammad Sharif Khan, who had been sent to the prince's court to convince Salim to return to his father but instead had chosen to remain in Allahabad. Now he was recompensed, appointed vizier and given the rank of five thousand, with the highest grade of title, *Amir al-Umara*, the Commander of Commanders. Previously marginalized groups found favour with the new emperor. While some members of the Turco-Persian elite mistrusted their Afghan colleagues, after his accession Jahangir attempted to strengthen his base by bringing increased numbers of Afghans into his court, in particular the young Pir Khan, later entitled Khan Jahan, who would write: 'He [Jahangir] gave so much attention to them [the Afghans] that they gave up their hostile attitude and bound themselves in submission and attachment to him even at the sacrifice of their lives. By their distinguished service, they raised themselves to the ranks of great nobles and became worthy of being admitted to the Emperor's company.'[3] In the midst of this bout of strategic generosity, Jahangir also was finally able to promote and reward Bir Singh Deo, the assassin of Abu'l Fazl, whose last few years had been spent avoiding Akbar's long reach. Awarded a *vatan jagir* (or *al-tamgha jagir*), semi-autonomous rule over his ancestral territories, Bir Singh would become one of the richest and most powerful men of Jahangir's court.

Even Jahangir's dealings with his younger sons demonstrated less the behaviour of an affectionate father and more a determination to strategically bolster his grasp on power. Underlining and reinforcing Khusraw's recent political humiliation, Jahangir publicly promoted the claims of his second son, Parvez. Prince Parvez was made much of, volubly praised at court and favoured with a robe of honour, and gifts of valuable jewels, elephants, as well as Persian and Turkish horses. Jahangir then hastily declared a military campaign against the as yet unconquered kingdom of Mewar, appointing Parvez as the commander of an army of twenty thousand. Jahangir arranged that the prince would be accompanied on this march by many of the most powerful noblemen at the court, several of whom had been closely allied with Khusraw. If successful, the campaign would bring glory to the new king, for even Akbar had been unable to subdue Mewar. If on the other hand the campaign failed, the operation offered Jahangir an opportunity to weaken Khusraw's base of support by removing a great many potential malcontents from the imperial court.

As for his third son, Khurram, while Jahangir lavished praise on him, his celebration of a beloved child seems to have been primarily aimed at undermining Khusraw's most fundamental argument for his own sovereignty, that Akbar had preferred him to his father. Jahangir wrote that in fact it was not Khusraw at all, but Khurram who had been his grandfather's favourite, superior to all of his brothers. 'Many times, he [Akbar] said, "There is no comparison between him and your other sons. I consider *him* my true son."'[4]

Legitimate rule

Having been witness to the success of the extraordinary image-making machinery at his father's royal court, the newly enthroned emperor turned to an array of references and symbols that could affirm his succession as not only legitimate but even divinely mandated. The nucleus of his claims lay in the story of his birth as prophesied by the Chishti Shaykh Salim, a legitimizing narrative that had been tailored specifically for him. This personal origin story supported any number of claims, political and sacred, and was such a critically important reference point that Jahangir would begin his memoir with its retelling. He reported other auspicious events, sharing a family legend reinforced by the other great religious allies of the Mughals, the Naqshbandi Order of Sufis, in which Shaykh Husayn Jami of Lahore dreamed that the line of shaykhs had transferred power to Jahangir, warned him to be prepared and described him as divinely chosen.[5] Not only did both of the great Sufi orders of Mughal India, the Chishtis and the Naqshbandis, affirm his place as the annointed heir, even the Jesuits reported multiple omens, signs and prophesies of the prince's coming ascension, telling the story of a Jain holy man who prophesied a short reign for the new king and was suddenly struck down with an other-worldly case of leprosy.[6]

For Jahangir, enthronement was an opportunity for personal public reinvention, including the creation of a regnal name: he would be Salim no longer – in part, he claimed, to avoid confusion with the two Ottoman sultans named Salim. Instead, he would take a name that reflected his new role. As the business of an emperor was to grasp hold of the globe, he would henceforth be known as *Jahangir*, He Who Seizes the World. In a further effort to align his succession with prophesy, Jahangir claimed to have heard that the 'sages of India' foretold that the successor to Emperor Akbar would be named *Nur ud-din*, the Light of Religion. The reference was in deliberate accord with his father's close identification as a sun king, and the Islamic ideal of 'a light-filled Perfect

Man', and it became a simple matter to thus enrich his self-awarded appellation: Nuruddin Muhammad Jahangir.[7] For the remainder of his reign, he would award the name Nur to both property and people of highest importance – his imperial gardens, some of his most intimate followers and even to his last and favourite wife.

An emperor's name was central to the public affirmations of legitimate kingship in the Islamic world, in being announced in the Friday prayers and minted onto the face of new coinage. Immediately after his ascension, his regnal name in place, Jahangir ordered a series of new coins, in purest gold and silver. Directly evoking his claims of divine light, he gave his new coinage titles, including the *nurshahi* (the Light King), *nursultani* (Light Sultan), *nurjahani* (Light of the World), as well as one named for the king directly, the *jahangiri*, which was engraved with a line of poetry, 'The face of gold was made as luminous as the color of the sun and moon by Shah Nuruddin Jahangir son of Akbar Padshah.'[8] The coins of highest value reiterated a sunrise motif: 'The world became illuminated by this coin like the sun; "The sun of the kingdom" is the date.'[9] His regnal name was used in an accessional chronogram, composed by the courtier Maktub Khan, which described the new emperor as a second Sahib Qiran, the dynastic reference to Timur, the Lord of the Auspicious Conjunction:

> King of kings Jahangir, a second Timur
> Sat in justice on the victorious throne
> Success, fortune, victory, pomp and triumph
> Are wrapped around him to serve with joy
> This is the date of his accession,
> When fortune puts its head at the feet of *sahib qiran-i sani*.[10]

His father's footsteps

The new king's relationship with his father had for many years been a fraught mixture of resentment, rivalry and admiration. As a prince, even before his rebellion, he had provocatively posed as a viable political alternative to Akbar, deliberately drawing the support of a large and varied base of disaffected outsiders. Yet for all that their relationship had been extremely complex and competitive in life, upon Akbar's death Jahangir expressed unreserved pride in his father's personal and political legacy. From the very start of his reign, Jahangir pivoted unequivocally to a policy of public devotion and emulation of Akbar, in what could be described as a political strategy of filial piety. Yet while Jahangir's public statements of support for Akbar's popular policies were politically expedient for the new king, his professions of admiration went beyond mere rhetoric, carrying a distinct tone of sincere reverence. The death of the king had freed his son to publicly demonstrate his admiration and affection.

In the first year of his reign, Jahangir wrote a glowing and highly sentimental description of Akbar, who, his son effused, had a 'radiant countenance', and the broad chest of a lion. Jahangir wrote of an endearing 'beautiful fleshy mole, about the size of half a chickpea' on the side of the emperor Akbar's nose. 'For those who study physiognomy', he added, 'such a mole is considered to be a sign of great good fortune'.[11] He briefly described his father's early inheritance of the throne and his outstanding success in battle, focusing on Akbar's courage and bravery, his honourable behaviour, his humility and sincere spirituality. No book, claimed Jahangir, even disregarding their relationship as father and son, could contain even a fraction of his father's good qualities.

Although his accession had fully converted Jahangir to his father's defence, it is unsurprising to find that the praise he offered his father would remain tempered with a competitive edge. When Jahangir described his Akbar's peerless skills as a huntsman, he was compelled to add that he himself was the inheritor of this gift, a passionate hunter of anything that could be shot with a gun. The fulsome approval he offered of his father's famed religious tolerance began with a description of his own religious debate with local pundits, which he claimed to have soundly won. Yet even implied criticism of Akbar would remain rare throughout his son's reign. In a masterful act of reputational rehabilitation, the former rebel would throughout his reign demonstrate consistent and enthusiastic adherence to Akbar's regnal model, particularly on issues of piety and charity, impartiality and even-handedness.

Jahangir struggled to explain the most sensitive of issues, his own acts of cruelty and rebellion against Akbar. Had we imagined that Jahangir's memoir was intended as a private confessional document rather than a deliberate and very public effort to assert and defend his sovereignty, the very first chapters quickly disabuse us of that notion. In the early pages of his memoir, he defended even the murder of Abu'l Fazl, who he described as an untrustworthy miscreant anxious to undermine the relationship between father and son. The assassination served a higher purpose, Jahangir claimed, allowing for his own eventual reunion with Akbar, after which their mutual mistrust and animosity were resolved.[12] At the time of his defeat of Khusraw, Jahangir ruminated on legitimate kingship, his own inheritance and his earlier disloyalty towards Akbar. Explaining that he had been advised by 'short-sighted men', he proudly added that using his own intelligence and knowledge, he ultimately had rejected the advice of those 'weak-minded people' who encouraged insurrection. He had, after all, eventually surrendered, and returned to the fold, quickly followed with public homage to his father, his guide and symbolic *qibla*.[13] It was through this act of humility, Jahangir claimed, that he deservedly 'got what he got', the emperor's throne.

Religious policies

At the time of Jahangir's ascension, there were many who felt great uncertainty over the direction of the new king's religious policies. Akbar had not merely tolerated religious differences but embraced them. By the final year of his reign, however, his rebellious son Salim had been widely reported to support a more conservative Muslim faction at the court, allying himself with those who had long resented Akbar's exceptional intellectual curiosity and endorsement of diverse religious communities. Rumours floated that the new emperor would pivot to a more conventional adherence to Islamic 'norms'.[14] The Jesuits in residence at the Mughal court, who had some years earlier held high expectations that Prince Salim was 'almost a Christian' now claimed that he had gained support for his contested succession by offering 'an oath to the Moors to uphold the law of Muhammad'.[15]

Immediately upon taking the throne, however, Jahangir made it very clear that any alliances he had offered to those who resented his father's imperial policy of religious liberality had been motivated by simple political expedience and would be rendered void with the new king's ascension. Careful to affirm his allegiance to Islam, Jahangir went on to offer an immediate and full-throated statement of advocacy for his father's model. Proudly contrasting his empire from those of his contemporaries – the Safavids, Uzbeks and Ottomans – Jahangir touted Mughal religious diversity, publicly upholding his father's notorious equitability and state protection of non-Muslim communities within his territories. Jahangir announced that followers of all religions – carefully enumerating Sunni and Shiite, Hindu, Frank and Jew – had a place within his kingdom.[16] Even those subjects whose religious views were less than perfect, he declared, were welcome, while sectarian discord and animosity were banished.[17] On appointing a new chief justice, Shaykh Ahmad Lahauri, the emperor publicly proclaimed that Mughal imperial policy rejected enmity and maintained peace with all religions, adding that he would make a personal effort to keep the name of god forever in his thoughts, as had his exalted father.[18]

The insecurity that had descended on many religious communities upon Akbar's death was relieved by the new king's public alignment with his father's policies. On learning that their monthly stipend, which had been initiated by Akbar, would be continued by Jahangir, the Jesuits of Lahore wrote: 'The king began at this time to show himself much less of a Moor than at first. He declared it was his intention to follow in his father's footsteps; and his actions confirmed his words.'[19] Akbar's model of benevolent acceptance would remain official Mughal religious policy throughout his son's reign. Years later Edward Terry, who became the chaplain for Sir Thomas Roe's English embassy at the Mughal court, described what he saw as Jahangir's commitment to this ideal, describing him as a king under which 'all Religions are tolerated and their Priests [held] in good esteem'.[20] Europeans, whose own early modern royal courts were famously intolerant of religious diversity, expressed nearly universal admiration for the high degree of liberality and accommodation at Jahangir's royal court. Thomas Coryat, an independent English traveller, wrote of the emperor that 'He speaketh very reverently of our Saviour, calling him in the Indian tongue Isazarat eesa (Hazarat Isa) that is, the great Prophet Jesus; and all Christians, especiallie us English, he useth so benevolently as no Mahometan prince the like.'[21]

It was in part because of his allegiance to a policy of toleration that Jahangir's piety and religious identity have been adjudged by many to have been insincere, earning him the reputation of an inconsequential dabbler. Some suggested that Jahangir's adherence to Akbar's religious curiosity and tolerance sprang not from principle but from indifference. In analysing the Jesuit texts, a commenter asserted that

> unlike his father, Jahangir had no feeling for religion ... he was in no real sense a seeker after the truth. The study of religious problems was with him nothing more than a hobby. Jahangir would have subscribed to no one set of doctrines as readily as to another; but he had very little use for any religion, and at none all for one that would not permit him as many wives as he wanted.[22]

That seems an unnecessarily cynical approach to Jahangir's spirituality, for there is plenty of evidence that Jahangir was sincere in his protestations of piety. Visitors to his court described Jahangir waking in the night and calling for impoverished religious scholars to sit with him, in conversation about God.[23] On another occasion, Jahangir's humble demeanour with a visiting beggar, likely a visiting Sufi shaykh, so impressed the British observer that he compared Jahangir's piety to that of Christian kings.[24]

The twelve decrees and the chain of justice

Within weeks of his enthronement, Jahangir announced the Twelve Decrees, a combination of trade laws, civil and religious edicts, and personal bequests.[25] Continuing his effort to calm the imperial elites and fulfil promises made during his succession negotiations, Jahangir's decrees not only confirmed the annual stipends paid to clergy, menials and to his father's favourites, but he notably doubled the incomes of the women of the family. Many of the decrees were aimed at public opinion and building support for the new king: eliminating non-Quranic taxes and alms that had been imposed by local administrators; forbidding disfiguring punishments, such as the cutting off of ears or nose; and ordering that hospitals be opened in the larger cities at the expense of the royal court. The emperor declared it illegal for local elites to seize the lands of peasants or force a householder to quarter troops and demanded that no one be allowed to interfere with the transfer of an inheritance. Jahangir decreed that trade tariffs be lowered and merchants' rights be protected, making it illegal to search their packs. He further ordered those who administered regions known for thieves and bandits, in either jagirs or royal lands, to construct wells, mosques and caravansaries; to encourage settlement; and to benefit merchants along the empire's highways. Later that same year, he would further demonstrate his support for mercantile activity by remitting all import and export duties on commodities for the two provinces of Kabul and Qandahar – both regions at the heart of Mughal imperial ambition and, not incidentally, bases for powerful noblemen of still unreliable loyalty.

Unexpectedly, the fifth decree called for a ban on intoxicants and liquor, although Jahangir's own alcoholism was publicly known and acknowledged by the emperor himself. Jahangir had made no effort to hide it, and even within the text of the decree itself the emperor commented that he himself had been drinking heavily for twenty years, since the age of eighteen. Describing his own struggle to reduce his consumption of alcohol, he proudly commented that he had managed to cut his intake to a third of his previous totals, now drinking only at night and for reasons of digestion!

Following the model of his charismatic father, Jahangir banned the slaughter of animals every year on his own birthday, as well as weekly on Thursdays, which was the day of his ascension to the throne, and on Sundays. Not only was Sunday revered as the first day of creation but Akbar had claimed that his own birth on a Sunday had added to the sacred character of the day, and Jahangir continued the weekly memorial veneration. The emperor added a request that every day the worthy poor be brought before him so that he might offer them assistance. Finally, the new emperor declared a general amnesty, releasing prisoners across the empire.

The decrees emphasized Jahangir's claims of just kingship, perhaps the most powerful trope of Persio-Islamic rule. The medieval courts of the Abbasid caliphs had retained many of the traditions and rituals of rule established by the pre-Islamic Persian emperors. Adherence to these ideals became even more evident after Ferdowsi's *Shahnama*, produced for the Turkish Ghaznavid ruler Mahmud, brought Persio-Islamic models of kingship as represented by the Sassanid kings Jamshid and Anushirvan, not only into the popular imagination but also to the royal courts of the conquering Turks and Mongols, for whom a reputation for justice would prove paramount in confirming sovereignty and right to rule.

Even as a rebel prince, Jahangir had shown allegiance to the model of the Just King. As emperor, attentive to his audience and quick to seize opportunities to reinforce his sovereign authority, Jahangir made public and performative efforts to demonstrate his adherence to imperial justice. On learning of tyrannical behaviour by the eunuchs of an important Amir, his response was to write immediately to chastise the offenders, claiming in his missive that his own 'sense of justice did not tolerate oppression and that in the scales of justice, greatness and smallness were not sanctioned'.[26] When Jahangir learned of two local leaders 'who made their living by tyranny and oppression', he sent one of the men to the gallows and imposed harsh financial penalties on the other, who was known to be rich. Having collected fifteen thousand rupees in this way, the emperor used the funds to establish soup kitchens, among other charitable institutions. Inspired by the success of his actions, he went on to order that soup kitchens be established across the empire, so that simple food could be given to the poor, as well as to pilgrims and travellers. Jahangir was insistent that his primary regnal responsibility was to serve as refuge and protector for his subjects in need. When advice literature gently suggested that the king must be the protector of Islam, promulgating religion and sharia, Jahangir completely disregarded the suggestion, returning his emphasis to themes of ethics and justice.[27] While offering us a glimpse of the religio-political discourses at his court, there is no clear evidence that Jahangir was influenced by – or even read – the advice literature composed for his patronage. The mere fact of it being gifted to the emperor or present in his library tells us little. In contrast, other of the palace library's volumes, such as that of Hafez, contain notations and marginalia that confirm the attention and interest of the emperor. Describing his own political philosophy, Jahangir made the direct link between the benevolence and concern of a Just King with the happiness and prosperity of his people.

In the first weeks of his reign, Jahangir made another powerful symbolic gesture to proclaim his allegiance to Persio-Islamic ideals. Following the celebrated model of perfect royal justice, the legendary Anushirvan the Just, 531–579 CE, who was known to have hung a bell outside his palace, allowing anyone who desired royal intervention to easily gain the attention of the king, Jahangir ordered a golden 'Chain of Justice' [*silsilla-i jambon* or *bastan-i zanjir-i adl*] strung with sixty bells and strung between a stone post set into the riverbank and the crenellations of the king's tower in the citadel at Agra. In theory, petitioners anxious to gain direct access to the ruler could stand on the riverbank outside of the citadel and pull on the golden chain. The bells would ring, catching the attention of the palace guards who could alert the emperor. Jahangir explained that his golden chain would allow the emperor's subjects, great and small, to bypass those public servants who were otherwise indifferent in offering justice to the needy and the deserving, and appeal directly to the imperial court in their time of need.[28]

It would be a mistake to dismiss the chain of bells as a myth or a merely symbolic gesture.[29] While Jahangir would never again mention them after the time of their installation (and in any case, the peripatetic nature of his royal court eventually made the bell apparatus in Agra superfluous), they are described by European eye witnesses, and paintings of the period included the chain of bells as a motif in imperial portraits of both Jahangir and his successor, Khurram/Shah Jahan.[30] It is in the symbolism of the gesture that its importance is found, and for Jahangir legitimate rule would continue to be deliberately reinforced by his deft use of easily recognized references and performances.

As for his sincerity, with or without a nearby 'Chain of Justice', Jahangir continued to make himself available to his subjects as a judicial arbiter, in sometimes surprisingly comprehensive and generous ways. On the occasion of a visit to Ahmadabad, Jahangir claimed to have made himself available every day for two or three hours, despite the heat and dust, to listen to his people and punish those who oppressed them. Complaining of pain and illness, the emperor dispensed imperial law in the most public and accessible of venues, on the banks of the river with no guards or walls separating him from petitioners. English visitors to the court would be struck by the regularity of emperor's public dispensation of justice. In 1616, Thomas Roe, the first British ambassador to India, who remained at the royal court of Jahangir for two years, wrote, 'On Tuesday at the Jarokha he sits in Judgement, never refusing the poorest man's

Complaynt, where he hears with patience both parts', remarking that the high degree of public access to the king put Jahangir in 'a state of reciprocal bondage'.[31] Roe emphasized Jahangir's forbearance, commenting on more than one occasion that the king 'sitteth in judgement patiently and giveth sentence for crimes Capitall and Civill', although he misconstrued the state of law in Mughal India, asserting that it lay entirely in the person of the king, writing, 'They have no written law. The king by his own word ruleth and his Governors of Provinces by that authority'.[32] Throughout his reign, Jahangir's assertions of allegiance to an ideal of justice allowed him to build a sovereign identity as the most charismatic of kings, comparable to the Islamic archetype of perfect kingship. A Jesuit at his court would write that 'His Majesty continued to show himself worthy of the name, "The Just King."'[33]

4

Filial rebellion

Khusraw's revolt

While Jahangir worked to stabilize his seat as emperor, his eldest son Khusraw seethed with impatience. Only five months after his father's ascension, on the 6th of April 1606, he launched a rebellion. Khusraw would justify his filial insubordination by pointing to his own father's years of rebellion, asserting, 'I shall certainly not become more criminal by taking arms against Jahangir than he himself was in revolting against Akbar. If I offend, it will only be by following the example of my father.'[1] Having previously been touted as a viable successor to Akbar, it is possible that Khusraw expected his uprising to be met with a groundswell of support, anticipating that former allies amongst the nobility would join with him. If so, he was to be disappointed. His rebellion did not attract any of the powerful men who had forwarded his claims while Akbar was still alive, and the effort immediately began to falter.

Having committed himself to revolt, Khusraw and his followers first looted sections of Agra, in search of money and supplies to support their rebellion, and then rapidly fled the city. The rebels moved northwest towards Lahore, plundering caravanserais and travellers, and sweeping up an ever-growing and increasingly unruly army along the way. The apprehensive city leaders of Lahore promised Khusraw funding and support if the prince could maintain discipline, but he proved unable to manage his provisional army, which looted the city for weeks until imperial armies appeared. The rebels fled, but Jahangir's troops brought no immediate peace, as they searched the city for supporters of the rebel prince, violently interrogating residents and sacking homes, leaving hundreds 'impaled or hanged, their bodies left to rot in the burning summer heat'.[2] Meanwhile Khusraw's army continued westward, trampling and burning crops, looting and extorting funds, as they devastated the countryside.

In the face of his son's revolt, Jahangir suffered a few days of panic, perhaps anticipating a rebel force equal to his own princely army, which at one point had swelled to over thirty thousand troops. He waffled briefly, unsure who should lead the imperial armies in pursuit. He expressed the vague hope that Khusraw might surrender if directly confronted by a powerful member of the nobility, although the emperor assured his generals that if the prince demanded a battle, they should meet him as a foe, ignoring any father–son sentiment, reminding them that kingship recognizes no family relationships.

As the indiscipline and aimlessness of Khusraw's army became clear in the early days of the revolt, Jahangir's self-confidence grew. He appointed Shaikh Farid Bukhari, who knew the region well and had allies in the Punjab, to lead one army, while he himself marched with another. Concerned that his rebel son might make his way to Central Asia or Iran where an offer of assistance could strengthen him, Jahangir determined to move quickly to block him from crossing the borders of the Mughal state. All the same, Jahangir paused to visit his father's tomb on the banks of the Yamuna river in Sikandra. Turning the brief rest stop into a pilgrimage, he claimed to seek assistance from the spirit of the late king. When one of Khusraw's supporters was captured almost immediately, he attributed that success to Akbar's intervention from beyond the grave, happily taking the event to be a good omen. Following the path of his son's army, he made another important stop in Delhi at the tombs of his grandfather, the Emperor Humayun, and the Chishti Shaykhs Nizamuddin and Nasiruddin Chirag, where he likewise distributed generous alms and publicly prayed for assistance.

As his confidence rose, the tone of Jahangir's complaints grew increasingly self-congratulatory and bitter. He wrote of his complete surprise at Khusraw's insubordination and, lamenting the suicide of the prince's mother, placed the blame squarely at the feet of her brother, Raja Man Singh. Jahangir scornfully criticized those of his noblemen who he felt demonstrated a certain lack of courage by not blocking Khusraw's path, and he lavishly distributed promotions and rewards not only amongst those who proved, however hesitantly, to support the king, but also those who as yet had taken no clear side. Jahangir spread abundant cash gifts, offering nine hundred thousand rupees in an effort to win over Jamil Beg, a tribal chieftain of Badakhshan, whose rival Badakhshani chief was allied with Khusraw. The commander of the second arm of the imperial armies, Shaykh Farid Bukhari, had been given a small fortune with which to reward local allies and tie them ever closer to the throne. Jahangir did not of course rely solely on the support garnered through generous gifts of cash. He proactively arranged for the arrest and imprisonment of anyone who might have a proclivity to rebellion, including the children of his uncle Muhammad Hakim, who had himself rebelled against Akbar. If a son could thus prove himself disloyal, how much less reliable would be cousins?

The king found a bitter humour in the situation. Outrageously pointing out that his own suffering in the noonday heat was made greater because he had missed his daily dose of opium, Jahangir seemed to suggest that Khusraw was more of an addict than himself, commenting, 'imagine what state that wretch must be in!'[3] When word reached Jahangir, in Sultanpur, that battle against Khusraw's army had at last been joined, he impatiently moved ahead of the army, initially accompanied by only fifty men on horseback. He later boasted of his rush to join the attack; although he had only just received his meal, he took but a single bite of his biryani, for luck, and headed out with no armour, bearing only a spear and a sword. On route, he received news of the success of the imperial troops. Khusraw fled the field, intent on reaching allies as he headed north, but the prince was captured quickly and, with a small number of loyal followers, was delivered in chains to his father.

The emperor later composed a verse condemning what he portrayed as his son's unrealistic aspirations:

> Who could have known that this youth of tender years
> >would in this way plot mischief against his elders?
> With the first goblet he brought forth the dregs,
> >bypassing my grandeur and his own shame.
> He burned the throne of the sun
> >in desiring the place of Jamshid.[4]

In the immediate aftermath of the rebellion, the emperor meted out vicious punishments. On Jahangir's orders, Khusraw's two remaining noble allies were sewn into the skins of freshly killed animals, one an ox and the other a donkey. Enshrouded in raw leather, each was mounted on an ass, facing backwards, and paraded through the streets. Husayn Beg, in the ox skin, lived for much of the afternoon but finally died of suffocation as the apparatus dried and tightened around him. Abdur Rahim, who was given water by sympathetic bystanders, would manage to survive his hours in the skin of the donkey. The aggrieved emperor then had three hundred of the captured peasant-soldiers of his son's army impaled or hanged, their bodies forming an avenue along the road into Lahore, through which Khusraw, weighed down with chains, was led on elephant back to review the anguish of his followers.

The aftermath of princely revolt

Jahangir seized the opportunity offered by his son's defeat to clean house. The complete destruction of Khusraw's claims had enhanced the emperor's authority and power, and he took immediate action to undermine those powerful noblemen who had shown themselves to be of inconstant loyalty, establishing reliable networks of loyal supporters in their place. Among those who had demonstrated a preference for Khusraw, the prince's father-in-law, Mirza Aziz Koka, was publicly humiliated by Jahangir, and forced to relinquish his lands and title. Although he would eventually recover part of his lost fortune and return to court, he would never entirely regain his former credibility or respect. The illustrious Raja Man Singh, the prince's uncle and former ateke, was also stripped of his power and position. He made a dignified retreat to his fortress in the district of Rohtas in Bihar, only returning grudgingly at the emperor's demand after an absence of more than a year. Jahangir took the opportunity to break the power of his entire Rajawat clan, moving Man Singh's immediate family to less-desirable positions in the service of the emperor, and promoting their tribal rivals to lead the Kachhwaha Rajputs in their place, with no reduction of overall mansabs, in hopes they would be steadfast in loyalty to Jahangir.[5]

Among the most significant victims of the emperor's wrath, although perhaps of little real consequence to Jahangir at the time, was the Sikh patriarch, Guru Arjun Singh (d. 1606). Passing through the Punjab, Khusraw had begged for financial assistance from the guru, who had offered the desperate prince a charitable gift of five thousand rupees. Jahangir saw this act as support for the princely rebellion and ordered the guru imprisoned, beaten and fined. On his refusal to pay the fine, Guru Arjun was promptly executed, in what would prove to be a disastrous and divisive moment in the history of Mughal–Sikh relations.[6]

As for the prince himself, Khusraw was initially imprisoned. Jahangir seems to have been unable to sustain his earlier outrage, however, and eventually allowed his son more freedom of movement within the confines of the royal court. The prince proved intransigent and only a few years later, in 1607, he would again become involved in a plot to overthrow his father. This time the emperor was informed of the conspiracy early, it was easily crushed and the ringleaders executed. Although reluctant to harm his son, after this second attempt at rebellion Jahangir agreed to have his son blinded, thereby making him forever ineligible for rule.[7] His memoir is silent on the blinding of the prince. Contradictory descriptions from the period claimed that the prince was blinded with a piece of wire or, alternatively, that poisonous plant juices were poured into his eyes, or that his eyes were burned when scorching hot bowls were placed over them. Some certainly expected that the technique would leave marks: a few years later, in 1610, an imposter claiming to be Khusraw pointed to scarring around his eyes as evidence of his identity.[8]

In this case, Jahangir immediately regretted his order, calling for the court doctors to repair the damage that had been done to Khusraw. His sight was at least partially restored and the prince would remain at his father's court. Khusraw's unrelenting melancholy provoked Jahangir's sense of injury, however, and he voiced resentment with his son, criticizing his unwillingness to throw off defeat and return to the routine of the court.[9] According to Jahangir, it was not his son's untrustworthiness but his depression that would eventually lead the emperor to eventually send him away, to the household of his ambitious younger brother Khurram (later the emperor Shah Jahan), where he died in 1622.[10]

While the rivalry and rebellion of his oldest son had been of deep concern to the new king on his ascension, Khusraw's complete defeat established the validity and propriety of Jahangir's inheritance and reinforced his authority. Jahangir pointed to his victory over his son as an explicit affirmation of a divine mandate to rule, writing: 'They [the followers of Khusraw] were, of course, unaware of the fact that the rule of empire and royal command are not something which can be carried out by a couple of intellectually deficient individuals. Whom does the All- Giving Creator consider worthy of this glorious and noble authority? And upon whose shoulders has he draped this *khil'at*?'[11] His son's rebellion had proven to be a golden opportunity for the new king. His success in confining and counteracting his son's claims confirmed Jahangir as Akbar's legitimate heir and as the sovereign ruler of Mughal India.

Babur's Kabul

In March of 1607, in the second year of his reign, Jahangir travelled north from Lahore to the Afghan city of Kabul. The timing of Jahangir's imperial visit, so soon after his son's rebellion was put down, suggests an effort to consolidate relationships with noblemen and family members who had supported the claims of his rebel son. Many of Khusraw's supporters were Afghans, Central Asian Badakhshanis and Uzbeks, who nursed a lingering regret and lack of confidence in Jahangir's leadership. In addition to the opportunity to reinforce old loyalties, the new king's physical presence in the region, as the centre of an impressive imperial entourage, would serve as valuable political theatre.

Perhaps most importantly, however, Jahangir's visit was inspired by dynastic nostalgia, for Kabul had a special place in the Mughal heart. When the Uzbek armies had swept through Mawarannahr in the early sixteenth century, driving the Timurids out of their ancestral capitals of Samarqand and Herat, Kabul had remained the last independent Timurid kingdom, ruled by Jahangir's great-grandfather, Babur. It was Kabul that served as the springboard for Babur's military forays into northern India, and even after he and his descendants had consolidated their power in Hindustan, Kabul continued to serve the dynasty as the imperial capital of the north, in the critical juncture between Safavid, Uzbek, Afghan and Mughal territories. Although intent on remaining as ruler of northern India, Babur had dearly missed Kabul – it was there that his children had been born, where he had caroused with his boon companions, picnicked in the hills with his aunts and sisters and first claimed the title *padshah*. In the last few years of his life, as conqueror of Hindustan, Babur wrote of his homesickness for Kabul's climate, gardens, grapes and melons. Little wonder then that his descendants would think of Babur's former capital with much more than simple affectionate regard. Kabul represented a strategic political and military site, but, more importantly, it was the core of Mughal political charisma. As the object of dynastic sentiment and nostalgia, it offered Jahangir a powerful backdrop for his imperial claims.

On 30 March 1607, at the auspicious hour determined by court astrologers, Jahangir left Lahore fortress, crossing the Ravi River to spend the first night encamped in the suburban Dilamez Garden. The journey to Kabul could be justified by geopolitical concerns, but Jahangir set a notably slow pace and it would be almost two months before the court progress would reach its destination, the imperial banners not entering Kabul until early June. The primary reason for the leisurely journey, as the emperor makes clear in his memoir, was Jahangir's simple delight in the beauty of the countryside. Marching down a riverbed just southwest of Rawalpindi, Jahangir admired the blossoming oleander bushes and ordered that his servants all put bouquets of the flowers in their turbans, thus turning the royal court progress into a mobile garden. Those who refused to play a part in the botanical display, he threatened, would have their turbans knocked from their heads. Coming to a lake with beautiful waterfalls in late April, Jahangir called a halt to the court progress for three days, time he spent drinking wine with his intimates and learning to fish with a local spinning net. Mastering the difficult technique, Jahangir proudly recorded having caught a dozen fish with his own hands. Susceptible to the tranquil and dreamy atmosphere, he had pearls placed in their noses and then released the bejewelled fish back into the lake.[12]

Jahangir's court progress was enormous, with tens of thousands of participants, and Kabul's small size and lack of resources could not support the entire imperial army. Jahangir ordered a large part of the force to hold back, remaining behind in a fortress built by Akbar next to the Nilab River, with instructions to join the emperor's contingent later. The emperor's more streamlined retinue crossed the rocky Nilab on shallow bamboo rafts supported with inflated skin bags, reaching the Khyber Pass on 20 May, and Kabul on 4 June. Entering the city at the hour determined to be most propitious, Jahangir scattered coins to the local populace, as his retinue slowly threaded their way to the royal garden named Shahr Ara, where the imperial tents were pitched.

In Kabul, Jahangir quickly became a tourist pursuing an itinerary of dynastic nostalgia. He carefully toured significant sites, including each of the city's imperial gardens. He listed them by name: the Shahr Ara (Adornment of the City); the Mahtab Bagh (Moonlight garden); the Orta Bagh (Central garden); another garden nearby which had been built by Jahangir's grandmother, the Surat Khana; and the largest garden in Kabul, simply known as the Chahar Bagh. Describing the Shahr Ara Bagh, Jahangir claimed it was so delicate that to walk on it in shoes would be a travesty, although it remained the site of his royal camp throughout his stay in Kabul. Spying a likely looking site nearby, he ordered the construction of yet another garden, and named it Jahan Ara, World Adorner.

Jahangir walked through one garden after another, listing those built by his great-grandfather, Babur, and his grandmother, Maryam Makani, and commenting, 'I don't remember ever having walked as much.'[13] His evenings in the Shahr Ara garden were spent in conversation with his close companions or the ladies of the harem. He described a delightful picnic, organized for the scholars and students of the local *madrasa*, who participated in noodle-cooking contests (after which the emperor awarded each of the cooks a robe of honour), archery contests and dancing. So magnificent was the setting that Jahangir could not resist sharing, and he ordered the chains removed from his rebellious son Khusraw.

In reading their two memoirs, it is striking to note the similarities between Jahangir's visit to Kabul and Babur's stay in Herat, another city of marked dynastic importance, which had taken place just a few years before the Uzbeks had driven him out of his ancestral territories. Herat, the former capital of the famed Timurid prince Sultan Husayn Bayqara, symbolized all that Babur had loved in the Central Asian Timurid courtly world, the lavish gatherings of boon companions in the city gardens, drinking wine and reciting poetry. Babur's journey, like Jahangir's, was heightened by nostalgia; in his memoir, the Timurid prince described with loving attention the various historic and cultural sites he visited, his sentimental attachment enhanced by his clear-eyed awareness of the threat posed by the invading Uzbek armies and the disappearing Timurid cultural world.[14]

Nearly one hundred years after Babur had ruled from Kabul, Jahangir would describe the city in terms of a memorial landscape. Basking in Kabul's dynastic connections, for Jahangir this journey became a part of his larger effort to publicly reinforce the inevitability of his own accession, and the suitability of his rule. Encamped in the Shahr Ara gardens, he named two great plane [*chenar*] trees, Farahbakhsh, 'the giver of joy', and Sayabakhsh, 'the giver of shade', and erected a marble stone between them, inscribed with his name and those of his ancestors, all eight generations back to the emperor Timur. In performance of his duty as a just King, he inscribed an imperial proclamation on the stone's other side, rescinding all non-Quranic customs duties, excise taxes or 'sums collected from God's servants', adding 'any of my descendants or successors who acted contrary to this would be subject to divine wrath'. He noted too the 'amazing coincidence' that the date of his entry to Kabul numerically equalled the year of the hijra [Thursday, the eighteenth of Safar, or *roz-i panjshamba bizhdah-i Safar*, yielding 1016] and ordered that inscribed on the stone as well. Attentive to charity as a requirement of kingship, Jahangir ordered one thousand rupees to be distributed to the poor each day when he was in the city.

Jahangir visited a stone platform south of the city, called the *Takht-i Shah*, King's Throne, which Babur was known to have enjoyed. A bowl had been carved from the stone itself to hold a vast amount of wine.[15] Babur had an inscription carved into the dais: 'The seat of the padshah, asylum of the world, Zahiruddin Muhammad Babur, son of Umar Shaykh Guregen – may God extend his kingdom forever – in the year 914 [1508–9]'. Jahangir's ordered a duplicate platform to be built immediately opposite, carved with his own name and that of the dynastic founder, their shared ancestor, Timur. Sitting on the platform, he ordered both basins filled with wine, which was then shared with his companions. A poet from Ghazni composed a chronogram for Jahangir's Kabul visit, reiterating his claims as a global ruler, 'Monarch of the countries of the seven climes', which the emperor ordered copied onto the nearby wall.

Reinforcing their important dynastic connection, Jahangir described seeing an original copy of Babur's memoirs written 'entirely in his own blessed handwriting'. As with the Takht-i Shah, Jahangir was compelled to leave his own mark, adding four additional sections at the end of Babur's manuscript, and an autograph. Although the court language of the Mughals was Persian, he emphasized his continued close connections with Babur by proudly asserting that he was 'not ignorant of how to speak or write Turkish'.[16] The day before his departure from Kabul, Jahangir treated as a holiday, arranging a traditional circle hunt, the Mongol *qamargha*, in the morning, and in the evening returning to Babur's stone platform where he drank 'many goblets' of wine with his companions. On 20 August, the imperial banners left the Shahr Ara gardens, Jahangir perched on an elephant, tossing small coins to those who had gathered on both sides of the road to watch the emperor's departure.

Jahangir's return to the Gangetic plain would be a slow-paced loitering journey. More major hunting parties were arranged, the emperor at times joined by his sisters and the women of the harem. His pleasure in the journey would be only briefly disrupted by information brought to him by his third son, the notably ambitious Khurram, that once again the eldest, Khusraw, was involved in sedition, this time a plot to assassinate his father as he hunted near Kabul. Although initially shocked and upset by the news, Jahangir quickly recovered his poise. The scheme had been discovered early, the co-conspirators quickly arrested, the emperor was unharmed. Even more importantly, Jahangir had grown confident in his control of the throne. Although professing a desire to torture the perpetrators, he was loath to disrupt the pleasures of the court progress and, in the end, Jahangir simply sent them off to be imprisoned or executed. In an interesting twist, among those suspected of support for Khusraw was Ghiyas Beg, the father of Mihrunnisa, the woman who would later marry Jahangir and eventually take the title of Nur Jahan. The emperor's future father-in-law was temporarily placed under house arrest but eventually accusations were dropped. The suspected ringleader of the plot, Sultan-Shah Afghani, was ordered shot in Lahore's main square, Khusraw was returned to chains and Jahangir continued hunting towards Agra.[17] The imperial banners entered the capitol at the end of February 1608 after an absence of almost three years.

Part Three

Agra, 1608–13

5

Relationships at the royal court

The nobility

Jahangir would remain in Agra for the next five years, consolidating his relationship with the Mughal nobility and establishing the patterns of royal life. In theory, the Mughal emperor was at the very centre of imperial power, from which position he directed a 'pervasive network of authoritative, hierarchical relationships', strategically assigning position and wealth and just as swiftly and unequivocally removing it.[1] The authority of the emperor was never absolute however, but remained a fragile product of careful and constant negotiation and mutual conciliation.[2] That becomes evident in Jahangir's relationship with some of the older notables at the court, whose long years of service to the dynasty gave them a perhaps startling degree of autonomy. When Raja Man Singh finally visited the royal court after having resisted six or seven earlier summonses, Jahangir compared him to Khan Azam, 'one of the adversarial old wolves of this eternal dynasty', adding, 'what these two have done to me and what I have done to them only God – and perhaps no one else – knows'.[3]

That Jahangir was aware of the fragile nature of his authority is indicated by his zealous guardianship of the attributes of kingship. Jahangir defended his sovereignty in both grand and petty ways. In his twelfth year, he described the special items of dress that only he was allowed to wear, including a long sleeveless jacket with front buttons, which Jahangir called the *nadiri*. That would be worn over the *qaba*, a long robe with a side-fastening, which was also set aside for kings. In addition, Jahangir claimed for monarchs a vest of Gujarati satin and a silk turban and cummerbund woven through with gold and silver threads. Confirming that Akbar had similarly imposed standards on the wardrobes of his elites, he added to the list the Tusi shawl, which had been his father's exclusive garment.

In his sixth regnal year, he was required to rein in the behaviours of Mughal frontier commanders. Stationed at a distance and thereby better able to circumvent imperial control, some had begun to perform certain court rituals and demand displays of obeisance that implied a degree of independent sovereignty. In response, Jahangir clearly identified the markers of kingship that he felt must be exclusive to monarchs, calling on the ancestral law code, the Chinggisid Tora, for support.[4] Issuing a set of decrees which he named his *Regulations*, he began by declaring that to sit in the *jharoka-i darshan* was forbidden to all but the emperor. In addition, members of a commander's retinue could not be given titles or be forced to salute him. They could not be made to walk in front of their commander, nor could they be ordered to make obeisance, *korunush* or *taslim*, before him. Elephant fights were forbidden, as was forcing elephants or horses to bow. Mughal commanders were forbidden to punish by blinding[5] or cutting off noses or ears. It was forbidden to force anyone to convert to Islam. The commander may not use a seal on his documents, or have drums beaten to announce his entrance or exit.

These markers of sovereign authority varied widely in their meaning, weight and resonance. Among them were rituals that affirmed the sacred character of a ruler, such as his appearance in the *jharoka-i darshan* and the performance of ritual obeisance, by man or beast. On the other hand, marking one's movements with drums and banners was a political performance that was at times transferrable by the king to a member of the highest nobility. Although jealous of his sovereignty, Jahangir would occasionally grant the rights to others, assigning his son, Khurram, and even some of his liegemen the right of drums and banners, in what would have been among the highest of royal tributes.[6] Famously, he would also appoint drums and banners to his favourite wife, Nur Jahan, thereby making a profound and public affirmation of her high political ranking at his court. And even the *darshan* was allowed to his sons, particularly to his favourite and successor.

Balancing the power of the old guard he had inherited, Jahangir came to the throne with a stable base of loyal courtiers who had remained with him in rebellion. He continually worked to attract others – often young men of long-established families with generational ties of loyalty to the Mughal dynasty. Understanding that his own authority and power were only as strong as the loyalty of the Mughal elite, Jahangir continually and ritually affirmed these ties of mutual dependence at his royal court. Even his lifelong dependence on alcohol could be justified as a means by which relationships with the noblemen at court were enhanced. At his regularly scheduled drinking parties, Jahangir carefully explained, his courtiers became 'intoxicated with the wine of loyalty'.[7] His very first Nowruz celebration at the palace in Agra had been a spectacular party featuring musicians, singers, dancing gypsies and 'and charmers of India, who could seize the hearts of angels with their blandishments'. There Jahangir had commanded that the party's participants were allowed any drink or intoxicant of their choice, with no concern for his recently passed decree which banned the use of alcohol.[8] He quoted from Hafez, the Mughal's most beloved poet, writing:

> Cup bearer, brighten our goblet with the light of wine!
> Sing, minstrel, for the world is working as we desire.[9]

At the crowded spectacles of the public audiences and in intimate evening gatherings with his favourites, the emperor distributed honours and promotions, lavished personal attention, offered access to privilege and power. The chronicles of the time describe a constant stream of arrivals and departures – noblemen and embassies, petitioners and devotees, all paying homage at the emperor's invitation or demand, in a recurring ritual reinforcement of loyalty, fealty and patronage. His handling of his notables proved effective. In the twenty-two years of his reign, the only uprisings he would experience, apart from the brief revolt of Mahabat Khan in 1624, came from princes of the royal blood.

Gifting

In the constant ebb and flow of visiting nobility, each arrival was accompanied by lavish gifting which affirmed fealty and patronage, a common practice at the royal courts of the Islamic world. Ceremonial gifting took place continually, with any new arrival from the provinces, embassy from a rival court, the military front or diplomatic exchange. Usually the gifting was public, often occurring at the third of the emperor's daily audiences, but an intimate might invite the emperor to a private gathering and there display gifts for his approval. At the Mughal court, the most prestigious of the gifting ceremonies came at the beginning of a new regnal year, marked by the Persian New Year [Nowruz], when the elites of the court 'attained the felicity' of performing *korunush* and *taslim*, the ritual genuflections required before the emperor that reaffirmed fealty. As a central part of their homage to the emperor, gifts were not only a mark of respect but also a reflection of the value placed on the relationship by both parties. As the Safavid ambassador explained in a dispatch from Agra, the gifts and presents he had carried to Jahangir were 'worthy of the rank of both giver and recipient'.[10]

The gifts brought to Jahangir's court were often of great monetary value, as Jahangir noted appreciatively in his memoir. At times the offerings must have seemed an onerous tax for those visitors coming before the king. Every official appearance required an offering; the more spectacular gifts could enhance the warmth of a visitor's reception, improve a nobleman's reputation, even profoundly impact his promotions and honours. When the emperor found nothing desirable among the gifts, on the other hand, the presenter was 'embarrassed', on at least one occasion sending those articles judged insufficient for the king as gifts to the women's quarters.

Jahangir clearly relished the attention and the largesse of visitors to the royal court, filling his memoir with lists of offerings: entire herds of elephants, Arabian horses, trained hunting cheetahs and birds of prey, quantities of fine gemstones and worked jewellery, luxurious textiles and works of art. Certain desirable gifts had been hinted at in advance, as when Jahangir received nine large hunting dogs, among other luxury goods, as a gift from the Shah of Iran. In particular, unique and glamorous foreign goods were welcomed by the emperor. Europeans struggled to find appropriately rarefied jewels and gifts for the emperor, but the Englishman Sir Thomas Roe claimed that cases of red wine would suffice, and also assured his supporters that large high-quality paintings, preferably those including many faces, would be welcomed.[11] When his father-in-law, the I'timaduddawla, hosted him in 1619, illuminating the lake around his assembly with torches and lanterns of every colour, among his offerings was a throne of gold and silver with legs in the shape of lions. Jahangir described it as superior to any offering he had yet received, and not only showed gratitude to the giver but also lavishly rewarded the European goldsmith who made it, giving him coins, a horse and an elephant and honouring him with a title: *Hunarmand*, the artisan.

Yet Jahangir was aware of the burden these extravagant tributes imposed on his courtiers, and he could be carefully abstemious when he chose to be. He described replicating the delicate interaction between Akbar and his courtiers, writing that during the seventeen or eighteen days of Nowruz one of the great noblemen of his father's court would host a daily reception, at which their offerings of jewels, textiles, elephants and horses would be made to their guest of honour, the emperor. Akbar would reciprocate that honour by attending the gatherings, selecting just a few gifts and returning the rest to the host. Jahangir claimed that he too was sensitive to the comfort and ease of his servants and, like his father, at times accepted only a few choice items 'in order to make the giver happy', returning almost everything else.

For those who were unable to offer rich gifts, Jahangir welcomed tribute that carried sentimental value rather than monetary worth. A Naqshbandi shaykh from the Uzbek territories, arriving before the king with a poem written in Babur's own handwriting, was treated with great reverence. Because the emperor was known for his interest in natural wonders, a visitor would arrive at the royal court with unusual animals, plants, technologies, even entertainment. When a courtier returned to the emperor's side from a tour of duty in the Deccan with a team of jugglers, the delighted emperor recorded his own reaction to their performance, wondering at their ability to juggle ten balls of various sizes.

No visitors were more laden with treasure than those who came from the royal court of the Safavid shah. At the end of March 1611, an embassy led by Yadgar-Ali Sultan brought a letter of condolence for the death of Akbar and gifts for Jahangir which included fifteen hundred pieces of precious fabrics, silk brocade and velvets, and rare black fox pelts from Russia, along with too many other choice items to list.[12] The gifts also included fifty horses from the royal stables of the Shah, bearing spun gold saddles, which were 'so fine and so rare that no king could imagine having more than one in his royal stable'. If the description of the Shah's gifts seems an exaggeration, we need only turn to another report, that of the English ambassador Sir Thomas Roe, who watched the arrival of the Persian ambassador at the Mughal court in October 1616, carrying an astounding array of gifts, including '3 tymes 9 mules of Persian and Arabia, this being a Ceremonious number among them, 9 mles very faire and lardge, 7 Camells laden with velvet... two chests of Persian Cloth of gold', as well as bejewelled daggers and swords, rubies, Venetian looking glasses and '21 Camells of wine of the grape'.[13] Roe too had brought looking glasses from Venice, but his gifts were so humble in comparison to those of the Safavids, that 'I was ashamed of the relation'.

Not all of the rarities and treasure that so delighted Jahangir were gifts. Like Akbar before him, the emperor was so anxious to have curiosities brought to his court that he commissioned his noblemen, stationed in a port city or sent on a buying trip abroad, to actively seek out odd or unique things.[14] Mughal craftsmen travelled with the hajj pilgrims to find new styles and carry them back to the royal court, along with foreign musicians and their instruments.[15] Safavid Iran proved a fruitful source by which Jahangir could acquire valuables for his collection. In his eighth regnal year, Jahangir sent his courtier, Muhammad Husayn Khan Chelebi, on an expedition through Iran to Istanbul, to locate and purchase jewels and rarities.[16] When his journey led him to the royal court of the Safavid king, Shah Abbas (1571–1629), the Mughal agent produced a literal shopping list of the items he had been ordered to purchase for the Mughal Emperor. The items listed, in particular turquoise and bitumen, were in some cases so rare that Abbas personally intervened to make sure that they could be supplied to the Mughal ruler, and gently scolded Jahangir for not having requested them directly from the Shah.

In 1616, Jahangir wrote to Adil Shah of Bijapur to request any particularly fine wrestlers or swordsmen he might have. While the Bijapuri fencers proved to be only mediocre, Jahangir was quite taken with the wrestler, named Sher Ali, who managed to defeat all of the Mughal champions. He became a member of the emperor's retinue, rewarded with an elephant and cash, as well as a jagir and the title *Pahlavan Paytakht*, Wrestler/Champion at the Foot of the Throne.[17] Jahangir had requests even for European monarchs. Manuel Pinheiro, a Jesuit close to the emperor, brought gifts from Jahangir to the Portuguese Viceroy, along with a letter asking for a set of European body armour. Philip III sent it as requested in 1611, one suit of armour to Jahangir and another to Muqarrab Khan, the governor of Surat and emperor's representative in Goa, writing to the Viceroy on which ship to look for them, explaining that they were 'both engraved and golden, but one is more exquisite'.[18]

Muqarrab Khan, the Mughal governor of Gujarat, acted as Jahangir's permanent liaison at the Portuguese port of Goa, authorized 'to purchase any rarities he could get hold of there for the royal treasury ... without consideration for cost ... [to pay] any price the Franks asked for whatever rarities he could locate'. In 1610, he brought Abyssinian slaves and Arabian horses, as well as longed-for European goods and oddities. An unpublished Jesuit chronicle claimed that in 1611 Muqarrab Khan held a brief diplomatic meeting with the Viceroy in Goa but failed to acquire a rare piece of furniture valued at thirty thousand cruzados. Jahangir is said to have been furious, and 'harshly criticized his advisor and friend'.[19] Among Muqarrab Khan's successes, however, was the purchase of a North American turkey, which so intrigued the emperor that he had his artists paint its image to accompany his memoir's text. Likewise, a zebra from Africa seemed to Jahangir as if decorated by the paintbrush of God. 'Since these animals looked so extremely strange to me', wrote the king, 'I both wrote of them and ordered the artists to draw their likeness in the *Jahangirama* so that the astonishment one has at hearing them would increase by seeing them'.[20]

Jahangir was particularly known to welcome dynastic memorabilia from Central Asia. The Mughal had long relied on their particularly charismatic lineage to affirm their authority as kings, and each generation toyed with the possibility of an invasion of the lost Timurid territories of Mawarannahr. Jahangir would justify the Mughal's inability to retake these territories by commenting that 'neither I nor my father, nor my grandfather, or my great-grandfather, Babur Shah, are as great as Timur; so we never allow ourselves to sit on his kingdom's throne in Samarqand'.[21] From the first days of his reign, however, Jahangir had expressed proprietary interest in lands he described as 'ancestral' and 'hereditary'. In 1608 one of his noblemen gifted the emperor a cup of white jade, which had been produced in Samarqand in the mid-fifteenth century for Timur's grandson, Ulugh Beg, whose name was carved along the exterior rim. Jahangir added his own name and that of his father to the inscription. Even more exciting was the arrival of a ruby, a gift from the Safavid Shah, also originating in the treasure of Ulugh Beg, inscribed with his name, his father's and his grandfather's. Once again, Jahangir had his name added, commenting that the presence of his ancestors' names on the item made its possession 'auspicious'.[22]

While the emperor was the recipient of institutionalized largesse, there was a high degree of reciprocity. In return for the treasures presented to him, his visitors and foreign courts received their own gifts from the king. Even the simple gift of apples to the Safavid ambassador Sayyid Hassan in 1620 was enhanced by Jahangir's assertion that they came from his own table and were the best apples he himself had ever tasted. The Safavid ambassador, bearer of extraordinary gifts, was returned home with an equally generous selection of jewels and wealth in rupees, and Jahangir's embassies to Iran may have even surpassed the Shah's for effect. When the Mughal ambassador Khan Alam entered Qazvin he led a procession of a thousand imperial servants, and in their train were 'ten huge elephants furnished with golden platforms... and all sorts of animals – tigers, panthers, Indian antelope and deer, leopards, rhinoceros, birds that could speak, and water buffalo that drew palanquins and carts'.[23]

For his own noblemen, Jahangir proffered promotions and honours, accompanied by jewels and treasure, beautifully caparisoned horses and elephants or jewelled swords and daggers, and honours such as to be accompanied by drums and banners, advantageous new titles, and positions in the imperial bureaucracy or military command. A common gift offered by Jahangir at the royal court was a robe of honour, or *khilat*.[24] The tradition of khilat is ancient, perhaps originating among the nomads of Central Asia, and was a well-established tradition in the pre-Mughal royal courts of India. Sultan Tughluq of Delhi is said to have ritually distributed two hundred thousand robes each year. Non-Muslim royal courts shared the ritual of khilat, as at the court of Vijayanagar in the sixteenth-century Deccan.[25] The gift of khilat was an acknowledgement of loyalty, and it was through that ritual offering that a ruler conferred honour and protection on a guest or a member of the courtly elite. Acceptance of the robes not only acknowledged the honour received by the recipient, but also established the reciprocity of the relationship. The robes themselves were often very luxurious – Jahangir mentions their embroidery with gold and silver threads – but the material value of the robe was not as important as the honour implicit in the presentation, reinforced by the public nature of the ceremony. Of greatest value were those robes that had been worn, or passed over, by the emperor himself, and that henceforth carried the charisma of the royal person, his *barakat* or blessing, and 'ritually incorporated' the recipient into the body of the emperor.[26]

The Mughals, like their predecessors in India and across the Muslim world, distributed khilat routinely. Abu'l Fazl reported that in Akbar's time a thousand robes were prepared each season, and 120 were on hand at any given time, 'for such occasions as the start of the solar and lunar New Years, and the king's solar and lunar birthday, Eid, the anniversary of succession, and important life-cycle ceremonies, promotion into the *mansabdari* system and promotion within it'.[27] Being offered the gift of an emperor's robe was a high tribute, tying the nobility even closer to their emperor in an intimate and inclusive bond that identified the recipient as an honoured member of the inner circle. Jahangir recorded dozens of khilat ceremonies at his court every year, on festival days and auspicious occasions such as military victories, birthdays or marriages, even to newly released prisoners. Jahangir granted robes of honour to visitors of distinction – ambassadors from the Safavid royal court, Sufi shaykhs from Samarqand, a particularly fine poet offering panegyric verse. Other garments of the king were often gifted, as in 1617, when Jahangir sent a gold-embroidered imperial *nadiri* vest to his son Khurram, then leading the Mughal armies in the Deccan. The gift was particularly significant because not only was the *nadiri* a garment reserved for the sovereign but, as the message sent with it explained, this particular vest had been worn by the king on the very day that Khurram had left Ajmer to take up the Deccani campaign.[28] Immediately afterwards, caught up in the display of personal generosity, Jahangir took off his own turban and gifted it to his vizier and father-in-law, I'timaduddawla, as a sign of the king's favour.

Not a public ritual, but often involving the greater nobility, the imperial weighing ceremony was an important gifting opportunity at the Mughal court. The weighing of the king had long been a tradition of Indian royalty. Rulers were weighed against a variety of luxury items, the sum of which was then offered as a charitable contribution, to the impoverished and the deserving, in a ceremonial demonstration of the authority and largesse of kings. Akbar, quick to take on the politically useful practices of other communities, adopted the ritual early in his reign because, as Jahangir explained, he was generous and 'appreciated the custom'.[29] Artists in the Mughal ateliers painted many detailed miniatures of the ceremony, illustrating the weighing mechanism. From Akbar's time, twice a year, on their lunar and solar birthdays, the emperor (and in turn the princes) were seated in an enormous pan suspended from the arm of a balance beam; a second pan, into which the goods were placed, hung from the other arm of the beam. According to his memoir, many of Jahangir's weighing ceremonies took place in the women's quarters, in the apartments of the emperor's mother. After his marriage to Nur Jahan in 1611, she would take charge of each weighing, both solar and lunar, a role that affirmed her powerful position. Jahangir would write that with his favourite wife making the arrangements, the charitable event became even more lavish. The results of the weighings were a truly extravagant act of imperial largesse, and often it was the women of the harem who took charge of its eventual distribution, thereby enhancing their own profiles and reputations.[30] At a solar weighing ceremony in his tenth regnal year, Jahangir was weighed twelve times, each time against a different material: gold, quicksilver, silk, and a variety of perfumes, such as ambergris, musk, sandalwood, aloes and others. In addition to the weighings, the charitable offering included a sheep, a goat and a chicken for every year of the emperor's life.

Weighings were considered to be propitious and could be staged as imperial efforts against misfortune. Jahangir recorded a weighing ceremony arranged for Khurram when the prince's health was not good, and on another occasion for himself to drive away ill omens. The weighing in 1610 had been an effort to counteract an inauspicious solar eclipse. The princes were weighed on their solar and lunar birthdays, like the king; and on rare occasions, the emperor even honoured a non-royal person with a ceremonial weighing. On receiving an optimistic diagnosis for his ailing grandson, Shah Shuja, Jahangir weighed the astrologer against gold, and send him home with the resulting sixty-five hundred rupees as a gift.[31] When Ustad Muhammad, an incomparable flute player, composed and performed a ghazal for the emperor, he was rewarded by being weighed against rupees. In addition, Jahangir gave the musician an elephant and a howdah, on which he and his rupees, in stacks around him, were paraded all the way to his home.[32] A poet was weighed against gold, which he then received, for his qasida about the Seljuk Sultan Sanjar.[33] On another occasion, the storytelling of Mulla Asad so amused the king that he was given a robe of honour, a horse, an elephant and a palanquin as well as the results of his weighing: four thousand, four hundred rupees. The emperor offered Mulla Asad a rank among his mansabdars, and even ordered him to keep himself available whenever members of the royal court gathered for a chat![34]

Viewings and interactions

The emperor's day was tightly organized around specific ritual appearances and interactions with his nobility. Carefully emulating the public audiences offered by Akbar, Jahangir made himself visible at a specific palace window, the *jharoka-i darshan*, each morning. Like the royal weighing ceremony, the ritual of darshan had deep roots in local devotional traditions. In Hindu worship, the viewing of the deity, or darshan, implies active and creative seeing: the worshippers take darshan (*darshan lena*), while the deity gives darshan (*darshan dena*).[35] The viewing is mutual, in that one sees the deity while being seen by the deity in an act of reciprocity that is at the heart of devotion.[36] For kings the darshan became an explicit affirmation of sacred rule. Akbar absorbed the powerful ritual of darshan into his complex of symbols and displays of divine sovereignty, making ritual appearances at the viewing window each day at dawn so that the general public might witness both sun and emperor, and receive the blessings of both simultaneously.

Like his father, Jahangir offered an 'auspicious viewing' at seven o'clock in the morning, posing in a specific window on the outer wall of the palace, facing a public courtyard. At noon, he showed himself again, but this event additionally offered the emperor an opportunity for entertainment: dancers, musicians and other performances took place before the darshan, including wild animal fights, which included 'elephants and gazelles jousting and men tempting their fate with lions'.[37] An English visitor described Jahangir's elephant fights, as 'the bravest spectacle in the world' in which the animals 'would exceedingly gore and cruentate one another by their murdering teeth'.[38] Another foreign observer expressed gentile discomfort at what he considered Jahangir's unseemly enjoyment of the combat.[39]

The emperor's third formal appearance took place at four in the afternoon, in the *divan-i 'amm* (the hall of public audience), and was an opportunity to not only be seen by the public, but also to interact with the attendees.[40] Staged around Jahangir at the *durbar* were his noblemen, carefully positioned by rank, so that the princes and those of greatest importance were closest to the emperor, within a red railing, with other liegemen and servants outside. There, in what Thomas

Roe would describe as a veritable theatre of power, the emperor accepted gifts, offered promotions and assigned honours.[41]

The Mughal emperors combined their public viewings with the royal dispensation of justice, allowing the public to not only pay obeisance but also to directly petition the emperor in a performance of perfect rule. As Abu'l Fazl explained, 'By their presence in this space ... the harassed and oppressed of the population may freely represent their wants and desires.'[42] Carefully maintaining his emphasis on Islamic strictures that a legitimate king offer justice, Jahangir's appearance 'every day as usual' allowed his subject to submit petitions, and receive imperial judgement. The emperor's daily schedule was closely limited by the requirement for regular scheduled viewings. Observers at the royal court commented that this was a heavy responsibility and a burden for the emperor, asserting that his failure to appear for more than a day or two would be seen by some as a reason for public unrest, even mutiny.[43]

At eight o'clock in the evening, after his supper, Jahangir would once again gather with his noblemen, this time in the private audience hall, the 'Guzel khan, a faire court with a stone throne in the middle'. This was a much more exclusive and intimate gathering, 'to which none are invited but great qualitye, and few of these without leave. Where he discourses of all matters with great affability'.[44] The English merchant Hawkins described 'a private roome where none can come but such as himselfe nominateth (for two yeeres together I was one of his attendants here)'.[45] There Jahangir would remain for a few hours, eating fruit and drinking wine, dealing with matters of state and conversing with his intimates. 'The course is unchangeable', Roe wrote. 'These is noe business done with him concerning the state, government, disposition of war or peace, but at one of these two last places, where it is publiquely propounded and resolved.'[46]

The wine of loyalty

There can be little doubt that his drinking affected the business of the court, although Jahangir carefully kept his consumption restricted to the evening hours. When Roe described the court's daily schedule, he carefully added a proviso, commenting, 'The course is unchangeable, except sicknes or drinck prevent it.'[47] The real business of the court was managed in the late afternoon and evening, but 'often the [durbar] time is prevented by a drowsiness which possess his Majestie from the fumes of Backus'.[48] Stories of the emperor's insobriety were not just hearsay. Although the emperor claimed to limit himself to six cups of wine each evening, an amount which Roe claimed increased the emperor's good temper, it would eventually put him to sleep on his throne, thereby ending his night audiences. An expansive Jahangir invited Thomas Roe to drink with him on his birthday. 'So drinking and commanding others, his Majestie and all his lords became the finest men I ever saw, of a thousand humours.... When he could not hold up his head, hee lay down to sleepe and wee all departed', wrote Roe. 'He had been very busy with his cups', Roe confirmed on a later occasion, 'and suddenly fell asleepe'.[49]

Alcohol had been a particular scourge of the Mughal dynasty, a history of which Jahangir was aware.[50] As we have seen, both of his brothers and an uncle had been killed by their excessive consumption of alcohol and Jahangir was quite public about his own struggle to manage addiction. In his memoir, the emperor straightforwardly depicted his own descent into alcoholism, describing the shift from wine to liquor, constantly increasing the quantities over a nine-year span.[51] By the age of thirty, he wrote, he was drinking so heavily and subsisting on so little food that his hands continually shook; he was so dissipated that he needed servants to help him hold the cup to drink. When Hakim Humam, one of Akbar's doctors, was finally called in, he did not mince words, warning the prince that his life was at risk and predicting he would last no more than six months were he to continue drinking at that pace. The prince was made to listen because, he wrote, the doctor's words were spoken in kindness 'and life is precious'. The remedy for his consumption of such enormous quantities of alcohol had been, Jahangir explained, not only to cut back, but also instead to shift to opiate-based cocktails, taking eight *surkhs* of opium in the afternoon, another six *surkhs* in the evening, in addition to the daily six cups of wine and cocktails.[52] Confining his drinking to the end of the day, he added the claim that he abstained on Thursdays (marking the day of his ascension) and the holy day of Fridays, although it is clear in his own record that Thursdays would in fact be regularly celebrated with drinking parties. When he turned forty-six, he claimed to have been maintaining this level of consumption for fifteen years. He would continue to reference his own regular use of opium and alcohol until his death. While Jahangir was willing to add controls to his drinking, and discuss it with a startling degree of openness, he remained an alcoholic and an addict for the rest of his life.

While having banned the consumption of alcohol in his early decrees, he swung between railing against alcohol and pushing copious amounts of it on his courtiers and family. Among those at court, he seems to have punished individuals who drank without his express permission (or personal participation). Roe would write, 'Though drunkenness be a common and a glorious vice, and an exercise of the kings, it is so strictly forbidden that no many can enter Guzelkhan... but the Porters smell his breath.'[53] Jahangir was aware that others at his court drank heavily, apart from himself. Amongst the most important of his nobles, Raja Bhao Singh of Amber died in December 1621 of an addiction to wine. Jahangir reported that the Raja's brother and nephew had both died as alcoholics.[54] He respectfully added that two wives and eight concubines of the raja immolated themselves on the Raja's funeral pyre. When his intimate companion Khan Jahan Lodi's addiction to wine began to ruin his health, the Khan made the decision to immediately and completely quit drinking. A horrified Jahangir begged him to reconsider, strenuously arguing that the safest approach would be to simply cut back, and drink in moderation. The nobleman ignored the emperor's advice, abstained and 'manfully' overcame his addiction.[55]

A family retainer who had been given as a slave to Humayun by Shah Tahmasp many years earlier and had served the Mughal emperors ever since was described by Jahangir, on the event of his death at age ninety, to have not for a single moment in his life been without the pleasure of wine.[56] When another long-time servant of the emperor died in 1608, Jahangir pointed out that man's vastly immoderate habits had always included drinking during Ramadan. His fatal mistake and the reason for his death, the emperor claimed, was the servant's decision to make up for his previous failings by completely abstaining from wine during the annual fast.[57] In 1621, the emperor recorded the death of servant whose task had been the safekeeping of the emperor's drugs. He would be replaced by two servants, one in charge of opium and another in charge of wine.

For all that its impact on his family had been so cruel, Jahangir himself described encouraging his sons to drink alcohol, even scolding the abstemious Khurram who at age twenty-four, though married and a father, had never tasted wine. Jahangir coerced his reluctant son, arguing that 'kings and princes have always drunk'.[58] The prince eventually acquiesced, although Jahangir complained that it had taken great persistence to convince him. Jahangir's second son, Parvez, would become a very heavy drinker. When Roe met with him in Burhanpur, where Parvez was serving as governor alongside Abdur Rahim Khankhanan, he brought the prince gifts, including a case of wine. Roe claimed that Parvez began drinking immediately. 'After I stayed a while', the Englishman wrote, 'I h[e]ard hee was drunck', and eventually a servant was sent to tell Roe to go home and make a new appointment for visiting Parvez.[59] Foreign embassies, including the English and the Safavid, quickly learned that the gift of alcohol would be well received at the Mughal royal court. 'There is nothing more welcome here, nor ever I saw a man so enamored of drincke as bothe King and the Prince [Khurram] are of red wyne', Thomas Roe would write, 'I thinck four or five handsome cases of... wyne will be more welcome than the richest jewell in Cheapesyde.'[60]

Punishment and clemency

Although he had famously committed notable acts of brutality while a rebellious prince, once enthroned, Jahangir would not be known for displays of exceptional cruelty. To be sure, it was a violent age and the emperor was not exempt from the standards of the time. The Englishman, Sir Thomas Roe, described Jahangir's sentencing of one hundred thieves, the chief among them torn apart by dogs and the others executed, their bodies displayed on the streets.[61] Jahangir was capable of a casual cruelty and callous disregard. Early in his reign, while travelling from Lahore to Kabul, the court progress passed a deep pond. On learning that locals believed it housed a man-eating crocodile, Jahangir decided to test the veracity of the tale and ordered a sheep thrown into the water. When the sheep managed to escape unscathed, the emperor ordered a servant to enter into the lake. To that servant's good fortune, the man-eater did not display himself and Jahangir declared the legend false.[62] On another occasion, a sanyasi was in a meditative state of extreme rigidity. Having had him brought to court so that Jahangir could observe his extraordinary condition, the clearly fascinated emperor decided to experiment by dosing the sanyasi with quantities of alcohol, suggesting that drunkenness might inspire movement. The holy man stayed rigid until, having had a great deal of alcohol poured into him, he finally lost consciousness and was carried away like a corpse. Jahangir took no responsibility for the experiment's potential ill-effects. When the sanyasi survived, the emperor blithely commended a merciful God.[63]

Jahangir exhibited a more egregious cruelty in response to a hunting incident, in which a groom and two palanquin bearers stepped too close and startled a nilgai just as the emperor was about to shoot.[64] The animal shied and escaped, and the outraged Jahangir had the groom immediately executed and the palanquin bearers hamstrung and paraded about on donkeys to warn his retinue of the price of carelessness. With seemingly no remorse, Jahangir ended the day hunting on horseback with hawks and falcons. On his visit to Gujarat, Jahangir told of visiting a beautiful garden where a gardener informed him that a servant of Muqarrab Khan had cut down several trees that overlooked the river. The emperor was outraged by the spoiled view. He investigated, found the story to be true and had the servant's index fingers cut off as a warning to others, adding that if Muqarrab Khan had known and approved of the desecration of the garden, he would have been punished as well.[65] All the same, Jahangir's orders do not stand out as exceptional. Akbar himself had offered similar punishments. In 1562, Akbar was at the village of Sanganir when it was reported that a *cheetaban* (cheetah keeper) had stolen a pair of shoes. The emperor's verdict was that the thief's feet should be cut off.[66]

For the nobility at the royal court, although the rewards for imperial service could be great, intimacy with a king was treacherous. Pelsaert, the Dutch merchant, would exclaim, 'A very small fault, or a trifling mistake, may bring a man to the depths of misery or to the scaffold... Wealth, position, love, friendship, confidence, everything hangs by a thread.'[67] Mutribi, the Central Asian Naqshbandi visitor to Jahangir's court, would write, 'Some people... employ themselves in well-wishing for kings from afar. Others throw their hearts and souls into danger and remain day and night in visible proximity around kings.'[68] Their comments can be understood as a universal trope of the pre-modern world rather than an indictment of a particular court or king. While he was clearly capable of insensitivity and malice, there is surprisingly little evidence that Jahangir was vindictive or unforgiving with the members of his nobility. His regular acts of benevolence and forgiveness notably appear not only in the king's writings, but those of his contemporaries.

Ruling over an imperial milieu that required loyalty to be continually reinforced and reanimated, Jahangir was quick to offer clemency. He not only ordered large-scale imperial amnesties to mark special occasions but also regularly offered reprieves on an individual level, even for those amongst his intimates who had caused him personal harm. Abdur Rahim 'the Donkey', who had been so cruelly punished for his support of Khusraw's revolt, was pardoned and returned to imperial service only a few years later, in 1610.[69] At the end of Khusraw's revolt, Jahangir publicly scolded Khan Azam for disloyalty, described by the emperor as unpardonable. His jagir was taken but his offenses were otherwise overlooked. It was not until the end of March in 1614 that Jahangir, suspecting that Khan Azam might undermine the military campaign against Mewar because of his lingering preference for Khusraw, ordered the nobleman imprisoned in Gwalior. After less than a month, however, Jahangir claimed that Akbar had come to him in a dream to ask for the release of his former milk-brother. Jahangir had Khan Azam moved to the fortress of Agra and by mid-April in the following year, the nobleman was allowed to return to court. Jahangir admitted to feeling a bit sheepish. While arguing that the punishment had been completely justified, he described feeling a great deal of personal embarrassment in meeting Khan Azam's eyes.[70]

Jahangir expressed regret and shame for his own actions on several occasions. One of his more well-known reversals occurred in 1618, and the story as told by Jahangir gives us an illustration of his understanding and application of justice within the complicated networks of his nobility. A young *khanazad*, Subhan-Quli, was accused of having planned the assassination of his patron, Islam Khan. The young man's relatives, all of whom were in service to the throne, argued that the accusation was unsubstantiated, the event had happened some time earlier and no evidence existed to prove his guilt. Jahangir agreed to spare him, but Subhan-Quli fled to Agra. He was quickly captured and brought before the court in chains, at which point Jahangir ordered him executed. His relatives again intervened, begging for clemency, and Jahangir once again agreed to spare the young man's life. By the time the order went out, however, the execution of Subhan-Quli had been completed. While quick to justify the death as well deserved, Jahangir described himself as deeply regretful. Conceding the potential for future errors in judgement, he ordered that henceforth any execution he ordered should be delayed until sundown. If the order had not been rescinded by then, the execution could take place as he had commanded.[71]

Jahangir wrote of his own remorse when an effort to interfere in the lives of his subjects backfired. A blacksmith came to ask the king to convince a widow he was courting to marry him; Jahangir off-handedly commented that he could prove his love by leaping from the window. The blacksmith immediately threw himself from the palace heights. The emperor ordered his own doctors to assist the dying man, but they could not save his life. An apologetic Jahangir described the event in his memoir, commenting: 'I regretted having spoken in jest and was dreadfully sorry!'[72] In both cases, it was the emperor himself who reported the tale, confided his error and expressed personal regret.

In contrast to his callous response when a hunt was spoiled by a servant's carelessness, Jahangir was magnanimous when another hunt was spoiled by a dangerous mishap of his own making. When members of his court were out hunting for game, a lion suddenly emerged and threatened the group. The courtiers made no effort to kill the beast, but sent for the emperor himself. Jahangir rushed to the scene, but his first shot merely wounded the lion, which turned to attack and maul a falconer standing nearby. At the emperor's second shot, the lion rushed a cluster of his servants, who collided in an effort to get out of its way. In their wild attempt to flee, they knocked the emperor down and ran over him, a few stepping directly on his chest in their panic. When the lion was finally successfully brought down, Jahangir punished none for their clumsiness and even awarded promotions to those individuals who had managed to demonstrate bravery, reporting the entire tale in his memoir.[73]

6

Divine kingship and the imperial cult

The Majalis

As emperor, Akbar, with the help of his amanuensis and panegyrist Abu'l Fazl, had set out to construct a sovereignty that was explicitly sacred in nature, establishing him as the ultimate royal and saintly authority. To support this goal, emperor seized upon the spiritual practices of other communities – praying with and using the relics and paraphernalia of Jesuits and Parsis, memorizing 1,001 names for the sun, practising fire worship with Brahmans and Zoroastrians, following tantric dietary principles and creating the particular sacred cult he formed around himself.[1] He was, as Moin has written, a *bricoleur*, 'an intellectual handyman', creating from a variety of materials and traditions a spiritual system uniquely his own, designed to buttress his claims both spiritual and profane.[2] To a limited degree, his ancestors had been similarly willing to engage in an eclectic spiritual sampling. Timur, for example, had established his own sovereignty through references to multiple cosmologies: Persianate, Turco-Mongol and Islamic.

By mid-reign, the public rituals of the royal court reflected his increasingly confident assertions of divinity, as when Akbar had himself declared the religious authority (*mujtahid*) of the age, when he demanded that his courtiers perform prostration (*sijda*) before him, and in his adoption of the viewing ritual (*darshan*), in the model of deities. His religious innovations were met by some at his court with accusations of heresy and transgression, even apostasy. A Jesuit observer wrote that 'the court is much perplexed ... because he seems to pay homage to the sun and the moon', and another confirmed that some 'considered the king to be mad'.[3] Ultimately, his detractors remained in the minority and proved unable to undermine the power or the divine status of their king. Akbar's claims were supported by both his establishment of a royal cult and the compendium of panegyric writings by Abu'l Fazl, who effusively established the emperor's status as the *insan-i kamil*, the Perfect Man.

Among Akbar's most celebrated spiritual-intellectual undertakings were his regular court gatherings for open religious debate. The assemblies were arranged around a diverse array of religious specialists – including the Brahmans and Jains who had begun attending the Mughal court in the 1560s after Akbar's conquest of Gujarat – all of whom were invited to argue particular points of interest before and with the king.[4] Akbar was not the dynastic originator of this ritual – as early as the thirteenth century his ancestors in the Mongol capital of Kara Korum had regularly organized religious debates before the ruler – yet perhaps none have presided over so regular and so diverse a forum as that of Akbar.[5] For his son and successor, Akbar's great legacy included not only rule over a massive and relatively stable empire, but also this carefully constructed ideological claim to imperial divinity. Jahangir's contested inheritance and the weak support he received from the Mughal nobility had made it immediately necessary that he should find a way to claim his father's divine status.

Emulating his father's religious debates even as a prince in Allahabad, Jahangir invited not only the diverse members of his own royal court, but also visitors from Iran and Central Asia, priests from the Jesuit mission and other Europeans – even those who were not religious specialists or scholars were expected to represent their religious communities. Jahangir commended a Jesuit for his frank comments. 'The Padre desires to shed his blood for his law and to be a martyr', Jahangir teased, 'that is why he has come from so far and speaks so freely, without any regard, what he knows against Maumetans and Gentiles.'[6] Confirming the open nature of these conversations, the Englishman Edward Terry, who remained at Jahangir's court for four years, would write that in Jahangir's kingdom 'every man hath libertie to professe his owne religion freely and, for any restriction I ever observed, to dispute against theirs with impunitie'.[7]

Beginning at the time of Jahangir's return to Agra in 1608 and continuing for the next three years, Abdus Sattar kept an account of 122 gatherings at the royal court, which he called assemblies, or '*majalis*'.[8] At the start of his chronicle, Sattar explained: 'The main reason for writing this book is that, since I have been at the service of Jahangir Shah for a long time and I have spent so much time with him, I made a vow to record forty reports of his nightly assemblies for the future generations. I asked him for permission in this regard, and he approved.'[9] A nobleman in the close circle of the emperor, Sattar represented the intellectual synthesis achieved at the royal court of Akbar and Jahangir. Multi-lingual and transcultural, Sattar had previously worked to translate Christian religious texts for the Mughal court. His scholarship, his facility with the languages and his familiarity with Christian works made him an invaluable aid to the emperor in these disputations with Europeans. His knowledge of Western culture was so intimate that some of the attendees at Jahangir's assemblies were led to suggest that Sattar was sympathetic to Christian positions, although Sattar quickly and defensively rejected that suggestion, clarifying his commitment to Islam.

As his chronicle confirms, the *majalis* gave the emperor a powerful platform on which to demonstrate his allegiance to his father's model and to appropriate his claims – most specifically, the mantle of divine kingship. Not simply reinforcing Jahangir's continuing alignment with Akbar's famous liberality, Sattar presented Jahangir as the Universal Manifestation [*Mazhar-i Kull*], the arbiter of all spiritual truth across all religions – a divine status previously claimed by Akbar.[10] Jahangir clearly relished the role of universal adjudicator. Sattar mentions regular occasions on which Jahangir defended the perceived quirks and particularities of non-Muslims. When his companions criticized doctrinal quarrels between Christians and Jews, Jahangir intervened to assert that those who followed Moses should be allowed their religion and those who followed Jesus likewise should be free to worship as they liked.[11] When the ulama at the assembly criticized ritual ablutions during lunar eclipses, Jahangir pointed out that Muslims prayed during an eclipse, and both prayers and ablutions were justified as acts of worship, a point for which Sattar claimed the emperor received general praise.[12] When Jahangir chose to describe and interpret his dreams during an evening session, Khan Azam claimed that as the emperor had been appointed by God, the dream was a form of guidance towards justice. Sattar went even further, adding that Jahangir was meant to sit on 'the throne of guidance' and 'to restore order to the spiritual and temporal worlds'.[13] He explained directly to the emperor that it was for him to decide right or wrong for, as the divinely appointed ruler, he held the scales of justice in his hand. A devoted subordinate, Sattar closed each debate with an assertion of Jahangir's infinite wisdom.

As Sattar's record explicitly confirmed, bonds of king and liegemen were closely tied in numerous ways, among which spiritual devotion was an integral component. The enlistment of personal disciples can be understood as the logical extension of Mughal imperial paternalism, harkening back to Babur's recommendation that his descendants socialize intimately with their retinue in order to tie its members ever more closely to the throne.[14] In such an eclectic milieu as the Mughal royal court, made up of Rajput nobles, Iranian intellectuals, Arab scholars, Turkish and Uzbek military men, local chiefs and caste leaders, diplomats, missionaries and merchants, Akbar's creation of an imperial cult based on not only fealty but spiritual devotion would supersede individual religious, ethnic or hereditary service loyalties, resulting in a body of intensely loyal courtiers.[15] Select disciples marked their initiation with a small portrait of the emperor: 'They looked upon it [the portrait] as the standard of loyal friendship, and the advance guard of righteousness and happiness and they put it wrapped up in a small jeweled case, on the top of their turbans.'[16]

Jahangir imitated his father's enrolment of loyal courtiers, positioning himself at the heart of a personal devotional movement within the royal household. This was a process he had begun in the days of rebellion, performing sovereign authority at his counter-court in Allahabad, where he had ordered his chief judge to vet potential candidates for discipleship and let the prince know to whom he should present a portrait.[17] Those chosen were warned to reject malice towards people of other faiths and to kill no animal outside of the hunt and war. The emperor claimed his disciples were themselves 'manifestations of divine light', to be exalted as each deserved.[18]

In the *Majalis*, Sattar identified himself as one of Jahangir's 'humblest disciples', and the king his *pir*, spiritual master and guide. Another member of the Mughal nobility, Mirza Nathan, would write of his experience in being made a disciple of Jahangir.[19] A *khanazad*, 'son of the house', in hereditary service as the scion of a Persian family that had served the Mughals for three generations, in 1607 the young Mirza Nathan travelled with his father to Bengal, where he fell seriously ill. In his dream the emperor spoke to him: 'O, Nathan! Is this the time for the Tiger to lie down? Arise! We have granted you security from pain and trouble by our prayers.'[20] He awoke in perfect health and shared his dream with his commander, who passed the information to the emperor. Jahangir then enlisted Mirza Nathan 'as one of the disciples of the sublime Court… [who] honored himself by observing the formalities of obeisance and prostrations of gratitude'.[21] Nathan would receive a tiny portrait medallion of the emperor, which he affixed to his turban, just as Akbar's followers had done a generation earlier.

In formally enlisting disciples and regularly presiding over religious debates, the emperor Jahangir experimented with claims of divine rule. The record of these efforts, the *Majalis-i Jahangiri*, was in many ways a collaboration between courtier and king. Jahangir was not simply aware of Sattar's record-keeping; he encouraged and assisted in the composition of his manuscript. Demanding that his work continue well beyond the forty chapters Sattar had originally planned, Jahangir regularly checked Sattar's entries, suggested edits and even made certain that Sattar would be present to take notes on especially important nights.

If Sattar were forced to miss a gathering, other noblemen present, either Khan Azam or I'timaduddawla, were told to share the details with him afterwards so that they could be written into the record.

As scholars have noted, even with Jahangir directing and correcting Sattar's work, there is a stark contrast between Sattar's *Majalis* and Jahangir's own *Nama*.[22] Although consistent in his assertions that he was appointed by God, the emperor's memoir made no reference to the evening assemblies, nor to any messianic claims or identification with the sacred and divine. Sattar himself would describe the relationship between the two manuscripts as a thematic bifurcation, calling his own record *Shabnamcha*, a nocturnal account of sacred and spiritual discourses, and referring to the emperor's memoir as *Ruznamcha*, a daily account of Jahangir's public and profane existence. It is possible that this separation was not always or entirely intentional. Sattar at one time expressed hope that 'some of the choicest episodes recorded there might even be selected for inclusion' in the emperor's memoir.[23] In the end, however, nothing of the *Majalis* made its way to the *Nama*.

Yet assertions of a stark division between the two manuscripts are, at least on Sattar's side, exaggerated. While Jahangir very deliberately kept the religious discourses and claims of divinity out of his own official record, Sattar would not remain entirely limited to the sacred, including in his record many wide-ranging and eclectic conversations that at times came close to bawdy. The *Majalis* reveals that the discussions at the emperor's assemblies regularly veered into rambling chats on any number of topics. To be sure, if the assemblies were originally intended as sacred and spiritual discourses, the fluctuating population of participants and contributors invited to attend Jahangir's evening assembly would have severely undermined that effort. The emperor included in his evening assemblies any visitor to court who captured his attention, regularly inviting not only scholars and travelling poets, but foreign ambassadors and often even merchants.[24] Reading their various records and commentaries, one wonders if Jahangir included the English simply for the amusement of watching their bumbling rivalries with the appalled and competitive Jesuits at his court. A further impediment to a disciplined focus on Jahangir's sacred nature was the amount of alcohol he consumed throughout the assembly; he himself described a ration of six cups of wine each evening. It is no surprise then that while they confirmed, with fascination, the liberal religious discourses at the assemblies, European visitors described the emperor chatting merrily with the assembled company on 'all matters, with great affability'.[25]

Jahangir used the assemblies as opportunities for personal self-aggrandizement in many areas, proudly demonstrating, for example, his own erudition. Sattar recorded whole sessions of the *majalis* devoted to literary discussions, with the emperor proffering his own poetry, requesting original verses from the assembly and sometimes beginning a verse for the gathered elites to finish.[26] Although at one point Jahangir proudly announced that he had memorized the classical literature and was willing to be tested on his knowledge, he quickly retreated from his lofty claims, with the concession that he may have forgotten a few texts or may have missed reading some of the more obscure books![27]

In the multifarious and motley company he had assembled, Jahangir hashed out diplomatic strategies and discussed the status and scandals of imperial rivals. As always, the personality of the Safavid emperor, who both intrigued and repelled Jahangir, was the object of much discussion. The emperor gossiped about claims of the shah's illiteracy, commented on cases of Safavid oppression and, with little self-awareness, expressed disapproval regarding Abbas' relationship with an unworthy son.[28] Another regular topic of conversation in the *majalis* was the proper and appropriate use of opium, Jahangir weighing in with his own experiences and preferences.[29]

And just as the *Majalis* did not entirely reflect the careful separation and protection of a divine space that some, including its author, have suggested, even membership in Jahangir's imperial cult does not seem to have demanded discipleship in all cases. While the emperor was busy establishing relations with loyal devotees such as Mirza Nathan, it is also true that Sir Thomas Roe, the British ambassador and trade negotiator to the Mughal court, was indoctrinated into Jahangir's circle, even receiving the ceremonial portrait of the emperor to wear as a symbol of allegiance. Roe had not developed a devotional relationship with the emperor nor did he fully understand the honour he had received, admitting that its purpose confused him.[30] Roe's inclusion suggests that Jahangir was perhaps not completely serious about his own protestations of divinity, and that membership in his devotional cult was independent of belief in the emperor's sacred character.

In fact, while Jahangir actively emulated his father's cult, and was surely very serious about the valuable ties of fealty it created with intimate companions like Sattar and young noblemen like Mirza Nathan, his actions suggest a degree of scepticism about his own claims. It seems that at least by mid-reign, if not before, Jahangir was more pragmatically interested in binding courtiers to him in vows of earthly loyalty and esteem than in presenting himself as a God-King. Instead, Sattar's record confirms the ideological explanation Jahangir most regularly and confidently offered for his rule: not the emperor's own divine or sacred status, nor even religion more generally, but his having been selected by

God to establish the Perso-Islamic model of *adalat*, justice. We have already seen Jahangir's commitment to performances and portrayals of imperial justice. In the *majalis*, Jahangir regularly returned to the argument that he had been ordained to protect his subjects, and thereby ensure their peace and happiness.[31] The greatest of sins, Jahangir would point out, was doing harm to people.[32]

Sattar's record of the evening sessions confirms that through his years in Agra, Jahangir experimented openly with the concept of sacred kingship established by his audacious father. The praise and accolades composed by Sattar, a self-proclaimed devotee, were as close as Jahangir would come to commissioning a regnal panegyric on the model of Abu'l Fazl's record of Akbar's kingship. Yet Jahangir's interest and appreciation for Sattar's record faded and after only three years the project was terminated. It would not be revived, nor would another court favourite take on the role of panegyrist. Jahangir continued to compose his own account of his reign, but carefully avoided making any direct claims of a sacred nature. While visitors to his court confirmed that Jahangir continued to hold evening assemblies, in the absence of a written record the audience for his performance would include only the small number of companions who were expressly invited to participate. Any claims of a divine nature made by the emperor at the evening assembly would, by design, go unrecorded and uncelebrated. Describing Jahangir's efforts to emulate his father's construction of sacred rule, Sattar's *Majalis* in fact demonstrated the emperor's ability 'to conciliate his messianic claims with a strong engagement with reason'.[33] Regular displays of self-awareness, scepticism and even humility suggest that Jahangir was uncomfortable adopting wholesale his father's millennial and messianic pretensions. In contrast to Akbar, while Jahangir may have seen himself as a King of Kings, he was clearly much less confident that he was in fact a Saint of Saints.[34] Arguing that he was divinely chosen, the emperor resisted assertions of personal divinity. His efforts would remain self-conscious, inconsistent and, for the most part, private.

Images of the divine

Ultimately, whatever visions of divinity Jahangir might have had would be most fully displayed not in his memoir, and only inconsistently in Sattar's *Majalis*, but much more profoundly in the so-called 'allegorical paintings' of his imperial workshops. Many of these paintings were produced while the royal court was in Ajmer, 1615–18, soon after the cessation of Sattar's writings, and they perhaps sufficed as a replacement for the emperor's one attempt at a panegyric chronicle. The most extravagant of these paintings would be produced in collusion with only a small number of artists in Jahangir's atelier; their works would illustrate the fullest expressions of the emperor's claims of sacred kingship.[35] These are at the very least highly political paintings, created in support of Jahangir's kingship and power, including elements that made explicit claims of divinity. A younger court painter, Bichitr, would produce some of the most technically flawless and brilliant scenes, but most are credited to Abu'l Hasan, the 'Nadir of the Age', who had remained with Jahangir since the earliest days of his rebel court in Allahabad. The collaboration between artist and emperor exemplified Jahangir's remarkably innovative aesthetic, in which highly realistic portraiture was overlaid with symbols and icons from all available sources, in an effort to assert claims of dominion over the world, *Jahan*. What went unsaid in the more modest *Jahangirnama*, and would be only inconsistently emphasized in the *Majalis-i Jahangiri*, was boldly portrayed in the emperor's fantasy dreamscapes. Modern scholars question the meaning and justifications for the paintings. In their natural realism and emphasis on individual identity, were these images intended as more than simple allegory, and did they in fact contain cosmological significance? Azfar Moin has suggested that Mughal painting 'constituted a space where Jahangir performed his miracles', ritual acts that might protect and guard his dominions.[36]

As an increasingly popular genre at Akbar's court, portraits of the individual personalities at the royal court had long been recognized as more than an important act of memorialization but even a kind of revivification. Abu'l Fazl wrote of Akbar that 'his majesty himself sat for his likeness, and also ordered to have likenesses taken of all the grandees of the realm' as a means by which one might circumvent death and loss. 'An immense album was thus formed', added Abu'l Fazl, 'those who have passed away have received new life and those who are still alive have immortality promised to them.'[37] While their contemporaries in Safavid Iran and the Ottoman Empire were inconsistent in their production of portraiture, anxious not to be seen as ignoring Islamic strictures against the painting of living things and occasionally throwing up their hands and closing their ateliers for a generation, the Mughals were relentless in their pursuit of the mimetic portrait. Jahangir, in close collaboration with his artists, further accelerated the Mughal celebration of the individual. Traditional and innovative symbols and motifs would of course enhance the power of the image, but the quest to discover and display the unique qualities of specific persons was powerfully expressed in explicitly natural portraits. The idiosyncratic personalities who inhabited the Mughal court were portrayed with increasing accuracy, so that even in the active and crowded scenes of the imperial durbar or the royal hunt the figures who populated the paintings emerged from the page as individuals.[38] The significance of portraiture went far beyond the emperor's pleasure in realism. For masters like Abu'l Hasan a 'sense for intricate, superbly executed detail... [was] used to stress elements of character', and sympathetically reveal something of the internal psychology of his subject. The result was the deliberate creation of a sacred talismanic object which allowed the pure essence of the subjects personality to remain and to be accessed.[39] While there exists no explicit written commentary on the meaning and significance of this close attention to mimetic accuracy, Jahangir himself suggested that portraiture offered a window into the soul. When Adil Shah's representatives visited his court, Jahangir sent them home with a portrait of himself, on which he wrote:

> Our merciful glance is always in your direction
> Rest assured in the shadow of our felicity
> We have sent you our likeness
> So that you might see our inner self through our external appearance.[40]

Realistic, naturalist portraiture became so important at Jahangir's court that when a Naqshbandi scholar, Mutribi al-Assam, travelled from Uzbek-held Samarqand to the Mughal court in 1626, the emperor took the opportunity to show him paintings of the Uzbek rulers Abdullah Khan and Abd al-Mu'min and questioned him closely on the accuracy of the portrayal. When Mutribi pointed out that a chin should be more crooked and a face made thinner, Jahangir had his portraitist Abu'l Hasan summoned. Corrections were made to the paintings on the spot.[41] On another occasion, Jahangir sent Bishan Das, among his most highly favoured painters, to accompany an embassy to Iran so that on his return to India he might paint truly accurate portraits of the Safavid Shah Abbas.[42] He would be rewarded on his return with the gift of an elephant from the emperor's stables. In 1609, Muqarrab Khan brought a portrait of Jahangir's illustrious ancestor, Timur, which the Portuguese of Goa claimed had been painted by a Byzantine Christian present at Timur's defeat of the Ottoman Sultan Bayezid, in 1402. Jahangir rejected the portrait, explaining that it could not have been true to life, as promised, for it looked nothing like Timur's royal descendants. The emperor, well known for his fascination with dynastic memorabilia, wistfully commented that had it in fact been a true portrait it would be the most valuable item in his collection.[43] Even in his determined pursuit of imperial souvenirs, it was not simply the reminder of dynastic power that interested Jahangir, nor concerns for an honest provenance: it was the mimetic accuracy of the portrayal that gave it the greatest value and drove the emperor's interest in acquisition.

Unceasing in his efforts to collect ancestral portraits, Jahangir was not always so sceptical. In January of 1620, a Mughal embassy returning from the Safavid court of Shah Abbas brought with them a painting of Timur pictured in battle against the Delhi sultan, Iltutmish. Also portrayed were the 240 of the great Amir's sons and commanders who participated in the battle. Negotiations for the paintings acquisition were tense, but finally Jahangir's ambassador was able 'through his auspicious ascendant' to convince Shah Abbas, who 'knew how intent we were upon such rarities', to gain permission to bring the painting from Iran to the Mughal court.[44]

If indeed Jahangir believed that mimetic and naturalistic portraits offered the viewer a glimpse into the inner self and even a sort of immortality, surely the hyper-realism of Abu'l Hasan's allegorical paintings carried even more elaborate consequences. It is in portraying the emperor astride the globe that the allegorical paintings gave truth to those aspirations that were in fact unachievable on the mundane earthly plane. In one painting, Jahangir is shown shooting an arrow into the head of his nemesis, Malik Ambar.[45] In another he embraces Shah Abbas, in both cases physically overwhelming his diminished and seemingly insignificant companion.[46] Perhaps his own obsession with the hunt inspired Jahangir's favourite self-portrayal, astride a lion and a lamb or more tellingly for an Indian monarch, a calf, a veritable Solomon the Just Lawgiver who 'brings inimical nature to a peaceful co-existence'.[47] In portraiture Jahangir is inevitably haloed but in paintings by Bichitr and Abu'l Hasan he is additionally surrounded by layers of coded insignia not only of the Islamic world, but also boldly culled from local and Western Christian iconography.

One is tempted to suggest that for Jahangir the value of his imperial portraits may have been in the static nature of their presentation, in contrast to the sustained and relatively public performance of wisdom and judgement required of the emperor at the *majalis*. In any case, it was through the visual arts that Jahangir was most able to explore visions of his own sovereignty, like his father, the '*bricoleur*', pulling visual symbols and sacred icons from all available sources to illustrate messianic dreams of dominion over the spiritual and the material worlds. The highly naturalistic quality of Jahangiri portraiture may explain, however, why even in the most fantastical dreamscapes, although haloed and enthroned, the emperor is not represented as an idealized icon. His presence retains an undeniable physicality. Portrayed in middle age Jahangir displays a visibly thickened form, double chin, thinning hair and a slightly more furrowed brow. For Jahangir and his artists, flaws were accepted and admitted. Amongst all of the paraphernalia of kingship and divinity in the allegorical portraits, the naturalism and veracity of the portrayal remained paramount. Rejecting pretences of perfection, even in the portrayal of a dream, the emperor was unwilling to forego his very real corporeal presence.

By the end of Jahangir's reign, the realism of the portrait and its emphasis on the specific identity of the subject had begun to take precedence over technique and artistry, even naturalism. In large paintings, crowded with faces, not only was each individual carefully distinct and idiosyncratic, but even the names of those portrayed were inscribed directly onto their images, above or across their bodies. In the royal durbar, the attendees are prevented from merging into the greater backdrop of magisterial splendour and the deft illusion of the scene is lessened, all for the sake of the visual identification that was reinforced – insisted upon – by careful labelling. It is clear that the extraordinary naturalism of Mughal portraiture was not simply enjoyed as a visual trick or illusion, or a demonstration of considerable artistic skill but, in the Mughal ateliers, accurate identification of the subject had become paramount.

The well-known mid-sixteenth-century work known as 'Princes of the House of Timur', illustrating a crowded garden party, was originally painted at the court of Humayun.[48] One hundred years later, it would be re-discovered and re-imagined by Jahangir, who ordered his court artists to add to the scene the figures of himself, his father Akbar and his sons – the painting's three unrepresented generations. The stark realism of their portrayals is wildly out of place among the classical Timurid images. Perhaps in an attempt to minimize the contrast, an effort was made to repaint some of the faces of the painting's anonymous individuals. Unsatisfied with the effort, and obviously frustrated by the thorough anonymity of the figures, names were inscribed across their bodies, assigning identity to the unidentifiable. And just whose identities were appropriated? The original picnickers, whoever they may have been in Humayun's time when the painting was originally made, were in Jahangir's ateliers labelled with the names of scions of the dynasty, reaching all the way back to Timur's grandson Ulugh Beg. Taking advantage of the figures' complete unknowability, Jahangir created a powerful genealogical portrait. Affirming Abu'l Fazl's exhortation that to be fully memorialized promised immortality, Jahangir's atelier not only illustrated an occasion and marked the passing of a life, but powerfully commemorated the unique individuals who made up the Mughal royal family and populated its court.

While the imperial artists of the Mughals were impacted by the physicality of traditional South Asian fresco and sculpture, exposure to European art powerfully influenced the efforts towards realism in their ateliers.[49] Jahangir himself wrote almost nothing of the Europeans who came to his court, but their letters and memoirs describe an emperor fascinated by the artistic idioms of the West. Muqarrab Khan sent European canvases from Cambay, and visitors to Jahangir's court were encouraged to bring European paintings as gifts. Often these paintings were the source of experimentation and emulation by the artists of the imperial atelier. Sir Thomas Roe, always concerned that his gifts were despised, had quickly realized that paintings, and in particular portraits, made a welcome gift for the king. He wrote to his sponsors in England to send paintings that were dense with portraits.[50] In 1616, Jahangir forced Roe to hand over the small portrait of his fiancée to the emperor's 'Cheefe Paynter', the owner's reluctance to part with it only overcome by the promise that it would be quickly returned. Jahangir did indeed return it, and was very proud to later show him five copies of the portrait, made by his artists, which Roe admitted were very fine.[51]

Jahangir was particularly interested in Christian iconography. Jesuit visitors reported that even as a prince, Jahangir admired images of Jesus and the Madonna and 'employed the most skilled painters and craftsmen in his father's kingdom in making him the like'.[52] The Jesuits supplied many images, and even created picture books of the gospels, in order to attract the king's attention and even facilitate his conversion. On the emperor's orders, the imperial painters Basawan and Manohar experimented with Christian themes, copying angels and ascetics and studies of the Madonna and child, while experimenting with European perspective, shading, design and structure. In confirmation of Jahangir's admiration for Christian religious iconography, a painting of his royal court indicates that several images of Christ and Mary were at that time displayed on the wall behind the throne. The Lahore garden palaces he built are described by eye witnesses as having been painted with Christian religious themes in some cases.

Jahangir encouraged his artists to cover the palace walls with images, many of them portraits. The English merchant William Finch, on visiting the new Mughal palace in Lahore described seeing lavish paintings in the palace, including images of mythological angels and monsters ('Banian dews'), as well as portraits of the king's ancestors and even paintings of Westerners.[53] When Jahangir visited Srinagar in the spring of 1620, he renovated Akbar's garden and renamed it Bagh-i Nur Afza, having the garden buildings decorated with figural paintings and even setting aside one of them as a *khana-i taswiri*, picture gallery.[54] On the upper level, he explained, were paintings of Humayun and Akbar, opposite portraits of Jahangir himself and the Safavid Shah of Iran, Abbas. Then were painted images of his uncle and great uncles, and his two deceased brothers, Danyal and Murad.[55] The second floor was decorated with portraits of various of his courtiers and noblemen, while the outside of the building was covered with detailed paintings of the stations along the road to Kashmir, arranged in the correct order. Jahangir's palace in Agra also included a gallery of portraits of European leaders and sovereigns, including the pope, King Philip II of Spain and the Duke of Savoy. Sir Thomas Roe visited Jahangir's throne room in Ajmer in 1616, on the celebration of the Nowruz, and found it to be 'sett out the pictures of the King of England, the Queene, my lady Elizabeth, the Countesses of Sommersett and Salisbury and of a Cittizens wife of London; below them another of Sir Thomas Smythe, governor of the East India Company'.[56] Surrounded as he was by the images of his contemporaries, whose portraits were a reflection of their soul and representation of their presence, when the peripatetic emperor Jahangir visited one of these properties, he 'presided over the assembly of the kings of the world that he convened'.[57]

7

International diplomacy and war

Europe

Seventeenth-century travellers made their way to India from across the globe. The port cities of the Mughals boasted a diverse crowd of adventurers, slaves, itinerants, mercenaries and merchants, mendicants and missionaries from Ottoman Turkey, Safavid Iran, the horn of African and the Arabian Peninsula, Baghdad, Khorasan, Bukhara and Balkh. Many never reached the royal court, but South Asian society was enriched and enlivened by their presence. Increasingly, those who did make their way to Agra or Ajmer to meet the emperor included arrivals from Western Europe, seeking a share of the generous royal patronage of the Mughal king and in search of religious converts or trade advantages.

In 1498, nearly thirty years before the Timurid prince Babur defeated the Lodi armies at Panipat, thereby establishing the Mughal dynasty in India, the Portuguese explorer Vasco de Gama had reached Calicut. The Viceroyalty remained there only briefly, transferring from Calicut to Goa in 1510, from where the Portuguese governed their string of coastal forts and trading centres throughout the Indian Ocean world. Their first contact with the Mughals came only after Akbar had conquered the Sultanate of Gujarat in 1572–73, giving that descendant of land-locked Central Asian warlords his first glimpse of the sea. The Mughal Empire would further expand its maritime element in the 1590s, with the conquest of Orissa (and the Ganges delta) and Sindh (with its northern coastline on the Indian Ocean), but its interests remained solely mercantile; there would be no imperial navy.[1] Concerned for the safety of the empire's shipping and for Indian pilgrims travelling to Mecca, the Mughals treated delicately with the Portuguese, agreeing not to harass Portuguese territories in exchange for safe passage for Mughal ships. While interest in an embassy was occasionally voiced, the Portuguese never managed to establish a representative at the Mughal court. Instead, it was the Jesuits of Goa who received an invitation to Akbar's court in Agra in 1579, and readily accepted the offer.

When the first Jesuit mission arrived in 1580, they found a small Portuguese community already residing in Fatehpur Sikri and even a number of Christian Europeans serving in the Mughal army. Over the next twenty-five years, three Jesuit missions would establish themselves in turn at Akbar's court. The Jesuits would maintain an excellent relationship with the emperor, participating in his religious debates, serving as translators for his massive literary projects and even tutoring the princes, but their hopes of converting Akbar to Christianity were quickly dashed. In the end, they would have no discernible impact on Mughal religious identity. They were nearly as unsuccessful with conversion outside of the royal court, and described working with 'unreliable' locals to create a congregation to be like 'building with bad timber'.[2]

Jahangir had close associations with the Jesuits at his father's court. On his ascension, Jahangir inherited the Jesuits of the third mission, led by Father Xavier, who had been at the Mughal court since 1595. Although, as we have seen, the Jesuits were initially fearful that he would remove imperial support from their mission, the new emperor made no changes to diminish their status. Jahangir not only confirmed the pension his father had allowed them, but he increased it by fifty rupees a month, and then added thirty more for their church. He allowed them to continue public religious rituals, even to set off celebratory displays of fireworks from the church courtyard, and was so interested in their Christmas decorations that he personally sent candles and flowers to enhance the nativity scene. 'These things', a Jesuit of the mission commented, 'could not have been done more openly in a Christian country.'[3] On another occasion, Jahangir sent candles to the Jesuit mission, the gift inspired, he claimed, by his having seen Jesus Christ in a dream.[4] In 1627, Jahangir once again fully funded a lavish Christmas crèche, sending one thousand crusados to the Portuguese church.[5] The Jesuit records confirm their continued participation in the evening gatherings of Jahangir's royal court to the last year of his reign, although their earnest attempts to promote Christianity were for the most part dismissed.[6]

With few exceptions, the activities of the Portuguese in India were ignored by the Mughal emperor who was for the most part simply uninterested in the Indian Ocean world. When mercantile rivalries resulted in a British-Portuguese naval battle at the Battle of Swally [Suvali] in 1612, during which four Portuguese galleons were run aground, Jahangir was impressed and delighted at having the Portuguese put in their place, particularly as it was rumoured they had been poised to seize Surat. As a reward for their success, he agreed to grant the British a long-awaited trade agreement. A further political crisis for the Portuguese began in 1613, when their agents in Surat seized a Mughal trading vessel returning from Aden. Although the Jesuit mission at court had long struggled to separate themselves from the Portuguese mercantile interests of Goa, in this emergency they were forced to exert diplomatic pressure. Eventually the Portuguese were forgiven and allowed to resume operations. Apart from these few political/commercial mishaps, Jahangir treated the Portuguese as little more than a source of welcome novelties and an occasional irritant. As merchants and adventurers from England began making their own way to the Mughal throne, both Portuguese merchants and their Jesuit allies at court found their positions as influential European cultural arbiters increasingly threatened and their power waning.

Among the first of the English merchants to come before Jahangir was William Hawkins, who arrived in India in 1608 as a representative of the fledgling East India Company.[7] Hawkins landed first in Surat, where the goods he had brought as gifts and for sale were seized by Jahangir's agent in Goa, Muqarrab Khan, who was not scrupulous in his quest for curiosities and valuables to bring to his emperor. Hawkins eventually managed to make his way to Agra, where he presented himself as the English Ambassador and delivered a letter for the Mughal ruler. It was addressed to Akbar, for the English had not yet learned of the king's death before setting out for India. All the same, Hawkins was well received by Jahangir, in part because he was able to speak Turkish and could communicate directly with the emperor, who was not only curious and interested but also surely enjoyed the presence of yet another oddity at his court.[8] The Jesuits at court who saw the English as both heretics and mercantile rivals were appalled and, in an effort to marginalize Hawkins, they belittled the English to Jahangir, describing King James as a 'King of fishermen' and England as impoverished and inconsequential. They were not entirely wrong.

Yet while Hawkins' inability to produce any gifts of consequence seemed to give proof to the Jesuits' counsel, the brash Englishman would manage to remain at court for three years, competing ferociously with the Portuguese (who he claimed made several attempts to assassinate him) not only for trade rights but also for the favour and the ear of the emperor. For a time, Jahangir seems to have enjoyed his presence, paying his expenses of more than £3,000 per year and even arranging Hawkins' marriage to a local Christian Armenian woman, Miriam Khan. Hawkins' position at the royal court would, however, be weakened by the actions of a compatriot named William Finch, who had arrived in India on the same ship. In an effort to buy indigo for export to England, Finch had carelessly bid against the agent of the Queen Mother, which caused her to lose the sale and make a formal complaint about the English to the emperor. In the end, Hawkins' downfall seems to have been self-induced. He was rumoured to have appeared at the royal court smelling of alcohol, and much as Jahangir himself was a heavy drinker, he was prudishly offended by signs of drunkenness in others.[9] Hawkins fell quickly out of favour and was dismissed.

English merchants continued to make their way to Jahangir's court in a steady trickle. All were similarly interested in international trade and personal profit, and all proved equally unimpressive and ultimately insignificant. There is no doubt that Jahangir at times found a certain amusement in their presence. When Paul Canning was sent to Jahangir as representative of a group of English merchants who had reached Surat in 1612, he brought with him two musicians, Lancelot Canning, who played the virginal, and Robert Tully, who played the coronet.[10] After a difficult journey of seventy days, they arrived at the Mughal court in Agra in April 1613 to perform for the emperor at the royal court. Jahangir showed no interest at all in the virginal, but the cornet was a resounding success.[11] The emperor himself tried unsuccessfully to blow the horn and demanded of his artisans that they produce six more. Their efforts were unsuccessful and although Tully agreed to train one of Jahangir's musicians to play the cornet, that man died of an illness a fortnight later. As Tully vehemently refused to teach cornet to any of the rival Jesuits, he remained the only cornet player in India and a popular favourite at the court, although he complained bitterly at being underpaid by the king.[12]

After several missions to the court of the Mughal had failed to acquire the emperor's permission to establish factories in India, the East India Company and King James I agreed to send an official ambassador. They settled on Sir Thomas Roe. In contrast to those who had gone before him, Roe was a gentleman. He had been knighted in 1605, was Oxford educated and well connected, a 'gentleman of civell behaviour, of good breeding, personage, and very good parts', all of which was understood to equip him with the skills to properly represent the English king and serve in India as a desperately needed 'cross-cultural courtier'.[13] Although his specific objective was nearly the same as Hawkins, to establish English trade hegemony in India, he was chosen for and proved highly sensitive to the difference in their relative status and anxious to defend his own, and his nation's, dignity.

Sir Thomas Roe arrived off the coast of Surat in 1615. Aware that his predecessors had left the English reputation in tatters – referring to Hawkins as a 'vayne foole' – his priority was to force a shift in the Mughal perception of English (in)significance. Firm in his belief that trade rights would go to those with greatest dignity and authority, he arranged to be landed under ceremonial rounds fired from the 'forty-eight pieces great ordinance' discharged from the English fleet at harbour, 'all handsomlye fitted with their waistcloths, ensignes, flagges, pendants and streamers'.¹⁴ He theatrically rejected the standard searches by imperial agents at the port, deliberately marking the very great difference between himself and his immediate predecessor, Edwards and his crew, who had arrived the previous year and complained that they had been 'verie familyarle searched...to the bottom of our pockets and nearer too modestlie to speak of yt'.¹⁵ Roe defiantly displayed his brace of pistols in protest of the pat downs of his subordinates being attempted by local officials. Negotiations continued all along the route to Surat, and indeed, throughout his stay in India, for Roe never abandoned his demand for the respect he felt was owed to himself, as ambassador, as well as to his country and his monarch.

Roe would remain at Jahangir's court for three years, following in the emperor's wake as he travelled from Ajmer to Mandu and into Gujarat, in a constant state of prickly egoism, general physical misery and pained awareness of his ambassadorial failures. In fact, lacking substantial authority, he would prove unable to fulfil his own boasting promises of English largesse and wealth, and his commission ultimately proved to be little more than 'an exercise in royal fiction-making'.¹⁶ His single real success was that for a time he captured the imagination and even the friendship of the Mughal king. Jahangir seems to have been charmed by the haughty and high-handed personality that came to his court, although it is hard to imagine that Roe was much more to the Mughal emperor than a distraction and a diversion. In letters to England, Roe claimed that Jahangir was 'very affable, and of a cheerful countenance, without pride', and later as 'gentle, soft, and good of disposition'.¹⁷

Roe's appearances before the emperor seem, however, to have been little more than exercises in humiliation and embarrassment. In the very public gifting ceremonies before the gathered noblemen and ambassadors, he was unable to offer the emperor anything of real value or interest. Although an accredited ambassador, his gifts proved to be worse even than those of some of the independent English merchants who had preceded him. He himself complained that his gifts were 'extreamly despised by those who have seene them'.¹⁸ Jahangir seems to have felt some sympathy for Roe and made a pleasurable fuss over the gift of a carriage, complete with English coachman, that Roe brought to the court in 1616, although it had visibly suffered on the long passage from England and its Chinese velvet upholstery was worn and faded. The emperor in his enthusiasm immediately had himself pulled about before the gathered nobles, making a sport of the gift. Roe felt he had done well, and it was only later that he learned that once he had departed from the court audience, Jahangir had turned to the Jesuits to ask 'whether the King of England were a great Kyng that sent presents of so small valewe'.[19] Perhaps more humiliating, the emperor ordered the carriage dismantled and renovated beyond its original pretentions, with the English coachman now 'Clothd as Rich as any Player and more gaudy', and the ruined Chinese velvet upholstery replaced with 'riche Stuffe, the ground silver, wrought all over... with flowers of silk... and instead of the brasse Nails that were first in it, were Nails of silver put in their place'.[20]

Mughal court dynamics befuddled and enraged Roe. He misinterpreted the reciprocity of court gifting, resentfully describing it as an outrageous 'Custome of daylye bribing'.[21] His efforts to marginalize the Portuguese and establish trade monopolies for the English were met with long delays and obfuscation, which he quickly blamed on Mughal greed and corruption. He particularly suspected the machinations of a court faction surrounding the queen – her brother Asaf Khan, his son-in-law the crown prince Khurram, her father I'timaduddawla and Nur Jahan herself – who Roe claimed were actively subverting the emperor's authority against him. Yet Mughal unwillingness to throw in with the English seems much more likely to have been a deliberate and official policy of 'vacillation... using the English to displace the heavily-entrenched Portuguese in Gujarat... and refraining from a full commitment to the EIC in hopes of soliciting gifts and increased economic concessions'.[22] After a year in Ajmer, Roe was forced to recognize that he was unable to further English trade interests. Trailing along in the court progress, complaining bitterly of his discomfort, he and his compatriots had become little more than minor supplicants at Jahangir's throne. Throughout his three years in India, Roe persisted in demanding equal status for himself and his king and the English continued to be completely outmatched by the cosmopolitanism and sheer wealth of the Mughals and their allies.

That Roe is remembered as significant at all is due to the rich record in letters and a diary he composed while in Jahangir's retinue. His writings are of mixed value. Like other Europeans who had made their way to Mughal India in search of wealth, souls, escape or adventure, his understanding of the events and personalities around him was narrowly limited and ill-informed. Roe proved to be utterly constrained by his sense of aggrieved dignity and wounded pride, and his insistence on demonstrations of respect made him obdurate and indifferent to the subtleties of local diplomatic courtesy and culture. Even in his official role as ambassador, he made little effort to improve his grasp of the local. Roe felt strongly that, no matter how practical, dressing as the Mughals did and learning to speak and understand court Persian would diminish his carefully constructed performance of English superiority. He seems to have made no effort to develop close relationships at court. Yet while this self-imposed ignorance meant that his interpretations and analysis were often erroneous and, one suspects, always self-serving, his richly detailed visual observations offer a layer of complimentary detail to the sparse contemporary record of Jahangir's royal court.

The Ottomans, Uzbeks and Safavids

Much more important to Jahangir were his relationships with his Muslim contemporaries in Central and West Asia, the Ottomans and Uzbeks and, most of all, the Safavids of Iran. Their complex diplomatic and cultural exchanges were driven by territorial rivalries but also by a high degree of shared social and cultural identity. The Ottomans, the first leg in the great Islamic imperial triumvirate of the age, had passed through West Asia and entered Anatolia before the Mongol advance and were influenced, but unlike the Safavids, not forged by Ilkhanid-Timurid power. Timur's defeat of the Ottoman Sultan Bayazid at the Battle of Ankara in 1402 would lead the later Timurids to confidently dismiss the power and importance of the Ottomans. Even in the Ottoman camp were those who argued that Timur's lineage boasted greater legitimacy than that of the Ottomans, and openly accepted late Timurid cultural superiority, even as Timurid political and military power were rapidly disintegrating across the region.

Direct contact with the Ottomans was very limited. Babur had benefitted from the presence of a few rogue Ottoman artillerymen whose efforts to build cannon for his campaign into Hindustan were only occasionally successful, but there is no evidence of any interaction between the royal families. By 1527, however, with their defeat of the Mamluks, the Ottomans claimed sovereignty over the most holy pilgrimage sites in Sunni Islam, the cities of Mecca and Medina. Although at one point supportive of South Asian pilgrimage to Mecca, Akbar quickly paled on the relationship, and essentially removed the Ottomans from the Mughal orbit. Jahangir would do nothing to bring them closer.

In 1609, an emissary arrived at Jahangir's court in Agra, claiming to be a representative of the Ottoman sultan. Jahangir considered the man's credentials to be fake, and the self-proclaimed emissary was told to leave, but not before the Mughal emperor commented bitterly that after Timur's defeat of the

Ottomans, he had returned Anatolia to that dynasty, taking only tribute and one year's revenue from the defeated province. In the face of this extraordinary generosity on the part of his ancestor Timur, Jahangir asked rhetorically, why is it that the Ottomans have never yet sent an ambassador to the court of Timur's descendants in Hindustan? Apart from that brief expression of grievance, Jahangir mentioned the Ottomans rarely and only when the comparison served to embellish his own image. As his personal experience with ambitious princes had done much to heighten his sensitivity to problems of succession, it was the relationship of the Ottoman Sultan and his sons that would occasionally pique his interest.

Less significant on the world stage, but important to the Mughals both for proximity and as a site for dynastic nostalgia, was western Central Asia, in particular the regions of Mawarannahr [Transoxiana], Badakhshan and Balkh. When he had first taken the Mughal throne, Jahangir referred to Central Asia as 'our ancestral homeland' and described a plan to eventually conquer the region. Although that campaign was never seriously under consideration, Jahangir referenced the heartland of Timur's former empire with ancestral pride and longing. His early interest in the pursuit of a campaign to the north had been piqued by the weakness of the Uzbek leadership, which was facing a series of rebellions and succession disputes. In reality, however, the Mughal emperor had a princely rebellion of his own to put down, and the campaigns in Mewar and the Deccan pulled his attentions south. By the time his own immediate crisis had been dealt with, a pair of Uzbek brothers, Imam Quli Khan and Nazr Muhammad Khan, had managed to seize control of the northern region, ruling jointly in Bukhara and Balkh/Badakhshan, respectively. Uzbek stability made the frontier a less attractive target for the Mughal king, and Jahangir would not return to the discussion of a military campaign to regain the Timurid ancestral territories. Regarding his dynasty's inability to recover the region, Jahangir commented that as neither he, nor his father, his grandfather Humayun, or great-grandfather Babur, were as great as their ancestor, the Amir Timur, in humility, they could never allow themselves to sit on the throne of his kingdom in Samarqand.[23] For the next ten years, Jahangir would have no contact with the Uzbek rulers.

It was the Mughal-Safavid relationship that would most engage Jahangir, politically and personally. Within a year of Akbar's death and his son's ascension, Safavid forces made the attempt to seize Qandahar, a long-contested territory. Their forces were defeated by the Mughal armies and the first Safavid visitor to Jahangir's court, Husayn Beg, arrived in Lahore in 1607 to apologize and explain away the entire affair with face-saving stories, blaming rogue local commanders in Herat, Sistan and Farah for having instigated the attack. Jahangir, distracted by filial rebellion and a new throne, was congenial and conciliatory. He accepted the apology, blaming the governor of Farah and others in the region who, he agreed, must have imagined that Akbar's death had weakened the Mughals and undermined the ability of their armies to defend their territory. Writing in his memoir, he fulsomely excused Shah Abbas (1571–1629) who, he was sure, understood that the attack was 'improper', and had ordered the Safavid troops to withdraw 'because the affectionate relationship between our [Safavid] noble fathers and the sublime dynasty of Jahangir Padshah is ancient'.[24]

The pattern of the relationship had been set. Whenever possible, their territorial and dynastic arch-rivalry would remain hidden beneath regular professions of familial love and lavish displays of mutual regard. At the end of March 1611, a major Safavid embassy arrived led by Yadgar-Ali Sultan, bringing gifts and a letter of condolence for the death of Akbar.[25] The letter affirmed the Shah's love for Jahangir in terms that gave him great pleasure, describing him as 'the goal that had been hidden behind the veil of destiny for years... that splendid light of the imperial assembly' and 'he who shines in splendor in the Sahib Qiran's [Timur's] meadow'.[26] Gifts included 1500 pieces of precious fabric, silk brocade and velvets, fifty horses with spun-gold saddles, goods from Russia, from China and from Europe, totalling so many choice items 'that would take so long to enumerate'.

Relations between the two monarchs would remain cautious due to their ongoing contradictory claims to Qandahar, but on a personal level they were forever deeply entangled by ancestral indebtedness and unrelenting mutual fascination. For both Jahangir and Abbas, this was not just a struggle over land but a contentious and intimate sibling rivalry. Abbas, who had taken the throne of Iran in 1587, was older, deeply experienced and much more personally powerful than Jahangir, but the connection between them was explicitly fraternal, each referring to the other in the most familiar of terms, as a brother. Both were aware that in the Turco-Mongol imperial milieu a brother might be one's greatest rival and enemy.

The ties that bound Safavid and Mughal dynasties dated back centuries. Iran had been a critically important core territory within the greater Timurid Empire. After Timur's death, his successor, Shah Rukh, had moved the imperial capital from Timur's Samarqand further west, to the far more cosmopolitan Iranian city of Herat (incidentally, the place of Shah Abbas' birth), emphasizing the region's status as a cultural and political centre. Herat increasingly defined the Timurid worldview, as its Turco-Mongol aristocracy oriented itself towards an urban

Persianate aesthetic. Yet with the collapse of broader imperial power after the deaths of Timur's immediate successors, much of the greater Iranian heartland fell from Timurid control, leaving only the region of Mawarannahr under their direct rule.

In the void left by the Timurid retreat, political power in Iran became highly fractured, dominated by the Qara Qoyunlu and Aq Qoyunlu Turcoman tribal confederations. It was in this fifteenth-century Turco-Persian milieu that Safavid political ambition arose through a marriage between Shaykh Junayd, the leader of the influential Safaviyyah Sufi order of Ardabil, and the sister of Uzun Hasan, ruler of the Aqqoyunlu. Their son Haydar would go on to marry his cousin, Uzun Hasan's daughter, born of a Pontic-Greek princess, in an alliance that welded together diverse and powerful local lineages.[27] After the murder of his older brother by an Aq Qoyunlu rival, their younger son, Ismail, would inherit the increasingly powerful dynastic unification of temporal and spiritual power. Threatened by assassination, Ismail spent his early childhood in hiding, not emerging until 1500. His appeal was intensely spiritual, an intoxicating blend of local Alid/Shi'i expressions, messianic claims and militant millennialism. In poetry written under the pen name *Khata'i* (Sinner), Shah Ismail made claims of divinity, arguing that he was the embodiment of the Divine Truth (*haqq*), of Ali and Jesus, the twelve Shi'i Imams, and the hero-kings of the *Shahnamah*. Appealing to the Turcoman tribes of Azerbaijan and Eastern Anatolia, Ismail gathered an army and defeated his rivals, the Aq Qoyunlu, taking their capital of Tabriz as his own. By 1502, Ismail had claimed the title of Shah and over the following ten years he unified Iran.

As contemporaries, sharing equally grandiose aspirations to kingship, Ismail and Babur had become mutually aware. Among his many military accomplishments, Ismail defeated the Uzbeks at Merv, resulting in the death of Shibani Khan, Babur's nemesis, in 1510. In the aftermath of that battle, Ismail took possession of Khanzada Begim, Babur's full sister, who had long been a hostage of the Uzbeks. The Shah immediately and respectfully returned her to her brother's royal court. Babur, who had spent a lifetime attempting to reunify and rule the Timurid heartland, and was possessed of a relentless ambition, turned for help to this new regional power and potential ally. Ismail met Babur's request with generous offers of military assistance. The price was a steep one, however, for when Babur and his borrowed Safavid troops finally managed to take power in Samarqand in 1511, in Babur's third conquest of the city, he ruled not as an independent Timurid prince, but as a liegeman of the Safavid shah. Babur's subordinate relationship was made explicit by his acceptance of the distinctive turban, the Qizilbash taj, which identified Babur as a disciple of the militant, messianic Shah. Babur's subsequent inability to protect the Sunni population of Samarqand from brutal Safavid efforts to impose adherence to their particular brand of Shi'i law led to their rejection of him as their ruler, and Babur was forced once again, and for the last time, to flee the city of his dreams.

Shah Ismail's power would not last long. Within just a few years, the foment Ismail had caused among the tribes of eastern Anatolia would lead the Ottoman sultan, Selim I, to move against the Safavids. The Ottoman's resounding victory against the Safavids at Chaldiran in 1514 was a cruel humiliation to the young Shah, who had for years successfully convinced his troops, and himself, of his invincibility. Having seized Ismail's capital of Tabriz, and even Ismail's favourite wife, the Ottomans found themselves to be overextended. They withdrew almost immediately from Iran, leaving Ismail to reconstitute much of his territories. Yet while his defeat had cost him neither his crown nor his kingdom, Ismail was broken. Increasingly, he hid himself away, drinking heavily and leaving governance to others, dying ten years later at the age of thirty-six.

As for Babur, his allegiance to the Shah and the early Safavid construct of ecstatic messianic Shi'ism did not survive the loss of Samarqand. For a brief period of time, Babur had continued to cooperate with Safavid military actions in the region, but within the year he cut all ties to his temporary Safavid masters and retreated to his base at Kabul, from where a decade later he would lead his troops into northern India, far from the centre of Safavid power. All the same, however briefly he had accepted Safavid supremacy, it would permanently impact relations between the Timurid-Mughal and Safavid dynasties. Both were aware that 'Timurid sovereignty [had been] severely undermined by Babur's discipleship to the Shah Ismail'.[28]

Timurid-Mughal sovereignty would be further undermined, and relations with the Safavids made even more complex, by the actions of Babur's eldest son and successor, Humayun. Babur would die only four years after his initial defeat of the Lodi rulers of north India at Panipat, leaving Humayun to rule a deeply unstable empire. For reasons as varied as the strength of his Afghan challenger, Sur Khan (later, Sur Shah), the impatient rivalry and the disloyalty of his own brothers, as well as his own acknowledged addiction to opium, Humayun proved unable to maintain control of the empire he had inherited. By 1540, he was in flight, crossing the deserts of Sindh and Baluchistan. By 1544, Humayun had lost his wealth and territory, his followers and even his son. Reaching the borders of

Safavid Iran, in a gesture oddly parallel to that of Babur, Humayun requested the support of the Shah of Iran, Ismail's son, Tahmasp.

Like his father, Humayun came to the Safavid shah as a supplicant. While he was treated with the respect due a royal scion, Humayun was required to publicly submit to the Shah. Just as Babur had claimed to accept Ismail as both temporal and spiritual leader, so too Humayun agreed to don the Qizilbash taj, publicly professing Safavid discipleship.[29] The Safavid nobility, gathered to witness the submission of the Mughal king, cheered and prostrated themselves before their Shah. Tahmasp, describing Humayun to the Ottoman sultan as formerly 'one of the greatest kings of the world', proudly added, 'From Hind came Humayun, my slave to be.'[30]

Just as Ismail had loaned an army to Babur, Tahmasp offered troops to Humayun, with which he could, at the very least, re-take the Afghan territory held by his brothers, whose jealous rivalries had cost him his throne. In exchange, Humayun would first lead his borrowed troops to Qandahar, which had become part of Babur's empire in 1522 and was currently held by Humayun's brother Askeri. It was agreed that he would win the region for the Safavid crown. In 1545, accompanied by a large company of Safavid troops, Humayun attacked Qandahar. After a six-month siege, during which time the borrowed Safavid troops had begun to bleed away, Askeri finally surrendered the fortress. Humayun took control of Qandahar in the name of the Shah, his good intent proven by immediately sending the captured treasure directly to Tahmasp.

Having handed over the fortress, and no longer commanding a Safavid army, a directionless Humayun and his followers hovered nearby. When Tahmasp's infant son, Sultan Murad Mirza, who had been sent with Humayun to serve as titular ruler of Qandahar, suddenly died, a relieved Humayun hastily resumed command of the fortress, forcing out the Safavid occupying force. In the ensuing years, Humayun managed to re-take Kabul and eventually reclaim his Indian empire, at which point Mughal control of Qandahar had become a *fait accompli*.

Although the two monarchs had continued a polite diplomatic relationship, Humayun's opportunistic allegiance to Tahmasp had lasted only as long as the assistance of the Shah was necessary. Following his triumphant resumption of control over Afghanistan and India, Humayun's assertions of kingship were unambiguously independent. The Safavids would remember his claims of fealty, however. When later Shah Abbas II (d. 1666), the seventh Safavid shah, built the beautiful small palace, the Chihil Sutun in Isfahan, he ordered it decorated with wall murals, one of which humiliatingly depicted Humayun as a lessor guest at the Safavid court of Tahmasp. It was intended to illustrate the historical superiority of the Safavid dynasty before such Mughal visitors as their regular embassies and the occasional rebel prince or disgraced courtier.[31]

Humayun would die only one year after regaining his lost South Asian patrimony, in 1556. His successor, the young prince Akbar, scrambled to gain control over his fragile newly unified kingdom, but was unable to retain Qandahar, which the Safavids hastily seized. Unlike Humayun, Akbar made no pretence of friendship, and for the next twenty years rebuffed any Safavid attempts to restore diplomatic ties. Tahmasp's death in 1576 introduced an era of deep discord in Safavid politics – his successors had short and bloody reigns. Finally, in 1588, Tahmasp's young grandson Abbas overthrew his father, the blind Shah Khodabanda, and took control of the unstable and deeply turbulent state. Having spent his childhood witnessing unrestrained and vicious political conspiracy, Abbas devoted the first decades of his rule to imposing control over the Turcoman elites and establishing powerful personal rule over the kingdom. Combating the traditional sources of Safavid military and political power, both the Turcoman tribes and the Sufi order of Ardabil, Abbas stepped away from the messianic Alid claims of his father and grandfather, moving instead towards the establishment of ulama-directed Twelver Shi'ism. A further challenge to Abbas were the machinations of external foes; in the chaos of his predecessors' reigns, the Ottomans and the resurgent Uzbeks, Iran's rapacious empire-building neighbours, had claimed large swathes of Safavid territory, which Abbas would devote his reign to recovering.

Relations between Abbas and Akbar reflected an intense personal rivalry. Both were young teens when they inherited fragile kingdoms near collapse, which required not only military innovation but also profound political-spiritual interventions. Both devoted a great deal of time and attention to defining their inheritances and honing claims to sacred kingship. As one might easily imagine, the relationship between the neighbouring monarchs was highly guarded. Their rivalry was exacerbated by continued competing claims to Qandahar. In the 1590s, having consolidated his rule over northern India, Akbar was secure enough to take on the contentious issue. His early efforts were unsuccessful but in 1595, with the Uzbeks posing an immediate threat in neighbouring Khorasan, the Safavid governors of Qandahar, brothers Rustam Mirza and Muzzaffar Husayn Mirza, surrendered the territory to Akbar, and accepted rank in the Mughal nobility. Abbas, still enmeshed in the struggle to strengthen and unify his own fragile inheritance, was unable to prevent the Mughal advance. Forced to bide his time, the Safavid shah maintained delicate diplomatic negotiations and a policy of deliberate patience. Safavid embassies continued to arrive at Akbar's court, although the Mughal emperor remained dismissive of the Shah, his chronicler describing Abbas as behaving 'like a dutiful child'.³²

Shah Abbas began to develop a relationship with prince Salim a few years before he became emperor. When the Mughal prince sent an agent to Iran to purchase rarities for his household (in what would become a constant quest for the odd and extraordinary at his royal court), Abbas personally arranged for the shipment, writing a letter to Salim in which he gently chided the prince for not having appealed directly to the Shah for the objects of his desire. Having already spent nearly twenty years on the Safavid throne before Jahangir's accession, the experienced Abbas was clearly playing a long game with the likely successor to the Mughal throne. When, in the last few years of Akbar's life, Salim had moved into open revolt, Shah Abbas was quick to seize the opportunity, preemptively expressing his own sympathy for the rebel.³³ In his letter to Salim, Abbas openly criticized Akbar and his treatment of a Safavid ambassador, a move that may well have enhanced his image in the eyes of the restless prince, whose response was affectionate and warm. It seems that Shah Abbas hedged his diplomatic bets by also initiating a correspondence with Akbar's younger son, Danyal. As for one of Abbas' notes to Salim, the original recipient may have been his brother, and was simply re-addressed to Salim after Danyal's early death.

Once emperor, Jahangir's protestations of friendship with Abbas became more self-aware and calculated. He had learned to be cautious, having received a critical lesson in the meaning of Safavid friendship immediately after his accession to the throne. With his attention entirely focused on the pursuit of his rebellious son, Khusraw, in May of his first regnal year, Jahangir learned that Safavid troops had besieged Mughal Qandahar. The new Mughal king was fortunate in that his governor in Qandahar, Shah Beg Khan, had the fortitude – and adequate supplies – to withstand the siege of his fortress for nearly a year, until support and reinforcements from India arrived. According to Jahangir, the governor's strategy for survival included not only daily raiding forays from the fort to engage the Safavid aggressors, but also public demonstrations of confidence and nonchalant unconcern. Positioning his court where it could be observed by the enemy laying siege below the fortress, 'not only did he not gird his loins, but he reveled and caroused, bareheaded and barefoot'.³⁴ The Iranian army finally fled at the approach of Mughal reinforcements led by Mirza Ghazi Beg Tarkhan, in January of 1607.

Although he had quickly accepted the excuses and apologies of Shah Abbas' dignitary, Husayn Beg, in that same year, it is highly unlikely that Jahangir was unaware of Abbas having encouraged the attack on Qandahar. The Shah's apologies had – somewhat obviously – been delayed until after it was clear that the Mughal military response would be a success. For the remainder of his reign, though never less than warm and intimate in his dealings with Abbas, Jahangir was intensely protective of Qandahar, in recognition that the city and its environs remained the object of Safavid expansionist aspirations. An English traveller, Richard Steel, described the fort housing 'a Garrison maintained by the Mogoll, of twelve or fifteen thousand Horsemen, in regard of the Persians neighborhood to the North'.[35]

While Qandahar would continue to be closely guarded, the arrival of Safavid embassies at the royal court of the Mughals were highly anticipated spectacles and the letters exchanged by the two great kings remained invariably effusive and loving. Jahangir remained fascinated with his arch-rival. On learning that the Shah had executed a son accused of insurrection, Jahangir questioned everyone coming from Iran about the incident. Nothing he heard completely satisfied Jahangir's curiosity and no explanation justified what he considered an extraordinarily disgraceful act.[36] Abbas continued to work hard to maintain an intimate relationship with Jahangir, who responded with nothing less than enthusiastic warmth but never quite let down his guard. Encouraged by their warm welcome, there were times when multiple Safavid emissaries were at the Mughal court concurrently. At least thirteen visitors from the court of Shah Abbas were mentioned by name in Jahangir's record. The Mughal emperor's guarded diplomatic relationship with the Shah proved entirely successful until, in the last few years of his reign, yet another princely rebellion would make the contested territory of Qandahar once again vulnerable to Safavid armies.

The Deccan and Malik Ambar

In a rare divergence from his expansionist father, Jahangir was not driven by territorial ambition. During his reign, the Mughal armies would remain employed on multiple fronts but much of their energy was devoted to protecting existing borders and suppressing local rebellions, particularly in Bengal. Akbar had defeated sultan Daud Khan Khurrani in 1576, declaring Bengal a *subah* in 1586, but the northeast was never completely subdued. Military campaigning remained constant, as Jahangir's armies were forced to combat a variety of local powers in West Bengal and Bihar, push back against the expansionist Ahom kingdom in Assam and defend the coastline from Portuguese and Arakanese piracy.[37] In 1608, Jahangir established a Mughal capital in Dhaka, appointing Islam Khan Chishti, Jahangir's childhood playmate and the son of Shaykh Salim Chishti, as governor, and renaming the city *Jahangirabad*. The gesture did not mark the resolution of the Bengal campaign and Mughal forces would remain committed to the region with little hope of acquisition, in an endless effort to prevent territorial loss.

Those expansionist campaigns Jahangir chose to pursue were invariably directed against states that Akbar had not been able to defeat: most notably, the Deccani states, Kangra and Mewar.[38] While he would ultimately find success in the latter two campaigns, no military aggression would prove more frustrating and no victory more evasive than in the Deccan, where the Ahmednagari general, Malik Ambar successfully resisted the Mughal imperial armies for decades. Ultimately, like his father, Jahangir proved unable to permanently defeat Ambar and their long years of unresolved rivalry in the Deccan was a source of frustration throughout Jahangir's entire reign.

The origins of the two men could not have been more different. As a child, Malik Ambar had been captured or sold into slavery, likely from one of the communities in the Harari highlands of eastern Ethiopia that supplied both Muslim and Christian kingdoms with slaves.[39] Contemporary accounts claim he had eventually been purchased for eighty Dutch guilders in the Red Sea port of Mocha and taken to Baghdad, where his obvious intelligence and aptitude led his owner to educate him, convert him to Islam and change his name, from Chapu to Ambar (*amber; ambergris*). Still a young man, he was finally transported to the western coast of India, one of thousands of Ethiopian slaves, known as Habshis, who were carried from the Persian Gulf or the Red Sea to serve the Deccani sultanates as soldiers. There he was purchased by the chief minister (*peshwa*) of Ahmednagar, Chengiz Khan, himself an Ethiopian and a former slave, whose own rise illustrated the potential for advancement for the elite slave soldiery in the 'politically unstable and socially fluid contexts' of the northern Deccan.[40] By the time of Ambar's arrival in the region, local rulers fielded entire armies of Habshi slave soldiers, many of whom would eventually become freed men, almost always remitted on the death of their owner, if not before. In turn, in 'a remarkable pattern of upward mobility', a successful commander, once freed, might purchase a slave regiment of his own, as had Chengiz Khan.

Malik Ambar loyally served Chengiz Khan for twenty years until the commander died in 1594, at which point Ambar briefly served the ruler of Bijapur. Soon after, he declared his independence, leading a mercenary force of

Ethiopian and local Maratha soldiers in the service of the ruler of Ahmednagar against the armies of the expansionist Mughal emperor Akbar. Although the Mughals were able to conquer Ahmednagar in 1600, a large territory remained independent and Ambar had been able to escape with his troops. The details are obscure, but by 1601 Malik Ambar had married his daughter into the local nobility and become king-maker and regent in Ahmednagar, placing on the throne and protecting the prince, Murtaza Nizam Shah II. Ambar and his chief rival, the general Rahu Deccani, both supporting the Nizamshahi ruler, split the kingdom into two spheres of influence. The north, to the borders of Gujarat, was controlled by Raju Deccani, while the area bordering on Bijapur and Golconda was ruled by Malik Ambar.

Akbar's imperial armies had continued to conduct operations in the region and, led by Abdur Rahim Khankhanan, were able to defeat Malik Ambar at Nander. A treaty was agreed to which allowed Ambar to retain power in Ausa, Dharur and parts of Bir, but disagreements between the feuding generals of the Mughal forces, Abdur Rahim and Abu'l Fazl, who was leading the second arm of the imperial forces in the Deccan, undermined negotiations and the treaty was abandoned. Instead, in 1602, Malik Ambar made a settlement with the Mughals which led them to remove their troops from the region. There are some claims that this included an agreement that Ambar would pay homage at the Mughal royal court. Raju Deccani continued to fight the Mughal armies for a few more years, but a settlement was reached in 1604 which left him to compete with Ambar for control over Ahmednagar.

In 1607, just two years after Jahangir had ascended to the Mughal throne, Ambar was finally strong enough to defeat his rival, taking full control of Ahmednagar, including the regional capital of Daulatabad. Having become the region's most powerful commander, Malik Ambar would considerably reform his military forces, which not only reinforced his defence of the Deccan but created the conditions and context for the later Maratha military successes under the Bhonsles. Ambar was a master of guerrilla tactics, what the Mughals called *qazzaqi* (*qazzaqlik*, in Turkish, the term Babur had used to describe his own military efforts) and Maratha speakers called *bargi-giri*. The term was used to describe a light cavalry made up of Maratha-speaking warriors, trained by the state and paid from the state treasury. Avoiding direct confrontation with opposing forces on the battlefield, they chose instead to harass and surprise their enemies in the steep and heavily wooded ravines of the Western Ghats, with dire consequences for the bulkier and slower Mughal armies. Malik Ambar used far more Maratha cavalry than other Deccani armies. Increasing their numbers five-fold in the years of his leadership, to fifty thousand men, he developed a joint Habshi-Maratha force which was trained to avoid open battle, instead emphasizing the harassing guerrilla tactics for which these Deccani forces would become known. It was this strengthened and empowered force that would successfully undermine Jahangir's aspirations on the southern border.

In 1608, the Mughals had begun a new offensive in the region, Jahangir assigning the generalship of the forces to the previously successful Abdur Rahim Khankhanan and, indicating a renewed commitment to the Deccani front, to his son Parvez, with Asaf Khan serving as his ataliq. The imperial forces were unsuccessful however and ultimately forced to retreat to Burhanpur. Ambar's armies were clearly formidable. In 1610, William Finch claimed that Ambar led fifty thousand men: ten thousand 'of his own caste' [Habshis] and forty thousand Deccanis, presumably Marathas. While Jahangir was clearly hoping that the sheer scale of the Mughal army would supply him a quick victory, his generals were in disarray and often at each other's throats. Each saw the other as rival, rather than partner, as Parwez and Asaf Khan accused Abdur Rahim, who had spent years developing local relationships in the Deccan, of conspiring with Ambar. Jahangir sent Mahabat Khan to retrieve him while a re-configured Mughal army, led by Khan Jahan and Abdullah Khan, along with thousands of new troops, renewed the attack. In 1611, they once again proved unsuccessful. Their failure allowed Malik Ambar to retake the fort of Ahmednagar and then Khirki, in a humiliating defeat that fuelled Jahangir's outrage. In 1612, Jahangir mused on the failures in the Deccan campaign, saving most of his fury for his own commander, Abdullah Khan, but commenting bitterly on 'the black-faced Ambar', who sent a massive force against the Mughal armies and deployed rockets and other explosives, then pursued and harassed them as they retreated to their base at Burhanpur.[41] Jahangir complained of the 'habshis who were acting like lords'.

Complicating Mughal claims in the region and a further goad to his frustration was the relationship, maintained by irregular diplomatic relations, between the Shi'i states of the Deccan and Safavid Iran. In the face of Jahangir's expansionist push southward, the rulers of Golconda, Bijapur and Ahmednagar reached out to Shah Abbas, claiming that the *ahl-i khilfat*, 'People of the Caliph', that is, the Sunni Mughals, were engaged in holy war against them and calling on the Shah to come to their aid. Their requests for help were couched in terms of loyalty and fealty to the Shah, and 'full of malice and ill-will' towards the Mughal king.[42] In 1609–10, during the Mughal campaign, Bijapur's sovereign, Adil Shah II, had written to Abbas, claiming to speak for all three local rulers, in calling for a Safavid army to be sent from Qandahar to join with them and conquer all of India, for 'the Deccani territories form as much a part of the Safavid Empire as the provinces of Iraq, Faras, Khurasan and Azerbaijan'.[43] On another occasion, he asked that the Shah consider him one of the Safavid provincial governors. It is highly unlikely that the Deccani rulers in fact saw themselves as less than sovereign kings, but they clearly hoped for a diversion. To Jahangir, who rightfully viewed Abbas as his most important rival, Deccani proclamations of fealty to the Safavid Shah must have truly rankled.

For the remainder of Jahangir's reign, Malik Ambar would represent imperial failure, re-emerging after every loss or signed treaty to harass the imperial armies and undermine Mughal ambition in the Deccan. It must have seemed that Amber would never be decisively defeated. In early 1615, Jahangir reported an attempt by certain Rajputs to assassinate Ambar, but the general's personal guard had rescued him and Jahangir could only storm at the missed opportunity. Within the year, however, the imperial armies defeated Ambar and what Jahangir described as his 'army of calamity'.[44] Even in victory, the emperor expressed deep frustration and indignation towards 'the ill-starred' Ambar, describing the two armies as forces of light and darkness, the Mughals as lions and the Deccanis as owls, considered to be creatures of ill-omen.[45] In his study of Malik Ambar, Richard Eaton explores Jahangir's expressions of increasing frustration and fury, referring to 'Ambar of dark fate' and 'the black-fated one'.[46] Others at the court referenced the lowly origins of the general by referring to him as 'Ambar Habshi'.[47] It is this tension that inspired one of the most remarkable of Jahangir's allegorical painting series, portraying the emperor victorious against Ambar, aiming an arrow into a diminished and defeated general's head.[48]

Always managing to somehow escape the Mughal onslaught, Ambar would reclaim his armies and his lands and rejoin his battle against the expansionist imperial forces. In the face of the continued failures of the Mughals in the Deccan, Jahangir became convinced that Abdur Rahim Khankhanan's understanding of the region and efforts at diplomatic outreach had in fact a proven a more effective strategy than the simple blunt force deployed by his other generals. The emperor promoted the Khankhanan, awarded him a robe of honour, a jewelled dagger, an elephant and Persian horses and reassigned him to the Deccani front, where he successfully coerced some of Ambar's staunchest generals to join the Mughal service, rewarding them with jagirs and mansabs. He also pursued close diplomatic relations with Ibrahim Adil Shah II, ruler of Bijapur, who cautiously manoeuvred between the Mughal armies on one side and Malik Ambar's forces on the other. While writing letters of submission that indicated his willingness to ally with Mughal interests, the Bijapuri shah continued to supply Malik Ambar with fresh troops for use against the Mughals, as did the ruler of Golconda.[49] Once again led by the Khankhanan, the Mughal armies remained unable to permanently defeat the Ethiopian general. In 1616, Prince Khurram was assigned to lead the Deccan campaign and was able to force temporary settlements on Ambar, but a final resolution would remain out of reach and the Deccani frontier would flare up into a new crisis in 1620.

8

Love and marriage

Marriage and the Mughal prince

In 1611, while still in Agra, Jahangir entered into a marriage that would in many ways come to define his rule. To this point, his many marriages had been primarily political and social alliances. The unions seem to have been successful, certainly to the extent of producing multiple children, including healthy sons to inherit the throne. At the age of forty-two, however, the emperor would marry for the last time. He chose the thirty-five-year-old daughter of Persian immigrants, already widowed and the mother of a child. She would become his closest companion. Although ultimately criticized and even reviled for her political role, the emperor's last wife, who would come to be entitled Nur Jahan, the Light of the World, would eventually and unapologetically act as co-regent, Jahangir's partner in a powerful marital alliance.

Imperial marriages in the pre-modern period served two primary purposes: to establish or reinforce political and diplomatic alliances, and to produce dynastic progeny. In the Islamic world, religious law limited marriage to no more than four women, which was certainly a more generous allowance than was given their Christian peers; yet for ambitious empire builders it represented an undesirable limitation on their power and on the potential for healthy heirs.[1] In response, rulers found creative means to compromise, most subsidizing legal marriage with a stable of slave women whose progeny could at times be accepted as legitimate heirs. In the face of religiously mandated marital limits and heightened political ambition, the Ottoman dynasty came to reject imperial marriage almost entirely, replacing it with a policy of anonymous concubinage. This allowed the sultan to have unlimited sexual partners, with the expectation of plentiful heirs, while freeing the royal family from the political drag and potential threat represented by ambitious male relatives of the bride.[2] They were unique in this; their Muslim contemporaries, while generally amenable to the presence of concubines, continued to make use of formal marriage as a diplomatic transaction.

Among the politically vulnerable and disputatious Timurid princely courts of fifteenth-century Central Asia, marriage arrangements were guided almost exclusively by the need for an alliance: to establish connections amongst rivals or to affirm ties of loyalty between the ruling dynasty and the nobility. The strategic significance of these marriages was further enhanced by the very real political weight attached to a woman's lineage. Women of the Turco-Mongol elite retained the charisma of their ancestry after marriage, even passing it on to their children, who could make demands of political power and tribal loyalty on the basis of their maternal inheritance. Famously, Timur had reinforced his own somewhat tenuous assertions of ruling legitimacy by marrying himself and his sons into the Chinggisid royal family, formally attaching his dynasty to that of Central Asia's greatest empire builder and claiming the title 'Guregen', the son-in-law. Marital alliance was so important a political strategy that, in dramatic contrast to his contemporaries in the Islamic world, Timur simply rejected Quranic marriage regulations entirely, accepting no limits to the number of wives a prince might have – at one time he was legally married to at least seven women.

Babur, who established the Timurids in India, would marry perhaps as many as eleven times. He wrote in some detail of the arrangements, describing his first marriage to a paternal cousin, Aisha Sultan Begim, daughter of Sultan Ahmad Mirza Miranshah, when he was aged sixteen, in 1499. The marriage had been arranged in his early childhood in a standard Timurid effort to tie together the elite families of the dynasty, but it was not a success. The young Babur did not warm to his wife and even complained of his mother forcing him to make conjugal visits. Eventually the marriage ended in divorce. Babur's second wife, Zainab Begim (m. 1504), a daughter of Sultan Mahmud Mirza, and fourth, Masuma Begin (m. 1507), another daughter of Sultan Ahmed Mirza Miranshah, were also his paternal cousins. In between he had married Maham Begim, his third wife, in 1506, while visiting the city of Herat. Although her parentage is obscure, it is clear that her origins were in the city's Timurid elite. His daughter wrote of the mutual regard between Babur and Maham, who was given the honorary title *Padshah Begim* (Lady Emperor). She was the leading woman of Babur's household, the mother of his eldest son and successor, Humayun, as well as foster-mother of his youngest son, Hindal, and daughter Gulbadan, both children of another of Babur's wives, Dildar Begim.

Babur would then marry Bibi Mubaraika, the daughter of an Afghan chief and rival, Malik Mansur Yusufzai. This was a marriage fuelled by a combination of political alliance and desire, arranged at Babur's request while he was establishing his hegemony over the Timurid-Afghan territories and negotiating local leadership with the Yusufzai chief. According to Babur's daughter, this marriage too seems to have resulted in a close and even loving relationship.³ Babur's eleven marriages, then, illustrate the classic Timurid pattern of diplomatic alliance within the ruling elite – forays into political marriage as seemed expedient, and the occasional marriage of the heart – and fully affirm his dynasty's common disregard for the Islamic injunction to limit marriages to four.⁴

With the dynasty's establishment in India, Mughal women came to be far less likely than Timurid women to marry outside of the small circle of the royal court. It was forbidden by Islamic law for a Muslim woman to marry a non-Muslim, which certainly reduced the pool of local rulers who might be seen as viable marriage partners. But Mughal women did not often marry into local elite Muslim families, nor were they sent to Central Asia or Iran to marry into other ruling dynasties, although a few elite Mughal women did marry émigré Safavid princes who served the royal court in India. Instead, the Mughal princess married exclusively within the extended royal family and closely affiliated local refugee elites, such as the Naqshbandi shaykhs of the Ahrari lineage, who had accompanied them into India and became a 'religious nobility'.⁵ Instead of establishing international diplomatic alliances, the marriages of princesses of the ruling dynasty in exile were entirely driven by the need to reinforce local and pre-existing loyalties, to shore up and unify the Mughal imperial elite.

Their brothers, however, retained the Timurid ancestors' extraordinary marital flexibility, which would set the Mughal princes apart from their contemporaries and rivals. Like the women of the family, Mughal men commonly married within the extended elite network, deliberately choosing marital partnerships that bound them closer to relatives and close allies within the fractious and competitive dynasty. In addition, however, they regularly arranged diplomatic and political alliances through marriage to the daughters of rival rulers. In both cases, their continued willingness to marry more than the proscribed four wives served as a useful tool to prop up individual and dynastic ambition.

Imperial marriage would famously come to take a new form in the third Mughal generation, in the reign of the emperor Akbar. Akbar's first marriage was arranged by his father when he was nine, to the daughter of his uncle Hindal, Ruqaiya Sultan Begim. In 1561, Akbar married his second wife, Salima Sultan Begim, who was not only a grand daughter of Babur but also the widow of Akbar's mentor and regent, Bairam Khan. Both women became powerful figures in the Mughal harem, although neither marriage produced surviving children. While his first two marriages reaffirmed Timurid ties, the second also aggressively asserted Akbar's increasing claim to power, combined as it was with newly independent kingship, the absorption of Bairam Khan's establishment and the adoption of his four-year-old son.[6]

Akbar would move outside of the Timurid pattern with his third marriage, however when, in likely the same year as his marriage to Salima Sultan, he married Harkha Bai (Hira Kunwari), the daughter of his closest Rajput ally, Raja Bihari Mal of the Kachwara clan of Amber. The raja had first established ties with the emperor when Akbar was only fourteen. Five years later, taking advantage of Akbar's presence at the shrine of the sufi shaykh Khwaja Moinuddin Chishti at nearby Ajmer, he proposed the marital alliance. It was an entirely political marriage, arranged to enhance the raja's influence at the Mughal court while dramatically extending Akbar's reach past the traditional circle of elites. As Abu'l Fazl would write, 'The rajah, from right-thinking and elevated fortune, considered that he should bring himself out of the ruck of landholders and make himself one of the distinguished ones at Court... [He placed] his eldest daughter, in whose forehead shone the lights of chastity and intellect, among the attendants on the glorious pavilion.'[7] Not only would his daughter marry Akbar, but his son Bhagwant Das would join Akbar's service, and a short time later they would be joined by his grandson, the eleven-year-old Man Singh, who would not only inherit the throne of Amber but also become one of Akbar's closest friends and greatest generals.

The ruling predecessors to the Mughals, the Delhi Sultans, had occasionally wed women of the Hindu Rajput elite. Over the decades of his reign, however, Akbar serially married into many of the elite families of Hindustan – Muslim and non-Muslim, Turk, Mongol, Persian and Rajput – in his effort to establish Mughal hegemony in the north of Hindustan. The marriages seem to have been mutually acceptable. There is a single mention, in the treaty confirming Akbar's conquest of Rambathore in 1569, that the daughters of defeated Rajput princes may have been demanded as brides or simple hostages or both, but no evidence of a state policy has been unearthed; political pressure and coercion are more likely. The treaty specifically exempted the chiefs of Bundi from 'that custom, degrading to a Rajput, of sending a *dola* (bride) to the royal harem'.[8] While his wives accumulated, Akbar's marriages were not solely about the assertion of imperial, or masculine, power. As was clear at the time of his marriage to Harkha Bai of Amber, the inclusion of Rajput women in the emperor's household was part of Akbar's larger effort to pull the fathers and brothers of his Rajput wives into the Mughal aristocracy, to serve as active allied elites, reliable players in his highly syncretic imperial milieu. As Ruby Lal has stated, 'What is most striking about these marriages is their range ... which went toward a grid of marital alliances'.[9] Akbar did not simply marry women, he married families.

There is sparse record of debate among the Mughals regarding their dynasty's rejection of marital limits in Islamic law. That they were aware of the legal standards is confirmed by the writings of Abd al-Qadir Badauni (1540–1615), a religious scholar at the Mughal court and author of *Muntakhabu-t-Tavarikh*, a history of the reign of Emperor Akbar. Badauni describes a series of conversations on the topic, in which Akbar, seeming increasingly concerned for the legality of his arrangements, sought not just clarity but absolution.[10] Having broached the question to his religious specialists, he received a variety of opinions from several jurists, none in support of unlimited marriage. At last, Badauni suggested that *mut'ah* marriages – which are made by private arrangement – might reasonably be seen to support the acquisition of any number of wives. He further assured Akbar that *mut'ah* unions were explicitly allowed by the famed Sunni scholar Malik ibn Anas, for whom the Maliki school of law is named. The relieved emperor immediately appointed a Maliki *qadi* (judge) who wasted no time in proclaiming *mut'ah* to be legal, thereby settling Akbar's brief doubts and confirming the sanctity of his marriages.[11] Having settled the issue to the emperor's satisfaction, the subject did not again arise.

In the latter years of his reign, Akbar's biographer, Abu'l Fazl, would claim that the harem contained five thousand women. These numbers do not reflect marriages or sexual partners. The Mughal harem, only starting to take formal shape during Akbar's reign, was made up of the extended family, not only wives, but also daughters, aunts and cousins, the children of the family, along with their servants, guards, teachers and others. Abu'l Fazl has been credibly accused of exaggeration, but even the much more conservative estimate of the Jesuit father Antonio Monserrate, a tutor to Prince Salim, confirmed that 'Zalaldinus [Akbar] has more than 300 wives, dwelling in separate suites of rooms in a very large palace'. It is possible that not all of his wives were actually the emperor's sexual partners; as Monserrate points out, 'when the [Jesuit] priests were at the court, he [Akbar] had only three sons and two daughters'.[12] Scholars have suggested that while a large female establishment served to enhance the authority of a pre-modern ruler, it was not unusual for rulers who presided over enormous harems to limit their sexual relationships to a small number of favoured women.[13] This was likely the case with Akbar and his successors, none of whom seem to have pursued relations with the potentially unlimited numbers of sexual partners available to them. For the most part, Mughal rulers remained serially monogamous. Even the active rumour mills of Agra and Delhi did not suggest sexual dissipation or unrestraint in the first several generations of Mughal rule.

Salim in love

Salim/Jahangir's romantic relationships have long been the object of speculation and rumour. Although he was married young and often – it is commonly estimated that he was married twenty times – Salim is popularly identified with a tragic love affair. Most versions of the legend assert that the young Anarkali was a member of Akbar's household, either in the harem as a favourite wife or a beloved concubine or a palace servant. The various accounts agree that on discovering the relationship between his son and Anarkali, the enraged and jealous Akbar had the woman entombed alive within a wall in the fort, an act of such cruelty that it was credited by some for inspiring Salim's rebellion.

The story, however, seems to be completely apocryphal. Not only is there is no historical evidence supporting it – no reference to it appears in Jahangir's writings or those of contemporaries at the royal court – but the behaviour of the central figures in the legend seems entirely out of character. Rumours of the affair may have originated with European travellers to Mughal India in the early seventeenth century, perhaps with William Finch, who visited Lahore in 1611, and described seeing there a 'sumptuous' tomb that he heard had been built by Jahangir for the murdered 'Immacque Kelle, or Pomegranate kernel... in token of his love'.[14] The enticing and romantic gossip became popular legend, and even today the story of Salim and Anarkali is widely believed, however unsubstantiated and unlikely.[15]

On the other hand, love matches did occur with some regularity among the Timurid-Mughal dynasts and among them can be counted Salim's final marriage, to Mihrunnisa, who would come to be known as Nur Jahan, the Light of the World. Mihrunnisa was the daughter of immigrants who, when faced with political and financial troubles at the Safavid court in 1577, made their way to Mughal India as part of a larger diaspora of Persians drawn to the beneficent court of the Mughal Emperor Akbar. The family is said to have struggled to survive the flight from Iran, their only daughter born enroute in Qandahar. Eventually her father, Ghiyas Beg, managed to come before the Mughal emperor, introduced by a fellow Persian immigrant named Malik Masud, and was given a minor position at Akbar's court, later receiving regular promotions. When she was seventeen years old, Mihrunnisa was married to Ali Quli Istajlu, another immigrant from Safavid Iran who had at one time been an attendant of Shah Ismail II. Ali Quli Istajlu served at the court of both Akbar and his son, Jahangir, who gave him the title *Sher Afkhan* after his acts of bravery in the Mughal campaign against Mewar. In 1607, however, Ali Quli Istajlu, who was serving in Bengal province, was accused of negligence in his duties. When Jahangir sent Qutbuddin Khan Koka to arrest him, Ali Quli Istajlu attacked and murdered him, and was killed in turn by Qutbuddin's companions.

By this time Jahangir had already promoted Ghiyas Beg to one of the highest posts in the administration, appointing him vizier of half the realm with the title of I'timaduddawla, immediately after his accession.[16] Jahangir's munshi (secretary) Mu'tamid Khan described him as a good tempered conversationalist, a decent poet and a man of piety, although he agreed that Ghiyas Beg was 'bold and fearless' in accepting bribes.[17] As the family members of an important Mughal nobleman, the newly widowed Mihrunnisa and her daughter Ladli Begim were sent for their safety and support to the Mughal harem, where Mihrunnisa for four years acted as an attendant to Sultan Ruqaiya Begim, Akbar's first wife and the daughter of his uncle Hindal.

Popular legend, once again drawn to the romantic life of the Mughal king, suggests that Jahangir had met and fallen in love with Mihrunnisa long before her husband's death, some versions even directly implicating Jahangir in his murder. These stories have no credibility. Had Jahangir been jealous of Istajlu's marriage to Mihrunnisa, it would be very hard to explain Jahangir's years of patronage and extravagant reward for the warrior, or the nearly four years between the death of her husband and her subsequent marriage to the emperor. Mughal accounts support the claim that Jahangir had met Mihrunnisa when she was a widow residing in the imperial harem, during the *Nowruz* festivities when the women of the Mughal family, joined by wives and daughters of the nobility, created a private *Meena* bazaar for themselves, selling small items to each other and donating the proceeds to charity.[18]

The Emperor Jahangir married Mihrunnisa on the 25th of May 1611. On the event of their marriage Jahangir gave her the honorific title Nur Mahal, the Light of the Palace, referencing his own name, Nuruddin, the Light of Religion. In his eleventh regnal year, he would enhance her title to Nur Jahan, the Light of the World, even more closely synchronizing her title with his own regnal name.[19] Jahangir never married again.

In contrast to the legend of Prince Salim's passionate love for Anarkali, his later marriage to Nur Jahan is generally treated by sceptical scholars as nothing more than a political arrangement, but that Jahangir trusted and loved his wife is obvious even in the spartan record of his *Jahangirnama*.[20] While her name rarely enters his record, that is true of all royal women, who would expect to be protected from the public gaze. Glimpses of an affectionate and trusting relationship between Jahangir and his last and favourite wife are however offered even by those who resented the queen's privileged position, and occasionally by the emperor himself. In his ninth regnal year, the emperor reported having been quite ill, yet he kept his condition hidden 'lest harm befall the country and the subjects'. After several days, when he finally confided his secret, it was to Nur Jahan, 'the one I thought had more affection for me than anyone else'.[21] Years later, in 1622, when he again fell ill, Nur Jahan again nursed him back to health, Jahangir claiming that her remedies were far superior to those of his doctors, in part, he confided, because of her affection for him.[22]

For all their love of gossip, travellers in India at this time recognized the close relationship of the king and his last wife. 'In wiving', speculated Edward Terry, in India from 1616–19, the emeror Jahangir 'respects fancie more than honour, not seeking affinitie with neighbor princes but to please his eye at home', clarifying that Nur Mahal was Jahangir's 'best beloved'.[23] Perhaps Jahangir's love and trust in her are most obvious in the degree to which the emperor brought her into every aspect of his life. Nur Jahan would be Jahangir's constant companion and political partner until his death.

Part Four

Elegant nomad, 1613–21

9

The peripatetic court

Ajmer and the campaign against Mewar

Having spent almost six years in Agra establishing the pattern of his relationships, both political and personal, Jahangir was restless. By 1613, the routine of the sedentary court had begun to oppress him. Complaining that he had little to do in the capital, he declared himself ready to lead the long-unfulfilled campaign against Mewar.[1] He commenced the journey at the beginning of September with a pilgrimage to his father's tomb just outside of Agra, which he called *Bihishtabad*, the Place of Paradise. He went on to make short visits to the palaces of his father-in-law, the I'timaduddawla and his brother-in-law, Asaf Khan, before started for Ajmer, where he planned to make a pilgrimage to the shrine of the great sufi shaykh, Khwaja Mu'inuddin Chishti, and personally deal with 'the damned Rana'.[2] As with his earlier travels in Kabul, the emperor did not hurry, lingering in garden encampments and halting the progress regularly to spend a day in hunting. He would reach Ajmer on 8 November 1613, entering the city at the hour determined by his astrologers. He immediately made his way to the Chishti shrine, where he ordered that all those present should pass before him so he might offer them charity 'according to their merits'.[3]

The Mewari conquest held special significance for Jahangir, as was evident from the start of his rule. Military success against Mewar had long eluded Akbar, and for Jahangir the defeat of Rana Amar Singh would be a resounding endorsement of his inheritance of Akbar's throne. In addition, a victory would perhaps assuage some personal guilt. As a prince, in 1599 and again in 1602, Jahangir had refused Akbar's demands that he lead the imperial armies against the Rana. His own spontaneous rebellion shortly thereafter had been a dangerous distraction that put an end to Akbar's final campaign against Mewar. In 1613 Jahangir would described the campaign as having been 'left half finished'.[4]

Shortly after his ascension he had sent Parvez with an army against the Rana, but, in an ironic twist, just as his own rebellion in 1599 had undermined his father's campaign, so too Prince Khusraw's rebellion in 1606 had distracted Jahangir and his armies. The emperor had been forced to order Parvez to settle with the Rana of Mewar as quickly as possible so that he might immediately march to Agra to protect the treasury and the family. As an added sweetener, Jahangir suggested that an obedient Parvez might take the mantle of favourite from his rebellious older brother Khusraw. When the Rana offered to send a younger son, rather than his heir, to Parvez to pay homage, the weak compromise was immediately accepted. The Mewari prince Bagha was sent under escort to the capital, while Parvez rushed to Agra, arriving there just after his elder brother's capture. Jahangir awarded Parvez a parasol and a jewelled sword, promoting him and increasing his jagirs. In 1609, Jahangir ordered Parvez to lead the imperial forces at the Deccani frontier, although the prince did not distinguish himself and the campaign became marked by lack of unity and communication, food shortages and deprivation. Meanwhile, Jahangir remained preoccupied with Mewar. The affair had not been satisfactorily settled and the brief truce arranged around the homage of Prince Bagha was quickly forgotten. Jahangir continued to send armies against the Rana, led by his most distinguished noblemen, always hopeful that he might achieve the victory that had long frustrated Akbar.

Although he had left Agra with the excuse of leading his own armies, on arriving in Ajmer in 1613 Jahangir almost immediately discarded his original plan and instead sent his third son, Khurram, who was proving to be a talented general. In late December 1613 Prince Khurram marched from Ajmer against Mewar with twelve thousand cavalry troops. In only a little over a year, early in 1615, Jahangir was able to trumpet the good news that 'my lucky son' Khurram had successfully forced the Rana to submit, agreeing to send his eldest son and the Mewari heir, Karan, to pay homage before the emperor.[5] Jahangir, revelling in the success of the campaign, was magnanimous in victory. 'Because it is our intention, insofar as possible, not to ruin ancient families...since Rana Amar Singh and his fathers were overly proud of the impregnability of their mountains and dwelling...and had not rendered homage to even one of the *padshahs* of Hindustan...I pardoned his shortcomings and showed him favor that would allay his fears'.[6]

It was in moments of military and diplomatic success that Jahangir demonstrated a particularly deft and foresighted strategy. Rather than impose humiliation on his defeated foes, Jahangir embraced them, in an effort to build a personal loyalty that might grow into imperial fealty. The first and best example of this strategy of victorious beneficence was in his campaign against Mewar. In February, the newly humbled Rana of Mewar himself paid homage to Khurram and presented him with a famous ruby, among other gifts. He was in turn shown great favour, was cradled and consoled by Khurram and gifted a 'sumptuous' robe of honour – along with another one hundred cloaks to be distributed amongst his entourage – as well as the gifts of an elephant and fifty horses from the imperial stables. He was not required to submit directly to Jahangir, but was released to go home, dignity intact, whereupon he sent his eldest son and chosen successor, Karan, to pay homage to Khurram and join that prince's retinue.

The treaty Jahangir negotiated with the Rana further demonstrates the delicate balance Jahangir carefully maintained with the elites of South Asia, in particular making allowances for 'ancient families', not only those who had long affiliated with the Mughals but even recent enemies and rivals. Jahangir graciously accepted the Rana's acceptance of allegiance to the Mughal dynasty and responded with enormous generosity, ordering the restoration of all of his ancestral territories, including even Chittor and lands seized years earlier by Akbar. The Rana's son and heir would be given a place with other young noblemen of the court within Jahangir's personal circle of followers. Jahangir made no effort to humiliate or undermine the Mewari dynasty, or diminish its regional charisma. In short, the treaty demonstrates a multi-generational strategy, which allowed the older Rana to retain his self-respect and autonomy, while pulling his son into the emperor's close circle where he would be expected to eventually culturally align with the Mughal political structure.

And indeed, the Mewari prince Karan was brought to court 'in all splendor and magnificence', where Jahangir claimed to have singled him out for kindness. Both Khurram and Karan were given gifts of royal robes by the emperor himself. Jahangir thoroughly enjoyed awing the Mewari prince, who he claimed was 'wild by nature', having been brought up in the mountains and away from royal courts. Jahangir gave him daily gifts over the course of the month, from falcons and swords to jewels and aromatics, and assorted textiles, from brocade to carpets. Karan was also given gifts, including a robe of honour, by Nur Jahan, an act of favour that left the prince, according to Jahangir, suitably impressed. In April, Jahangir visited the house of his victorious son, Prince Khurram, and was presented the famous 168-carat ruby of Mewar, valued at sixty thousand rupees. Jahangir expressed disappointment. It was not as large and fine as he had expected, but he had it inscribed with the date of the Rana's homage to the prince. Finally, intent on impressing the 'wild' prince of Mewar before returning him to his father, Jahangir took Karan lion hunting. The emperor described himself making a perfect shot in high wind, on a restless elephant – delighted to have not been humiliated in front of his new liegeman.

The walking commonwealth

Even after the Mewar campaign had been successfully concluded, Jahangir remained in Ajmer. Over the three years of his stay, by his own count, Jahangir visited the nearby Chishti shrine nine times, made eleven lengthy trips to Pushkar Lake, had gone on nearly fifty lion hunts and made thirty-eight visits to the nearby garden complex and hunting park he had built and named for himself, *Chashma Nur*. By 1616, however, Jahangir again expressed his boredom with sedentary rule. In particular, he claimed that the death of a beloved grandchild in May of that year had made the city unpalatable for him. Once again using a military campaign as an excuse to leave the city, he determined to personally lead the Mughal armies in a military campaign into the Deccan. Having sent his son Khurram ahead in the vanguard two days earlier, the emperor started out from Ajmer at the end of October. This would be the beginning of a years-long court progress.

All of the early Mughal kings had been highly mobile rulers, in part because of the military and strategic demands of their expansionist empire but also perhaps as a legacy of their semi-nomadic Central Asian heritage. Their travels allowed the Mughals to continually reassert their imperial powers, making personal and immediate the relationships of his allies with the king. Abu'l Fazl wrote of Akbar that

> when his majesty leaves court, in order to settle the affairs of a province, to conquer a kingdom, or to enjoy the pleasures of the chase, there is not a hamlet, a town or a city that does not send forth crowds of men and women with vow offerings in their hand, and prayers on their lips, touching the ground with their foreheads, praising the efficacy of their vows, or proclaiming the accounts of the spiritual assistance received.[7]

The design of the Mughal camp allowed the emperor to maintain the work of the royal court even while operating a near-continual court progress. As a mobile capital and seat of imperial authority, it contained 'all the essential components of the central administration, such as audience halls; the chancery; the treasury and mint; stables; artillery; a large portion of the main army; thousands of staff, servants, and porters; tens of thousands of domesticated and pack animals carrying equipment; and large bazaars'.[8] Until the eighteenth-century collapse of imperial fortunes immobilized the dynasty in the crumbling Red Fort in Delhi, the Mughal kings regularly toured their empire, warring against enemies and intimidating potential rivals with the vast size of the imperial armies, awing observers by the magnificence of their retinue.[9] Jahangir's grandson, Aurangzeb, emperor of the Mughals from 1658 to 1707, known as the last of the 'Great Mughals', might have been speaking for the dynasty when he warned his sons: 'As far as possible, the ruler of a kingdom should not spare himself from moving about; he should avoid staying in one place, which outwardly gives him repose but in effect brings on a thousand calamities and troubles' and 'It is bad for both emperors and water to remain at the same place. The water grows putrid and the king's power slips out of his control. In touring lies the honor, ease and splendor of kings'.[10]

The mobility of Jahangir's royal court was undoubtedly motivated less by political and military concerns than those of his ancestors, but his insistence on a constant court progress was readily accepted by the imperial nobility.[11] South Asian traditions of kingship had long supported a mobile royal court, asserting that a king should stride out to the four quarters of his territories, to establish himself as a true *chakrivartan*, a 'wheel turning ruler'. Ritually crossing his imperial territories, traveling to, touching and confirming his imperial borders, the ruler thereby centralized power in his own person. In addition, much of the Mughal nobility was descended from Persian or Turco-Mongol semi-nomadic warriors and empire builders, for whom the peripatetic court was a well-established and respected tradition of sovereign kingship. The mobility of the Mughal royal court, though it only loosely demonstrated the seasonal pastoralist pattern of their distant ancestors, was openly recognized by contemporaries as having Central Asian antecedents: 'This is indeed slow and solemn marching', wrote a later observer of the Mughal court progress, 'what we here call *a la Mongole*'.[12]

Even while travelling vast distances, Jahangir's life in camp was luxurious, as befitted a great king. Two identical tent encampments leapfrogged across each other, and as the royal court began their march in the morning, their destination camp had already been prepared for the emperor's arrival. In their turn, the tents they had just vacated, luxurious constructions of silk and linen, were hauled to a camping ground two days' march away, ensuring the royal company a well-prepared and comfortable halt. The road was widened and cleared for the court progress. The Englishman Edward Terry, who participated in the progress from Mandu to Ahmadabad in 1618, wrote of the thorough preparations for these 'journies in a wilderness where (by a very great company sent before us to make those passages and places fit to receive us) a way was cut out and made even, broad enough for our convenient passage; and in the places where we pitched out tents a great compass of ground rid, and made plain for them, by grubbing up a number of trees and bushes.' He added, 'That which seemed to me most strange was, that notwithstanding our marvelous great company of men, women, and children, there together, that must all be fed, and the very great number of other creatures that did eat corn… we had so many victuallers with us, and so much provision continually brought unto us, that we never felt there the want of any thing.'[13]

On the march, the sheer size of Jahangir's court progress was staggering. Foreign observers, unused to such a spectacle, wrote of their awe and astonishment. Terry had arrived in India in 1616 to serve as the chaplain of an East India Company fleet and remained to serve as chaplain for the embassy of Sir Thomas Roe. Participating in the Mughal court progress through Malwa and Gujarat in 1617–18, he reported:

> The number of people of all sorts is so exceeding great… first there are one hundred thousand soldiers, which always wait about that king (as before observed) and all his Grandees have a great train of followers and servants to attend them there, and so have all other men according to their several qualities, and all these carry their wives and children, and whole families with them, which must needs amount to a very exceeding great number.

So great was the crowd, wrote Terry, that it took twelve hours of steady march for the entire entourage to pass: 'When that King removes from one place to another… a broad passage is continually fill'd with passengers, and elephants, and horses, and asses, and oxen, (on which the manner sort of men and women with their little children, ride), so full as they may well pass one by the other.'[14] It was, he wrote, 'a walking commonwealth.'[15] Roe counted at least one hundred thousand horses, 'with infinite numbers of cammuls and elephants; so that with the whole baggage there could not bee lesse than five or six hundred thousand persons, insomuch as the waters were not sufficient for them.'[16]

Once a campsite had been chosen, the red tents of the king and his household were pitched in the centre. The largest tent was the massive *bargah*, which Abu'l Fazl claimed contained fifty-four chambers and could house up to ten thousand people. Next to that, the textile screen *gulalbar*, which contained the emperors administrative centre, including another massive rectangular tent, was divided into forty sections and hung with rich textiles. Akbar's personal tent pavilion, the *do-ashiyana manzil*, was a two-story structure containing his sleeping quarters and boasting a jharoka balcony. Adjacent were two dozen rectangular tents for the women of the harem. Immediately surrounding the emperor's tents were the white tents of his noblemen, each accompanied by his own establishment. Further out, camp followers and merchants assembled in assigned locations. Europeans were frankly awed by the organization of the Mughal royal encampment – even the stoic Roe described Jahangir's camp in nearly poetical terms, as 'One of the greatest rareties and magnificences I ever saw … like a beautiful city' with 'streets are so orderly [it] … may equall any towne in Europe for greatness'.[17] Hawkins compared it favourably to the English capitol, writing that when Jahangir 'rideth on progresse or hunting, the compasse of his tents may bee as much as the compasse of London and more; and I may say that all sorts of people that follow his campe there are two hundred thousand, for hee is provided as for a citie'.[18] Terry claimed its full impact could only be attained from a distance, writing:

> The infinite number of tents, or pavilions there pitched together, which in a plain make a show equal to a most spacious and glorious city. These tents I say, when they are altogether, cover such a great quantity of ground, that I believe it is five English miles at the least, from one side of them to the other, very beautiful to behold from some hill, where they may be all seen at once.[19]

While the wilderness served as a Mughal encampment when necessary, suburban gardens and hunting parks were the preferred staging grounds for the imperial court progress. The Mughal emperors invested time and labour into the design of their hunting camps: forested areas were cleared; lakes or rivers dammed or diverted; and tanks, reservoirs and even artificial lakes and formal gardens were constructed. The hunting parks were often an extension of formal imperial pleasure gardens, which had long been an important attribute of kingship and a demonstration of cultural prowess among the Mughals and their Central Asian ancestors. Most importantly, the imperial gardens and parklands of the Mughals 'served as nodes in an elite web of ceremonial movement'.[20]

The gardens of the Mughals were a legacy of ancient Persia. Lavish imperial projects of the Achaemenid court, gardens had been patronized by the wealthy and powerful and overlaid by representations of prestige and power over land, finances, labour and nature itself. Just as more permanent stone monuments were constructed in an effort to awe and impress, the imperial garden came to play a critical role in the public development of political identity and image, and displays of a fine aesthetic sensitivity. Hundreds of years later, the Turks and Mongols who came to rule the region recognized Persian pleasure gardens as a place to enjoy the prerogatives and privileges of royal life, as well as powerfully evocative instruments of religious and political legitimation.[21] It was under the rule of these semi-nomadic kings that the formal gardens of the Persian shah became integrated with camps and hunting grounds.

In the fourteenth century, Timur had surrounded the palaces of his capital city with pleasure gardens planted with orchards of fruit and shade trees, raised paths, artificial streams and herds of wild deer. Visitors noted that the royal family lived year-round in tent encampments within the royal gardens. For Timur and his descendants, the pleasure gardens of Mawarannahr became the site of public display and court ritual, the social centre for the literary and political elite, and eventually a symbol of the golden age of late Timurid society. When in 1526 Babur had arrived in northern India among his starkest criticisms of the conquest territories was the lack of formal pleasure gardens built in the Persian tradition.[22] Insistent on the need for formal gardens to serve as the political and social centre of his rule, he would build a series of walled gardens along the undeveloped banks of the Yamuna river, and gave tracts of riverfront land to his nobles for them to do the same. Building imperial gardens across the breadth of their territories, the Mughal conquest of India 'came to be expressed hardly at all in religious monuments but pervasively as the imperialism of landscape architecture, the civilized ideal of the Timurid period'.[23]

As Jahangir crossed the landscape of his territories, he created and renovated hunting parks and gardens. His gardens were more than just an enhancement of the beauty of the natural landscape. Jahangir would comment that the transformation from natural to manipulated landscape made the site 'a *real place*, the likes of which world travelers could not point to'.[24] On his first visit to Lahore as emperor, Jahangir established a hunting park in the western suburbs, Shaykhupura, adding a massive tank and minaret complex, called Hiran Minar. The complex would serve as a campground for the imperial court. He also commissioned a pair of imperial gardens in the city itself – one in the fort, a rectangular garden with pool, and the other added south of the city on the Ravi river, near the existing Mughal Dilamuz and Dilkusha gardens. A foreign visitor listed the fruits and flowers in the king's northern garden, the diversity and range unattainable in the Gangetic plateau explaining Jahangir's delight: 'very good apples... almonds, peaches, figges, grapes, quinces, orenges... etc., roses, stock- gellow-flowers, marigolds, wall-flowers, ireos [iris], pinkes, with white and red divers sorts of other Indian flowers'.[25] In 1614, while hunting nilgais in the Taragarh hills, Jahangir had discovered a natural spring, which he declared contained the finest water in Ajmer.[26] Appreciative of the beauty of the setting, Jahangir ordered site be developed into an imperial hunting park. The site, which he named for himself, *Chashma Nur*, would eventually boast eight intricately painted pavilions and a 30-meter square pool. Jahangir visited the park thirty-eight times during the nearly four years he lived in Ajmer.

Jahangir claimed pre-existing gardens for himself, including two major garden complexes outside of Agra. Both sites made comfortable camping grounds for the royal court progress and were close enough to the capital to be a destination for short excursions, for family picnics and parties. Babur had originally built the famous *Gul Afshan*, 'Flower scattering' (now called *Ram Bagh*, or Garden of Repose), on the eastern bank of the Yamuna River, the site of his successful efforts to transplant Afghani fruits to Hindustan. Jahangir used it regularly, his ownership marked by the new name he gave it, *Nur Afshan*, 'Light scattering'. Jahangir named a second garden just to its south *Nur Manzil Bagh*, 'Garden of the Abode of Light', and claimed to have spent two hundred thousand rupees on its structures and numerous fountains, for which water was pumped by teams of bullocks from a well just outside the wall. Finally, like rare and obscure objects, even a garden could be gifted to the emperor. Roe described a site just a few miles from Ajmer where Asaf Khan had built and given to Jahangir 'a house of pleasure' cut from two great rocks, and with it 'a handsome little garden with fine fountaynes...a place of much melancholy delight and securitye, only being accompanied with wild Peacockes, turtles, foule, and Munkyes, that inhabit the rocks hanging every way over yt'.[27] As for original gardens, Jahangir's legacy includes some of the loveliest of Mughal Hindustan, including large terraced landscapes that stretched for miles along the banks of Lake Dal in Kashmir, becoming synonymous with Mughal elegance and luxury.[28] Demonstrating the character and interests of its imperial patron, it would be built 'more for aesthetic and convivial purposes and secondarily as statements of power and dominion'.[29]

As had his ancestors, however, Jahangir used his gardens as imperial backdrops for the exposition of his own political power and military successes. Although sculpture was not a popular art form at the Mughal court, on the occasion of his triumph over Mewar, Jahangir had ordered statues carved of the Rana and his son, which were then erected in the palace garden in Agra, directly below the *jharoka-i darshan*. Their presence left the defeated Mewaris in permanent public attendance before the emperor. In this, Jahangir may have been inspired by Akbar who, according to Monserrate, had put up at a gate of the Agra fort life-size statues of vanquished Rajput chiefs on elephants.[30] Gardens were also displays for imperial memorabilia. When visiting his son's garden, Jahangir noticed a tree with a hole that he deemed ugly. Taking it as an opportunity to assert paternal power and to demonstrate filial pride, Jahangir had it filled with a slab of marble stone carved in his own name next to that of his father, King of Kings, Akbar.[31]

The fruits of empire

The very fruit grown in Mughal imperial gardens was for Jahangir a symbol of his own great political power and imperial reach. His notable passion for grapes and melons, cherries and mangoes can be seen as an inheritance from his influential great-grandfather, and in both of their memoirs fruit becomes an unexpected metaphor both for territorial acquisition and for homeland. Residing in Agra as the new king of Hindustan, Babur had complained bitterly about the poor quality of India's melons. In what he described as a state of exile, Babur had missed the fruit of Kabul so greatly that on one occasion when he cut open a melon that had been carried to him all the way from his former capital, the familiar aroma caused him to burst into tears of homesickness. Among the last entries in his memoir, Babur described his efforts to transplant the beloved fruits of the Afghan mountains to his *Hasht Bihisht*, Garden of the Eight Paradises, outside of Agra, successfully producing within just a few years what he pronounced to be 'very nice little melons and … rather nice grapes…. I was particularly happy that melons and grapes could turn out so well in Hindustan'.[32]

Jahangir wrote regularly and fulsomely of the fruits that came to his court from all corners of his territories. In his first years on the throne he evoked his great-grandfather Babur through his pleasure in the grapes and cherries, the melons and apricots of his Afghani territories, all of which he indulged to his heart's content while socializing in the gardens of the ancestral capital of Kabul, describing cherries growing on the branches in pairs, seeming like clouds of butterflies.[33] Several years after his return from the Afghan territories, and regularly thereafter, Jahangir received the gift of fifty camel-loads of melons from Kariz, an agricultural village in the vicinity of Kabul. They were 'better than any melon in Khurasan', claimed Jahangir. Having chosen a regnal name that described him as 'One Who Seizes the World', the emperor confirmed and described the vast distances of his imperial territories with the tray of fruit he was offered on that occasion, which included not only Karizi melon, but also 'melons from Badakhshan and Kabul, grapes from Samarqand and Kabul, sweet pomegranates from Yazd, apricots from Farah, pears from Badakhshan, apples from Samarqand, Kashmir, Kabul and Jalalabad (a dependency of Kabul), and pineapple, which is a fruit that comes from the Franks' ports'. Jahangir would add that, just as Babur had had grapes and melons planted in his gardens in Agra, so too pineapple was successfully being cultivated in the Agra orchards, which produced several thousand of the fruit each year. On a visit to Gujarat in early 1618, he was proud to show off by sharing Kariz fruits with the Shaykhs of Ahmadabad, whose melons, he was proud to announce, were not nearly so fine as his own. The caravan which carried the melons had taken five months to reach Gujarat but arrived undamaged and seemed fresh. Jahangir's oranges had travelled almost as far, passed from hand to hand by runners all the way from Bengal.

Having renovated Akbar's garden in Lahore, the Bagh-i Nur Afza, Jahangir had cherry trees planted, and he delighted in their success. Jahangir claimed to love cherries more than any other fruit because sweet cherries went so well with wine. He named each tree as it bore fruit: Shirinbar (Sweet Fruit), Khoshguvar (Delicious Flavour), the most prolific, Purbar (Fruitful) and Kambar (Little Fruit). His son's garden nearby had a fruit bearing cherry tree that the emperor named Shahwar (Kingly), and a new sapling in the Ishrat Afza Garden he named Nawbar (New Fruit).[34] The reader cannot doubt his very real sense of personal accomplishment and pleasure when he exclaimed that those cherries he had picked for himself had additional sweetness.[35] On the final day of cherry season, Jahangir reported that fifteen hundred cherries had been picked from the trees in the Nur Afza garden, and he went on to order that cherry trees be grafted in most of his Kashmiri gardens. Babur had once commented that while the mango of India was excellent, it was by no means equal in flavour to the melon. For Jahangir, on the other hand, much as he declared his love for the fruits of his Central Asian 'ancestral homeland' and for all that he welcomed the camel-loads of imported melons, his reader was assured by this proud South Asian king that Kashmiri cherries were superior to those of Kabul and none of the fruits of the north could equal the delicious Indian mango.

10

The itinerant king

From garden to garden

The pain of his granddaughter's loss, which Jahangir claimed had inspired his departure from Ajmer in 1616, did not linger. Nor did his resolution to personally lead the imperial armies in the Deccan. Almost immediately upon beginning the journey, Jahangir had reclaimed his pleasure in the open road. The emperor simply relished the experience of travel, describing daily hunts and regular halts at scenic locations. Jahangir would write that the journey was so pleasant that he never felt the difficulty of the road. He often based the length of each stay on the beauty of the landscape, confirming the laxity of the schedule with comments in his memoir that 'the place was so pleasant and the lake so fine that we stayed for four days' and 'it was so green and delightful that we stayed there for three days'. Hunting each day, their evening campsites were all in 'delightful places on the banks of lakes, streams, or large irrigation canals edged by trees, greenery, and poppy fields in flower'.[1] Heading towards Gujarat, the imperial retinue travelled to a mountain valley with a waterfall. Although it was the dry season, the stream had been strategically blocked for the emperor's visit. The water was released all in a rush so that he might admire it pouring down from the cliffs above. 'To chance on such a site is an opportunity not to be missed,' he wrote.[2] Afterwards, Jahangir and his retinue drank wine on the banks of the stream, in the shadow of the mountain. Arriving at last in Mandu at the beginning of March 1617, the emperor would famously exclaim that in the long months of travelling, 'the arduousness of a journey was never felt... it was as if we were moving from garden to garden'.[3]

The informality of the peripatetic court facilitated a relatively intimate and unconstrained social life for the king, and spontaneous stops for wine were not uncommon. The sheer beauty of his surroundings might bring on the urge for drink, as when on the road to Kabul Jahangir became enamoured by the clear air and delicate rain and called a halt for bowls of wine. From that point forward, he commented, the road was travelled in good spirits.[4] In the capital or on the court progress, Jahangir hosted regular drinking parties on Thursday evenings to which 'particular servants', those noblemen closest to the emperor, were invited. Bowls of wine and other unspecified intoxicants were shared amongst the partygoers as, Jahangir would write, his servants were 'made happy on goblets of joy'.[5] The emperor's wine parties were written into the calendar of the royal court, with the consumption of alcohol the central activity of the gatherings. Jahangir took great care in arranging that his wine parties take place in a perfect setting. The length of time in a given campsite might be shortened or stretched if the location was considered appropriate for a scheduled wine party – in particular, Jahangir required it be next to a river or a lake. On a Wednesday in the autumn of 1618, the royal court progress had planned to camp at Samarna, but with no lake in sight, and his thoughts on the wine party scheduled for the next evening, Jahangir ordered that they push on. The royal entourage continued its march from midnight to Thursday dawn, when they finally arrived at a large manmade pool in Bhagor. Jahangir's wine party took place by the waters that evening, as scheduled.[6]

On reaching Ramsar (Ransagar), a property the emperor had assigned to Nur Jahan, the king's massive company settled in for eight days and the lake was illuminated for Jahangir's regular Thursday evening drinking party. A week later, the emperor and his companions enjoyed their wine cups and then climbed into the boats that had been wheeled along on the court progress, ready for such an opportunity as this. Fishing with nets in the nearby lake, the imperial party proudly divided their catch amongst the courtiers. Spending his days in boating and hunting, Jahangir praised the beauty of the landscape and the verdant countryside. In mid-February, the royal progress had pitched tents in village of Sarangpur, about which Jahangir effusively wrote, 'What can one write of the beauty and delights of this place?'[7] Coming upon a massive banyan tree, marked with Akbar's handprint, Jahangir added a handprint of his own and ordered a marble monument to mark the spot. Hunting towards Haselpur, Jahangir waxed poetic on the local grapes and mangoes, the beauty of the rivers, the poppies in bloom.

The joy Jahangir took in travel would only increase throughout his reign; he would remain relentlessly mobile until his death. His bliss was not always shared by his companions. When Thomas Roe requested permission to join his court, the restless king had fervently asked how far he would be willing to travel. Roe, with high hopes for trade concessions, answered, 'To the world's end, if his Majestie did.'⁸ It was a promise he sorely regretted. In 1617, he would write to a friend, complaining bitterly of his discomfort and claiming that those who marched in the king's progress were in a state of misery. 'His own people, who almost know no other god', wrote Roe of the king's retinue, 'blaspheme his name'.⁹ On their travels to Ahmadabad in early 1618, Roe complained that the emperor 'continues without rest, by soe miserable ways as I believe never armie nor multitude ever went... I am entering into the Miserie and Charge of following'.¹⁰ Yet not all who journeyed with Jahangir were as uncomfortable. Terry, the English cleric who was also pulled along in the wake of the royal court, seems to have relished aspects of the journey. He wrote that winter of 'traveling with him [Roe] in progress with that King... 'twixt Mandoa [Mandu] and Amadavaz [Ahmadabad] nineteen days, making but short journeys in a wilderness where... we never felt there the want of any thing'.¹¹

Touring and hunting

The journey from Ajmer to Mandu would take the royal progress over four months, of which nearly every day was spent hunting, even as the royal court marched for forty-six days and rested in a series of camps for seventy-eight days, including the Mughal hunting parks of Bhimbar, Girjhak, Makhiyala, Jahangirabad, Sirhind, Salimgarh and Palam.¹² The hunt was woven into the court progress, summed up in the commonly used phrase *sair u shikar*, touring and hunting. Travelling with the royal court to Mandu, the Englishman, Terry, claimed that the length of stay in any one spot was predicated on water supplies, and when there was plenty the entourage would remain in place, allowing the king to 'find pastimes', the most important of which was the hunt.¹³

Jahangir was at all times prepared to hunt, travelling with 'divers kinds of hawks, dogs and leopards... and being thus provided for variety of sports, would fly at anything in the air, or seize on any creature he desired to take on the earth'.¹⁴ Jahangir would hunt along with his noblemen, in 'a very great company besides of Persian and Tartarian horsemen, his soldiers (which are stout daring men) would attempt to take some young wild elephant found in these woods... they likewise pursued on horseback lions, and other wild beasts, and killed some of them with their bows and carbines and lances'.¹⁵ The emperor kept a regular tally of the number and type of game hunted. Camping near Mandu in March of 1617, Jahangir reflected on the journey, regaling his companions with stories of past hunts and describing his own keen longing and avidity for the hunt.

Idly wondering if he might be able to compose a full list of all the animals he had hunted since the age of twelve (1580–81) and ordered that everyone who participated in the royal hunt, including the scouts, record keepers and overseers, bring him their count. The result was an astounding 28,532 animals, of which 17,167 had been shot by the emperor himself.[16] Jahangir carefully organized the list into three categories. Of quadrupeds, he counted eighty-six lions and nine bears, along with cheetahs, foxes, otters and hyenas and sixty-four wolves. As many of his hunts were directed at the antelope, it is no surprise that he counted 889 nilgai, along with two thousand other various deer and antelope. In the category of birds, he counted 13,964 of various kinds, including over ten thousand pigeons, and various hawks, ducks, herons and even crows. His final category was that of water animals and included only the ten crocodiles he claimed to have killed.

The Mughal dynasty boasted a lengthy hunting tradition – their Turkic and Mongol ancestors had been famed hunters – yet hunting was a prerogative of kingship among the royal courts of India as well. In the medieval world, the royal hunt was not primarily motivated by the search for food. It was instead a privilege reserved for the nobility and an opportunity to demonstrate skills of governance and warfare. A king might prove his worth as ruler through his performance in the hunt, as the temperament and skills required for both occupations were closely related. The hunt displayed their prowess with horse and weapons, strategic planning and an ability to control an armed cohort. Displays of hunting skill played a vital role nearly universally in establishing high social status. Kingship was closely associated with physical capacity and feats which are commonly attested by and projected through royal hunt. Among the ancestors of the Mughals, a successful hunter like Chingis Khan would attract a following when his skills had proved his worth as a leader of men. Centuries later, the royal hunt remained 'a heroic pastime', as an English witness to Jahangir's hunts would write, 'or rather a high and dangerous attempt at becoming great personages'.[17]

Jahangir filled his *Nama* with regular references to the circle hunt of ancient Turco-Mongol origin called, by both Mongols and their distant descendants the Mughals, the *qamargha*. Men in the tens of thousands participated in the Mughal *qamargha*. Witnesses describe up to hundreds of thousands in the emperor's retinue, and hunting expeditions fused with military campaigns so that the two became nearly indistinguishable in the eyes of observers. Hunters, soldiers and serving men would arrange themselves in a circle, as vast as their numbers would allow. Moving in unison towards the centre, the beaters would drive all wild game before them. Once the game had become densely packed within the circle, the ruler and noblemen of his choosing could ride into the ring to slay the animals of their choice. Jahangir participated in a week-long *qamargha* in his seventh regnal year, which he carefully described in his memoir – a hunt that would not have greatly changed since the days of his distant ancestors. Noting the large congregation of antelopes near Samugarh, the hunt was arranged. Beaters drove antelopes from every direction into a large central area which was then surrounded with cloth barriers, *sarapardas* and *gulalbaras*, which formed a sort of corral. When the hunting ground had been made ready for his entrance, Jahangir entered and on every day for the next week hunted with the women of his harem. On Sunday and Thursday, days he had determined not to shoot animals, they were instead caught in traps.

Jahangir counted 917 antelopes, male and female, hunted in that week. More than two-thirds of them were captured alive, however, and of that number, 404 were turned loose on the polo field at Fatehpur Sikri. In an act reminiscent of his fishing expedition outside of Lahore in 1607, he ordered that another eighty-four captured antelope have silver rings put in their noses, and they too were released on the polo ground. The meat of the nearly three hundred antelopes killed, by gun or cheetah, was divided among the members of the royal court: the women of the harem and their servants, as well as the emperor's *amirs* and courtiers. When Jahangir declared himself finally tired of hunting, his noblemen were allowed to enter the hunting ground to take what they liked of the remaining beasts.[18]

The Mughals used a wide variety of animals as hunting partners, not only horses and elephants, which were at times both vehicle and weapon, using tusks and feet to kill. Falconry was an elite sport in the medieval world, universally celebrated as a symbol of kingship, and Jahangir often had himself portrayed with a hunting bird on his wrist. Equally prestigious was the use of non-domesticated animals in the hunt, and the miniatures of the period as well as the *Jahangirnama* attest to the use of trained cheetahs to hunt alongside the emperors. Akbar had claimed to have invented a method of deer hunting that combined the Central Asian *qamargah* with the South Asian practice of hunting with tamed cheetahs. As Abu'l Fazl described it, 'The hunters lay in ambush near a place frequented by deer, and commenced the chase from this place as if it was a *qamargha* hunt. The cheetah is then let off in all directions, and many deer are thus caught.'[19] Akbar had a stable of as many as one thousand cheetahs and two hundred cheetah trainers and keepers, with as many as three or four men assigned to each animal. The cheetahs were each given a name, 'which indicates some of its qualities', and rank, travelling with the court progress on litters hung on each side of an elephant's back or on wheeled carts, with servants running alongside.[20] Jahangir's hunting cheetahs wore not only collars and leashes but rode horseback to the hunt on gold brocade saddlecloths and, like his father, he had them carried in the royal procession on wheeled carts, sometimes pulled by their personal handlers. The best hunters among Jahangir's imperial cheetahs were not only named but also given titles and even had their portraits painted. Lions were also used as hunting assistants, referenced in a single entry in the *Jahangirnama*, describing a day's hunt while on a journey to the ocean port of Cambay, and Jahangir wrote of one of his tame lions successfully taking down several large nilgai while on a three-month-long winter hunt in 1611.[21]

Jahangir wrote fondly and nostalgically of an even more unusual hunting companion, an antelope named Hansraj, who he claimed was unequalled in fights with other antelopes and tame enough to draw wild antelopes to the waiting hunters.[22] When Hansraj died at Jahangirpur, a favourite hunting ground, the emperor had a tower erected over the grave, on which the royal court's chief calligrapher inscribed: 'In this delightful open space came an antelope into the trap of the ruler of the world, Nuruddin Muhammad Jahangir. Within a month, it had lost its wildness and become the chief of the royal antelopes.' From the time of the death of Hansraj, and in his honour, Jahangir banned the hunting of antelopes on that plain, issuing an imperial decree that from that time an antelope's 'flesh would be like that of a cow for *kafirs* and like that of pigs for the Muslims'.[23] A gravestone in the shape of an antelope was erected in commemoration of this favoured hunting companion.

In creating specific hunting bans, Jahangir was following his father's model. Akbar had set Sundays aside, as the day of his birth, banning not only the hunt but even the eating of meat. Thursdays would be set aside as well, as the day of Jahangir's accession to the throne – although, to be clear, this was only a ban on shooting prey, and the insatiable Jahangir continued to hunt on Thursdays with cheetahs.[24] When the Feast of the Sacrifice fell on a day in which the killing had been forbidden, Jahangir forced the court to wait until the next day.[25] He himself then slaughtered three sheep to mark the occasion and then set off on another nilgai hunt.

Throughout the years of his reign, Jahangir hunted regularly with the women of the harem. Hunting together in mixed parties, the inner circle combined the physical energy and tension of the hunt with relaxed evenings, participating in parties and picnics in their encampments in the imperial gardens. Jahangir even described the women of the family as regular participants in the *qamargha*, in which they hunted with rifles, often from the perch of an elephant howdah – in later years, from a carriage. By the time of her first mention in the *Jahangirnama*, in 1614, three years after their marriage, Nur Jahan had become one of Jahangir's closest companions. She was widely recognized as a skilled marksman, which must have particularly endeared her to her husband. Jahangir allowed her to take on the sovereign act of the lion or tiger kill, even while jealously restricting it from his sons and closest courtiers. Her success in the hunt delighted him. When she shot four tigers with six bullets, none having missed its target, he proudly wrote of the occasion in his memoir, describing the exceptional marksmanship she displayed, shooting from the back of an elephant in a howdah. In reward, her doting husband scattered a thousand *ashrafis* over her head and gave her a pair of pearls and a valuable diamond.[26] In 1619, on the road to Kashmir, his huntsmen brought reports of a tiger in the area of Mathura. Arranging to have the animal's retreat blocked with several elephants, he mounted and went out with his attendants. As Jahangir had recently vowed to kill no animal by his own hand, once again it was Nur Jahan who fired the musket. Jahangir described the rank smell of the tiger and the restless elephant shifting under her, conditions which would have made the shot difficult even for one of his noblemen. He proudly confirmed however that Nur Jahan had been able to kill the tiger with a single bullet.[27]

In 1618, as he turned fifty, Jahangir recalled a vow he had made years earlier that he would give up hunting in that year. He delayed, making the determination that quitting at the year's end would be sufficient for the terms of the vow. He continued to hunt until in mid-October his grandson Shah Shuja, son of Khurram, became ill. As Shah Shuja's condition deteriorated Jahangir became increasingly distraught. He recalled hearing of a similar crisis, when he himself was as yet unborn and not moving in the womb. Akbar had commonly hunted with leopards but, according to Jahangir, the deeply concerned father-to-be vowed that if the child remained healthy, he would never hunt with leopards again on a Friday. In the same spirit, Jahangir efficiently chose to apply his older vow to his new circumstances and forswore shooting animals from that time forward, in hopes that his sacrifice would result in Shuja's recovery.[28]

Jahangir was further inspired to follow through on the pledge because his fiftieth year began with a new health crisis, leaving him struggling to breathe properly. After reaffirming the vow and making a pilgrimage to Akbar's tomb to ask his support, his felt that his health had begun to improve. Proud of his sacrifice, however delayed it had been, Jahangir quoted one of the most beloved of Persian poets, Sa'adi, writing in his memoir: 'Harm not an ant dragging a crumb, for it has a soul, and life is precious.'[29] In 1619, Jahangir arranged for another *qamargha*, in which seven hundred antelopes were captured, to be released on the polo fields of Fatehpur, thus satisfying his lust for hunting while fulfilling his promise to do no harm.[30] His vow notwithstanding, Jahangir would continue to describe participating in an unceasing number of hunting parties, offering no explanation for the seeming conflict. When Khurram finally went into rebellion several years later, Jahangir wrote that he felt free to call off his personal hunting ban, however incomplete his observance, given that it had been offered for the sake of the rebel's son.

Hunting was seen as a valuable public service performed by a noble monarch. An English visitor to Jahangir's India warned that although the landscape was lovely, 'lest this remote country should seeme like an earthly Paradise without any discommodities, I must needes take notice there of many lions, tygres, jackals... and many other harmful beasts'.[31] As a protector of the people, the hunter-king would rid the landscape of dangers and pests. The hunt could then be claimed as a royal duty, an act of arbitration, between the king's subjects and the forces of nature which only the king was competent to control. In the ancient Indian tradition, the 'rulers had to interact with the wilderness, placate, contain and appropriate its raw power', whereby the king gained religious merit, and the hunting ground became a ceremonial seat of royalty.[32]

Jahangir claimed that his hunt kept the wilderness in check, protecting his subjects and their property. In particular, the special qualities of the lion or tiger hunt offered the emperor an opportunity to affirm his sovereignty and demonstrate his own manifest nobility. In 1608, when lions were reported to be menacing travellers between Panipat and Karnal, Jahangir organized a *qamargha* of elephants with which to kill them, explaining that he had thereby 'eliminated their evil'.[33] On other occasions, he described himself having delivered his subjects of an 'evil menace' and a lion 'of its own evil nature'.[34]

As with other attributes of kingship, Jahangir jealously guarded his role as protector of his subjects. He rarely allowed others the opportunity to hunt lions or tigers, although as we have seen, Nur Jahan was made a regular exception. When in 1617 Sir Thomas Roe was threatened at home by a wolf and a lion that had breached the high wall around his property, he was required to wait for permission from the emperor before he was allowed to kill the lion, 'for that no man may meddle with Lions but the King'.[35] Having been granted permission, he was able to shoot it only after the lion had killed a small dog 'that I had long kept', although a household servant was allowed to kill the wolf. As the favourite son and presumed successor, Prince Khurram was given permission to lead the hunt against a man-eating tiger, but when the carcass was displayed at court,

Jahangir's insecure pride and competitiveness became evident, as he pointed out that although while alive the animal had seemed large, in death it proved to be thin and underweight – much smaller than large tigers he himself had shot![36]

Jahangir claimed to prefer this most dangerous of hunts to any other and would forego all other game 'as long as there is a lion to hunt'.[37] Even when the summons came on a non-hunting day, Jahangir fulfilled his duty. He responded to the request with alacrity, proudly announcing afterwards that he had taken the lion down with a single shot and adding that although he did not generally hunt with guns on Sundays and Thursdays, the danger to his subjects required his service.[38] The emperor even took responsibility for what he claimed was a shrinking population of dangerous animals, writing that under his own divinely appointed rule, the creatures of his lands had lost their wild natures and even lions had become tame and harmless.

Gujarat and the sea

A year after departing Ajmer, in October of 1617, Jahangir led his court progress towards Gujarat, professing a desire to both see the ocean and to hunt wild elephant. Along the route, the emperor welcomed a steady stream of visitors, continuing to hunt almost daily. Here the *Jahangirnama* begins to read like a travelogue, its pages filled with descriptions of landscapes and monuments, local history, legends of strange incidents and past kings. It was not until they neared Ahmadabad that Jahangir finally discovered a landscape he did not like. The emperor complained of the arid land, the thorn hedges and roads so dusty that travel in a cart had become impossible, declaring that Ahmadabad should have its name changed to *Gardabag*, City of Dust.[39]

His party reached the sea at last, arriving in the port city of Cambay in mid-December 1617. Although a passionate observer of nature, Jahangir seems not to have enjoyed the shore and remained only for a few days to make charitable contributions and offer honours to the local noblemen. On 30 December, the imperial banners unfurled towards Ahmadabad. His dislike of the landscape did not prevent Jahangir from remaining curious and open, exploring local specialties. He tasted kedgeree for the first time and enjoyed it enough to order that it be served on his 'sufi-like days' when he kept a vegetarian table.[40] Having spent only a month in the area, however, Jahangir began to prepare for a return to the lovely Malwa. Conditions were not optimal. It was already March, and the heat was intense, making the proposed journey difficult. Additionally, news had arrived that the plague was in Agra. Eventually he was convinced to wait for cooler weather in Ahmadabad, which was larger and had more resources than Mandu. Jahangir bitterly criticized the local weather and what he considered to be the foul air of Gujarat. He did admit that his distress may have been exacerbated by his enormous consumption of alcohol and opium. On his doctor's recommendation, he reduced his use of intoxicants, noting that it made a slight improvement.

The insalubrious climate and setting made his royal duties seem more onerous than usual. Jahangir complained that although it caused him great suffering, he had the responsibility to dispense justice and charity and 'had given to the needy night and day', never resting from his labours, which he claimed were his only consolation for the journey to Ahmadabad.[41] The miserable Jahangir was inspired to suggest even more alternative names for the city, bitterly and creatively suggesting *Samumistan* (Land of Pestilential Wind), *Bimaristan* (Land of the Ill), *Zaqumzar* (Thorn Patch), *Jahannamabad* (Hell City), adding that Ahmadabad 'has qualities of all of them'.[42] He felt trapped by the monsoon, claiming that were it not for the rains, he would ride away on a flying carpet, like Solomon, and composed a ghazal that reflected his mood:

> It is necessary to quaff a goblet of wine in the face of the garden
> There are many clouds, it is necessary to quaff much wine.[43]

Restless and in bad health, and thoroughly anxious to depart, he finally ordered the forward camp dispatched to Agra in late summer, but in the meantime the rains held him in Ahmadabad for two more weeks. On 2 September 1618, he celebrated his fiftieth solar birthday with a weighing ceremony, scattering pearls and golden flowers. Finally, the rains slowed and his imperial camp managed to shift a short distance, to the banks of the river in Mahmudabad. There they remained for eleven more days, waiting for the river to recede enough to allow a crossing. Jahangir was inspired to perform a scientific experiment, testing the pestilence of the air by hanging a dead sheep in both Ahmadabad and in Mahmudabad. As one might expect, given his dislike of the place, Jahangir claimed that the sheep's carcass rotted much faster in the airs of Ahmadabad.[44]

By mid-September, Jahangir had once again contentedly returned to the routine of the travelling camp, enjoying regular hunts and wine parties, making side trips for pilgrimage and sightseeing and the occasional public gesture of piety and justice. Camping at Ujjain, a *jagir* of Khurram, he visited an ascetic living in a hut next to the Kankriya tank. They talked for a long time, Jahangir would later write, because 'I am always ready to receive advice from dervishes'.[45]

Travelling onwards to Khurram's palace, he celebrated the birth of a grandson, Aurangzeb, sharing wine bowls with his intimates. Looking around him at the flourishing fields of millet, Jahangir was self-congratulatory, moralistically reflecting on the story of the gardener whose successful crops proved to be a reflection of the good intentions of a just and benevolent king.[46] By early December he had reached the fortress of Ranthambhor, where Jahangir toured the massive complex. Complaining that the rooms were airless and small 'by the Hindu fashion' he settled himself comfortably in a bathhouse next to small garden for the length of his stay. Finishing with the fortress he ordered that each of the prisoners held there be brought before him for royal justice and clemency. All but murderers and those adjudged potentially seditious were freed, and the emperor offered each a grant and robe of honour, in accordance with his station. Once again, Jahangir returned to the court progress, which wound through the hills to Agra.

An Enlightenment king of the east

The memoir written by his great-grandfather had given Jahangir a literary model that offered critical insights into kingship and dynastic identity, but it also included detailed descriptions of the physical landscape, which Babur had closely observed throughout the years of his ranging across Central and South Asia. Babur's emphasis on the natural world was surely an influence on Jahangir, who opened his own *Nama* with detailed description of India's landscape, its cities, its flora and fauna, adding several passages on the characteristics, history, climate and conditions of Agra, the de facto capital of the empire and the site of Jahangir's accession to the throne. In what would become a typical frame of reference, using very precise numerical measurements, Jahangir described the length and breadth of the city and counting the cost of its construction, not only in lakhs of Mughal rupees but also in the currency of Iran and Turan, not incidentally confirming that the emperor anticipated an international readership for his memoir. Throughout his reign, Jahangir continued to record the details of the landscape. His descriptions of natural phenomenon were patient and exacting, as he enumerated the birds, the fruits and flowers, their unique characteristics, their growing patterns, and always his own heightened sensitivity to the beauty around him.[47]

Jahangir remained fascinated by the rare and beautiful, the unique, inexplicable, or simply odd. Scenic landscapes were lovingly detailed in effusive prose as the emperor's notes became a travelogue, describing local places but more often local history and legend, strange incidents and past kings. At times, describing a curious article or event, from the appearance of a heavily bearded woman to the strange sound of the wind in the mountains of Kashmir, Jahangir explained that it was their very strangeness that justified their inclusion in his memoir.[48]

In addition, the emperor often made painstaking efforts to offer scientific observation and analysis. Jahangir carefully collected sometimes quite random and miscellaneous data, as he measured, weighed, compared and offered his reader detailed measurements of fortresses, pillars, animals hunted, the depths of ponds and the comparative weight of soils, and even water. In his seventeenth regnal year, he visited the waterfall at Uhar. Because the spring was renowned for its beauty and the quality of its waters, Jahangir ordered its waters weighed, and a comparison made with water from the Ganges and the Lar valley. Arguing that the quality of the water would be indicated by its weight, Jahangir found that Uhar water was heavier than Ganges water, and Lar Valley water was the lightest of all.[49]

For all the occasional seeming frivolity of his record keeping, he remained observant and at times deeply pragmatic. Travelling to Gujarat, the emperor noticed a clever wall design that allowed porters to rest their loads on the low walls to rest, before easily going on again. Admiring the practical engineering, Jahangir ordered similar walls to be constructed across the empire, at the expense of the royal court. At times the information he had collected could prove useful. When a quail with a single spur confused his hunting scouts, Jahangir identified it as a female. When the bird was split open, several embryonic eggs were discovered. Delighted at having his statement confirmed, Jahangir happily postured before his scouts (and his readers!), explaining that the female's head and beak were smaller than the male's, adding with a degree of personal pride, that his skill had come from a lifetime of patience and careful observation. Recording the story of his success, in his memoir the emperor smugly went on to add a thorough explanation of bird windpipes, types of bustards, and his own refined sensitivity to the differences in flavour between the most delicious fish in Hindustan.[50]

His travels were an opportunity for regional elites to pay homage, and knowing of the emperor's delight in oddities, they gifted him with the curiosities of their region, which had been carefully assembled for the occasion. Jahangir collected the obscure and unique whenever possible but if in his travels he happened upon a curious landscape the emperor took ownership in other ways: through meticulous measurements of scale and weight, by having an inscription carved, a garden or platform built, or ordering a likeness rendered by the painters he kept near him as he travelled. Their route taking them past a palm tree that he felt had an odd shape, the emperor stopped the progress to measure the height of its trunk and both forks of its limbs, and then the distance from the ground to the place where the branches and leaves began to emerge. The king's measuring continued beyond the obvious, from the place where branches and leaves were green to the very top of the tree, and then its circumference. The unusual palm tree so enthralled the emperor that he ordered a high terrace built around it and finally, because it was 'so very straight and harmonious' the emperor ordered his painters to draw a picture of it for the *Jahangirnama*.[51] As Ebba Koch has pointed out, Jahangir 'turned his observations of natural phenomenon into nature studies', combing visual and the literary to produce an exacting portrayal of regional natural history.[52] These paintings may have allowed Jahangir to assert his sovereignty over the natural world (*Jahan*), but this power dynamic in no way diminished the pleasure he took in discovery and observation.

The emperor's inquiring mind was at times only satisfied by the results of experimentation and analysis, demonstrating his tendency towards sceptical rationalism. In his fifth year as king, he described his experimentation with bitumen (a naturally occurring pitch or asphalt; the word 'bitumen' is of Sanskrit origin), which he claimed was known for healing broken bones. The doubtful emperor had a chicken's leg broken, then both fed bitumen to the chicken and had the substance rubbed on the break, keeping it on the leg for three days. In the end, after observing the effects of his experiment, the emperor concluded that the break was not at all improved and that bitumen was indeed not a miracle cure for broken bones.[53] On another occasion he had a tiger and a lion dissected, in an effort to determine if the physical placement of their gall bladders might determine their relative degrees of courage.[54]

The emperor was proud of his palace breeding operations, touting his own success in having mating pairs of leopards and lions, which he claimed his father had been unable to achieve. On occasion his observations combined sentimentality with scientific curiosity. Among the emperor's menagerie was a pair of *sarus* cranes.[55] A breed known for their devoted monogamy, Jahangir named his pair Layla and Majnun, after the tragic characters in the popular Persian romance. In 1616, after five years of captivity, the cranes mated and hatched two chicks. Jahangir, suffering the doldrums of Ahmadabad, thoroughly enjoyed the development and spent the next month closely observing the behaviour of the little crane family. In October, when two wild cranes appeared, having been attracted to the cries of his pet cranes, Jahangir had them caught. Putting rings in their noses and around their ankles, he released them.

While none of the Mughal kings, including Jahangir, attempted to develop a system of disciplined analysis, most were possessed of broad interests and relentless curiosity, demonstrating real scientific instincts. This period has been identified with a reinvigoration of the 'rational sciences', across the Islamic world: including logic, philosophy, mathematics and history.[56] Jahangir is often described as 'self-taught' but he had inherited a dynastic culture of observation.[57] Babur's *Vaqa'i* had contained marvellously detailed zoological and geographic observations, in particular during his passage from Afghanistan into Hindustan.[58] Akbar's chroniclers too had described the emperor's occasional experiments, such as his ordering that a group of infants be isolated from the spoken word, in an effort to determine whether language learning was innate (he discovered that it was not).[59] Jahangir's grandfather, Humayun, had dabbled in scientific exploration. In 1619, Abdus Sattar, Jahangir's devotee and author of the *Majalis*, brought him the marvellous gift of a miscellany of Humayun's writings, which included his notes regarding astronomical and other 'unusual' matters that he had resolved after experimentation. Jahangir expressed elation at seeing his grandfather's studies, claiming that no rare object or gemstone could equal Sattar's gift in value.[60]

Jahangir's efforts may have been inspired at times by eccentricity and passing whimsy, yet his spirit of inquiry and his efforts to label and organize his empire were not so very different from those of his European contemporaries, those men of the Enlightenment who similarly attempted to impose order and rationality on the landscape. The Europeans at his court created what they considered to be an encyclopaedic, organized body of texts, so too Jahangir took pains to collect and collate accurate and detailed data, to systematically observe and analyse his environment, creating out of wild nature an orderly and controlled cosmos. Jahangir shared the Enlightenment preoccupation with measuring and quantifying the natural world. In contrast to the Europeans in India, however, who sought not only to organize and impose order but were often influenced by a sense of cultural superiority, portraying India as both dangerous and primitive, Jahangir's data collection sprang from his own enthusiasm and delight in the beautiful, the curious and the obscure. Where his European travelling companions saw only a 'wilderness, overspread with trees', Jahangir described magnificent gardens.[61] That Jahangir's court progress was often aimless rather than directed at military or political goals allowed the emperor to experience his territories on the level of the local and colloquial. His detailed record of so many curious events, unusual plants and animals, stories of ancient rulers and local heroes, folk remedies and recipes offers the modern reader a remarkably rich and eclectic picture of early modern India.

Just as the *Jahangirnama* confirms Jahangir's personal fascination with the beauties and oddities of the natural world, so too does the guidance and direction he gave to his painters. Having taken his father's throne and inherited the imperial atelier, Jahangir continued the trend established at his princely court in Allahabad, in which individual master painters were commissioned to produce singular paintings, emphasizing naturalism and veracity of detail. Jahangir was attentive to the individual skills and style of each of his artists, asserting that he could recognize the hand of a particular painter even if the work were unsigned or the composition a collaboration.[62] As he moved across the South Asian landscape, enraptured by the scenery and creatures of his kingdom, he made regular requests to his painters that they keep a record of the sights. Tulips and lilies, a particularly magnificent falcon, the pair of pet cranes named Layla and Majnun, his tamed antelope – all were described in some detail by the emperor and made the subjects of imperial paintings at his command. Among the paintings, for example, is a remarkable study of a dodo, so detailed and accurate that modern scholars believe it to have been composed from life, 'sensitively, knowingly drawn, and painted with finesse'.[63] As Ebba Koch has written, the nature studies of Jahangir's ateliers 'emerge as exact natural history drawings which, in their best moments, are compelling works of art'.[64]

Of all his painters, Jahangir most often mentioned the artist Mansur, who had been with him at his rebel court in Allahabad.[65] Mansur's studies of wildlife and flowers not only delighted the emperor for their beauty but satisfied his leanings as a naturalist. On a visit to Kashmir in the early spring, Jahangir claimed that 'Ustad Nadir al Asir Mansur' had drawn more than a hundred flowers.[66] Mansur's images are as fine as any Audubon watercolour, portraying the exotic creatures brought to the Mughal court and the indigenous wildlife of South Asia in lines of extraordinary delicacy and detail. Yet as accurate and sensitive as are the nature studies painted in Jahangir's workshops, the emperor's own descriptions of the natural world are at times just as patient, detailed, and exacting.

Odd and unusual people inspired Jahangir to demand a painting. Perhaps the most famous example of the collusion of text and image in the *Jahangirnama* is that of the portrait of Inayat Khan. Inayat Khan had served as a paymaster for the Mughal emperor – Jahangir described him as among his closest servants and subjects – yet was so powerfully addicted to opium and wine that he had become severely debilitated.[67] Jahangir ordered his personal physician to treat Inayat

Khan, but the doctors soon announced that it was impossible to save him. Yet in 1618 when the dying man begged leave of the emperor so as to return to his home in Agra, Jahangir could not resist ordering him to remain. Inayat Khan's condition was so startling, his emaciation so complete, that Jahangir determined to have images made of the skeletal figure of his courtier, on the very eve of his death. His fascinated horror was surely in part fuelled by his own struggle with addiction. 'Skin stretched over bone', he would write, 'Good God, how can a human being remain alive in this state?'[68] Because of the extraordinary condition of his servant, Jahangir ordered his painters to make a record. On the very next day, Inayat Khan died.[69] Both the preliminary sketch and final painting of the dying Inayat Khan survive, painted by the artist Balchand, showing him propped up on several plump bolsters that dwarf his skeletal frame, gazing expressionless into space.[70] The images are excruciating in their detailed rendering of a dying man, affirming the emperor's fascination with the obscure and the shocking, as well as displaying a scientific curiosity and callous detachment.

Pilgrimage, shrines and holy men

As Jahangir traversed the South Asian countryside, he easily integrated the hunt and his efforts at scientific inquiry with the responsibilities of the royal court: welcoming the homage of local grandees, performing the regular business of promotions and tribute, contriving plans for military campaigns. Local religious and political leaders flocked to pay obeisance at the royal threshold and in exchange receive honours, charity and patronage. The peripatetic king was thereby able to learn of local conditions. Jahangir's interest was not only politically and militarily strategic but at times humane. On seeing a particularly fine stepwell in the pargana of Badnawar, he declared that all new wells should be of this design, only larger.[71] In Kashmir in 1622, having himself struggled to cope with the climate as he made his way through the mountains, Jahangir noted that the people suffered terribly from the cold. He ordered the revenue from a local village be used to purchase clothing for the poor and for heating water at the mosques so that the pious would be comfortable in their ablutions.[72]

As he and his retinue moved through the cities of his empire, they flung half and quarter rupee coins to the waiting crowds. Charitable giving was for Jahangir a critical aspect of kingship. Early in his reign, the emperor quoted the axiom: 'From the table of emperors comes relief to beggars,' and ordered that one of the officers in his imperial guard would distribute money to the poor every day.

Priding himself on his accessibility, Jahangir used his constant court progress as an opportunity to see and be seen by his subject people. He famously claimed to offer justice personally, accepting petitions from the lowliest of his subjects, but he also preferred to offer his charity directly to his subjects, face to face. In his fifth year as emperor, Jahangir had ordered that the needy and poor be brought before him in the evenings so that he might give them land, cash and clothing. Once again referencing the boredom and restlessness he had been experiencing in Agra, the emperor went on to explain, 'This would give me something to do and it would relieve their suffering. What better occupation could there be?' From among the throng, a specific individual would occasionally come to his attention. When one member of a crowd of supplicants informed the emperor that his name, *Jahangir*, was numerically equivalent to *Allahu Akbar*, Jahangir was delighted. Taking it as a good omen, he gave the man land, a horse and a robe of honour. Over the course of a year, Jahangir recorded having given 'from my own hands' thousands of rupees, gold and silver coins, thousands of acres of land, entire villages, farms and thousands of loads of rice.[73]

At times Jahangir's very movements seem to have confirmed the landscape of India as a sacred space, enacted through the emperor's constant performance of pilgrimage. His journeys allowed Jahangir to visit sites of devotional significance and individuals of noted piety. Jahangir remained most publicly affiliated with the Chishti Order of Sufis. When he fell ill in April of 1614, he had pierced his ears with pearl earrings in honour of the Chishti *khwaja*, clearly hoping that the act would compel a saintly intervention. His followers too began to wear pearl earrings, which the emperor himself supplied, although while his own earrings denoted his reverence for the Chishti shaykh, his noblemen wore pearls to mark their devotion to Jahangir. In 1615, for those who had pierced their ears 'as a sign of loyalty', 732 pearls were distributed for a value of thirty-six thousand rupees.[74]

The emperor's careful attention to the important Chishti shrines outside of Fatehpur Sikri, Ajmer and Delhi served multiple purposes. First, Jahangir's visits were overtly political acts that reinforced his lifelong allegiance to the Chishti order and their centrality to his own personal legitimizing narrative. The Chishti shaykh's premonition of his birth was, after all, at the base of Jahangir's individual claims of ruling charisma. Of equal importance, his visits to these sites reinforced the carefully tended continuity between his own reign and his father's. They were commemorative re-enactments of his father's performative pilgrimages and supplications. Finally, the Chishti shrines were inherently devotional spaces where one might 'quest for the sacred'.[75] Jahangir rarely mentioned attending formal religious ceremonies but described attending the *sema* at a Chishti dargah, in 1615, where he stayed late to watch the Sufis dance into an ecstatic state before him. Jahangir described a similar scene in Agra in 1610, where the respected Shaykh Husayn Sirhindi and Shaykh Mustafa arranged a *sema* of 'dancing and ecstasy' for the emperor.[76] Jahangir followed formal rituals of devotion at pilgrimage sites, circumambulating the tombs of the saint-shaykhs and reciting the *Fatiha*, followed by charitable contributions for the shrine and its residents, and scattering coins to the public. Notable mosque complexes were treated similarly, the buildings admired (and at times carefully measured!), but the emperor's attendance at formal prayers goes unremarked.

Among the sacred sites that Jahangir visited were the graves of his ancestors. Treated with great reverence, the Mughal graves were situated in classic imperial gardens. A foreigner at the court noted, 'Every Mahometan of qualitie in his life time provides a faire sepulcher for himselfe... The rest of the ground they plant with trees and flowers, as if they would make Elysian fields such as the poets dreamed of, wherein soules might take their repose'.[77] Akbar had planned his own tomb in Sikandra and work on the project had begun before his death, in 1604.[78] When Jahangir first visited the tomb on his return from Gujarat, he was so disappointed in the structure that he ordered the work be begun anew. The mausoleum was not finished until 1612–13, after which it became a site of regular dynastic pilgrimage. In 1619, Jahangir began a court progress to Lahore with a visit to Sikandra and described the women of the harem circumambulating Akbar's tomb in prayer, accompanied by a crowd of dignitaries and Quran reciters, and a performance of song and dance. On reaching Delhi, he and his retinue prayed at Humayun's tomb and at the shrine of Nizamuddin Chishti.[79]

Paying visits to local religious personages offered similarly devotional experiences for Jahangir. In Lahore, he visited the home of Shams Khan, who attracted the attention of the emperor not only because of his reputation for piety and spirituality, but also for his lifetime of avid hunting.[80] On another occasion, he paid his respects to Mawlana Muhammad Amin, who inspired the emperor with his poverty and devotion, his pleasant conversation, and sound advice. Both were rewarded with land and money.[81] When possible, whether in Agra or along the court progress, Jahangir called local religious leaders to his court, where he would stay awake half the night discussing topics of mutual interest. Abdus Sattar, his close companion, once brought to court an ancient Sufi shaykh, La'l Matta, who was said to have attended the *majalis* of Babur, Humayun and Akbar. He told tales of capture and abuse at the Safavid court of Shah Tahmasp, where he claimed to have been blinded by a blow to the head, although his sight had later been magically restored. His conversation was of great interest to Jahangir as it touched on almost every one of the emperor's favourite themes: a strange and magical event resolved by divine intervention, effusive praise for Jahangir's Mughal predecessors and sharp criticism of the Safavid shah. The emperor was so fascinated by the old man's stories, and so impressed by his piety, that in addition to money and a shawl, he paid for the Sufi's burial site and sent him a gravestone that, Jahangir claimed, bore the mark of the footprint of the Prophet Muhammad.[82] Other visiting religious figures were not so entertaining. When he invited Qadi Nasir Burhanpuri to court to speak with him, Jahangir respectfully described the qadi as exceptionally learned, but dry and no pleasure to talk with. The shaykh was rewarded for his piety and hastily sent home.[83]

Muslim luminaries had no guarantee of welcome or imperial support at the royal court of Jahangir. In Agra in June of 1619, Jahangir had the famed Naqshbandi preaching shaykh Ahmad Sirhindi arrested. The shaykh had long been a critic of Mughal religious liberality and, clearly stung by the criticism, Jahangir accused him of being an arrogant imposter and a charlatan who, with his followers, had spread hypocrisy, peddled mysticism, and hoodwinked a gullible public.[84] Insisting that the shaykh's writings were too impolite to repeat, Jahangir claimed that his 'nonsensical rhetoric' would lead to infidelity and apostasy. In punishment for his arrogance and 'idle talk', Sirhindi was imprisoned in the fort of Gwalior. Only one year later, however, a forgiving emperor ordered the chastened Sirhindi released from prison. The shaykh expressed gratitude for his freedom and remained at the royal court for some months in seeming amity with Jahangir.[85] He seems to have remained in the emperor's good graces afterwards, for when Jahangir was weighed against gold on his fifty-fifth birthday, Sirhindi was among the recipients of the imperial charity, receiving a gift of two thousand rupees.[86]

Jahangir's determination to remain true to his father's values is confirmed by the criticism levied at him by Sirhindi, but also by his continued generous and affectionate attention to the greater Naqshbandi leadership. His devotion to the order was more nostalgic than spiritual, driven by the order's close ties to the Timurid-Mughal lineage. Several years earlier, Jahangir had exchanged 'dueling verses' (*mojavabe*) with Khwaja Hashem Dahbedi, of Samarqand and had received from him the gift of a verse written by Babur for one of Hashem's ancestors.[87] When a follower of the *khwaja* made his way to Jahangir's court in 1620, the emperor enthusiastically claimed his own allegiance to Hashem.[88] Sending a charitable gift of ten thousand rupees to Samarqand, Jahangir asked that half of the money be set aside for the custodians at the Gur-i-Amir, Timur's tomb, and the rest given to a shaykh of the Dahbedi Naqshbandi lineage. When the Naqshbandi litterateur Mutribi al-Asamm of Samarqand decided to pursue imperial patronage at the Mughal court, he prefaced his journey with two years of research for an anthology of Central Asian poets he planned to bring as a gift for the emperor. Arriving in Lahore in 1616, at the age of seventy, he remained at Jahangir's side for two months before being released to return home with the rewards of his journey. During those months, Jahangir grilled Mutribi about the personalities and conditions of Central Asia, 'in the manner of a longtime expatriate, plying a more recent one for the latest gossip from home'.[89] Notably, Jahangir's questions for Mutribi had neither political nor strategic purpose but were 'entirely sentimental'.[90]

Over the years of his reign, Jain intellectuals became increasingly less visible at Jahangir's royal court. Jahangir had initially welcomed them, even following Akbar's model in offering them honorary Sanskrit titles. Perhaps unsurprisingly, he invented new titles which encompassed his own name, including entitling Vijayadeva Suri, the newly appointed head of the Shvetambara Tapa Gaccha, *Jahangiramahatapa* (Jahangir's Very Pious), and offering the Jain monk Siddhicandra two Persian titles, both *Nadirazzaman* (Wonder of the Age) and *Jahangir-pasand* (Favourite of Jahangir), after he complimented the emperor on his grasp of Jain doctrine.[91] Siddhicandra's writings expressed real anxiety, however, about the compromises inherent in accepting the patronage of kings, and he and Jahangir eventually had a falling out. Siddhicandra's reason for the collapse of the relationship is fantastical, involving a hotly contested debate over Jain doctrine, the public appearance of an intrusive Nur Jahan into the evening assembly, and finally the emperor's effort to force the Jain to marry under threat of death by elephant, finally resulting in a temporary ban on renunciants entering the cities of the empire. Truschke rightfully explains that the value of the story is not in 'its historical viability' but rather as a moralistic tale that upheld Jain religious commitments.[92] Although Siddhicandra's story ends with Jahangir's cancellation of the ban, the point seems to have resonated, 'namely that monks belong in the forest rather than at court'.[93] By the end of Jahangir's reign, the Jain leadership had left his entourage.

Jahangir often chose to visit pundits and ascetics. While he demonstrated a somewhat superficial understanding of local non-Islamic religious traditions, he expressed a general benevolence, as demonstrated by his regular and enthusiastic participation, along with members of his intimate court circle, in festivals such as Holi and Diwali.[94] In this, as in so many features of his rule, Jahangir modelled himself on his father, who 'conversed with the good of every religion and every sect and gave his attentions to each according to his station and ability to understand'.⁹⁵ When criticism of the Christian crucifixion was voiced, Jahangir countered that it was certainly no more difficult to defend than a belief in Krishna's impregnation of twelve thousand *gopis*. Yet when on another occasion some criticized ritual performance of ablutions during eclipses, the emperor pointed out that Muslims also prayed during an eclipse, and at least their ritual bathing kept the worshippers clean.⁹⁶

Using the movements of his court to seek out and debate with pundits, whom he referred to as 'the wise men of Hindustan', Jahangir claimed to be always on the hunt for 'a real fakir from whose conversation some great bounty might derive'.⁹⁷ Jahangir's respect and financial generosity was based on his measure of an individual's piety, which he identified with poverty, seclusion and prayer. Visiting the temple complex of Haridwar, Jahangir praised the devotion of the Brahmins and hermits whose lives of seclusion were spent in worship 'according to their religion'.⁹⁸ Just as he did at Sufi dargahs and mosque complexes, at local temple sites Jahangir offered alms of cash and goods to each of those present.

Jahangir was regularly drawn to the venerable ascetic Jadrup Gosain, a favourite of the Emperor Akbar. As the hermit could not be commanded to Agra, Jahangir sought him out in a barren wilderness where he lived in a hole so narrow that even a small child, the emperor would write, would find it difficult to enter. Mu'tamid Khan was present at this meeting and described the quite literal hole, writing that the lean ascetic had to stretch out his two arms and wiggle his body through the opening to enter or leave his narrow home.⁹⁹ Just as his visits to the major Chishti shrines were re-enactments of his father's spiritual quest, so too were Jahangir's visits to the hermit of Ujjain, but these were much more than simple filial performances. The piety and wisdom of Jadrup Gosain affected him profoundly, and Jahangir would travel to visit with him at least four times, declaring that in conversation with the ascetic he felt great contentment and strength.¹⁰⁰

Jahangir went on to make the claim that the science of Vedanta, as studied by the ascetic he described as a great *sanyasi murtazi*, was no less than the Brahmanical counterpart of Sufism.¹⁰¹ His companion, Mu'tamid Khan, agreed, 'He [Jadrup] confirmed his own mystical opinions as corresponding with those of the Muslims.'¹⁰² Followers of the Sufi tradition of Ibn Arabi, Jahangir and his milieu not only understood both Vedanta philosophy and Sufism to be inherently pantheistic, but were quick to conflate the two devotional systems.¹⁰³ Jahangir would quote the great Sufi poet Rumi to justify Jadrup Gosain's naked asceticism, describing what he called a shared 'idiom of dervishes'.¹⁰⁴ When discussing the last life stages of a Brahmin, Jahangir explained that his mind would be closed to all but god and blithely quoted the Persian poet Fighani in order to better explain Vedanta: 'There is one lamp in this house and from its rays in every direction I look an assembly has been formed.'¹⁰⁵ Mughal acceptance of a synchronicity between devotional practices in both Islam and forms of Hinduism would later be explicitly confirmed by the Sufi poet Bulleh Shah (1680–1757), writing:

> I will play Holi, beginning in the name of the Lord, saying bismillah.
> Cast like a gem in the name of the prophet, each drop falls with the beat of Allah, Allah,
> Only he may play with these colourful dyes, who has learnt to lose himself in Allah.
> 'Am I not your lord?' asked the Lover, and all maids lifted their veils,
> 'Everyone said, yes!' and repeated: 'There is only one God'.
> I will play Holi beginning in the name of the Lord, saying bismillah.¹⁰⁶

Jadrup Gosain was not the only non-Muslim recipient of Jahangir's praise. Searching for spiritual guidance, Jahangir sought out pundits and ascetics with whom he might hold discussions. On his return from Gujarat in 1617, Jahangir would visit a famed recluse at the Kankriya. Having spent some time in conversation with him, Jahangir declared that the sanyasi 'knew all about the principles of Sufism in his religion... It can be strongly said that no one of this type better than he has been seen'.¹⁰⁷ Again, Jahangir unhesitatingly conflated Brahmanical and Muslim devotionalism by referencing the sanyasi when claiming that 'I am always ready to receive advice from *darwishan*'.¹⁰⁸

His appreciation for piety, however, did not translate into uncritical acceptance any more than it did with Muslim clerics he found wanting. While on a hunting expedition at the Pushkar tank in 1614, Jahangir's party came across a complex of temples. Jahangir later wrote of his disgust with a black stone carved into in the shape of a man with a boar's head. He declared the religious leader of the site to be a false guru, manipulating a gullible public.¹⁰⁹ The emperor ordered the site destroyed and the yogi driven away. Jahangir's general acceptance of various local worship traditions makes this particular episode highly unusual, but in this case it seems that his vitriol was inflamed by prevailing political rivalries. The statue that so offended him had been carved on the orders of the local ruler, Rana Shankar, the uncle of 'that damned Rana', the ruler of Mewar and the current target of Jahangir's imperial armies. On other occasions he expressed censure but destroyed nothing. In Kashmir, he came across a temple that similarly vexed him. It was, he reported, filled with bats and owls and he described the temple 'from without as corrupt as an infidel's grave, from within the wrath of God'.¹¹⁰

For all his expressions of horror and scorn, in this case he passed by without interfering.

For the most part, Jahangir's criticism was reserved for any religious leadership which criticized the emperor and for those he felt were coercing the general public, which he considered to be easily fooled but essentially blameless. On hearing stories of a false Jewish prophet, Jahangir asserted that those who were misled were not at fault for their false beliefs and would not go to hell, but those leaders who did it for financial reward would be punished. 'If an individual believed that his religion was true and what he did was for the sake of God, his practices are counted as an act of worship; but if his deeds were because of his greed and hostility, indeed he has died for ever and is in the place of torment.'[111] He wrote contemptuously of the rarity of honest spirituality, comparing the truly pious to the mythical phoenix and the philosopher's stone.[112] 'All I saw', he wrote, 'was a flock of petty fools, and the result of my seeing them was nothing but mental confusion and obfuscation'.[113] And even in his criticism, Jahangir again confirmed that he regularly sought religious comfort from ascetics and pundits, describing his search for a yogi from whom one might derive some spiritual benefit, but finding only miserable ignoramuses.

Part Five

Kingship in crisis, 1619–27

11

Golden days

Kangra

By 1619, having ruled for fourteen years, Jahangir was relishing the freedom of his near-constant court progress and the successes of his reign. Soon after the Mughal victory against Mewar, he had ordered a campaign against another previously unconquered state, that of Kangra, just south of Kashmir. Led by the Mughal general Murtaza Khan, Jahangir's armies moved against a fortress that had previously proven impregnable to Akbar's armies. Among the troops assigned to the campaign was young Rao Suraj Mal, the eldest son and presumed heir of Raja Baso, who ruled the neighbouring district of Nurpur. Not incidentally, Rao Suraj Mal was a liegeman of the Mughal prince Khurram, his presence illustrating the emperor's willingness to take advantage of local allegiances and relationships in order to reinforce Mughal power. In this case, however, the young prince was insubordinate, leading Murtaza Khan to complain of his trouble-making proclivities. Suraj Mal professed innocence and Jahangir, sensitive to the young man's liege relationship with his son, allowed him to follow Prince Khurram, currently campaigning in the Deccan.

Early the following year, Murtaza Khan died and the campaign against Kangra faltered. It was in 1618, while travelling in Gujarat, that the emperor finally ordered Khurram to take control of the operation. Khurram assigned his general, Taqi, to lead a renewed attack on Kangra fortress and once again sent Suraj Mal to lead troops as part of the campaign. By this time, Raja Baso had died and, showing respect to his son's liegeman, Jahangir had allowed Suraj Mal to inherit his father's lands and title of Raja. The Mughal emperor's support, in the face of years of intransigence, did not improve Suraj Mal's reliability, and he bitterly fought with Taqi, complaining of the general's incompetence. Once again, we see Jahangir's willingness to absorb a degree of rebellion in the interests of closer ties with local elites. Rather than punish Raja Suraj Mal, he allowed Khurram to simply replace Taqi with his own close ally, Raja Birkramjit. Even this did not assuage Suraj Mal, who continued to undermine the campaign until eventually, in November of 1618, he went into open revolt, plundering the nearby parganas, most of which were the *jagirs* of Nur Jahan's father, the I'timaduddawla.

At last the Mughal armies were forced to respond, and early in 1619, pursued closely by Bikramjit, Suraj Mal was defeated, escaping into the narrow mountain passes while the Mughal armies destroyed his fortresses. His younger brother, Jagat Singh, was quickly located and given rank and the title of raja, and was rushed out to serve under Bikramjit, again demonstrating Jahangir's strategic support for local kingship under Mughal patronage. At the end of the following year, in 1620, a very proud Jahangir would claim victory over Kangra, rewarding his son with the imposing title of "Shah Jahan" (King of the World) to mark his military success.[1] Jahangir would lavishly describe the campaign as a 'ghaza,' claiming that it had been of central importance to him since taking the throne.[2] Contrasting his own success to the failed efforts of his father and previous rulers, dating to the first Muslim conquerors in Hindustan, he thanked God for allowing him the victory 'no other mighty ruler had been able to achieve, and which seemed unfeasible in the narrow view of the short-sighted.'[3]

Sikri, Agra and the road north

The imperial banners reached Fatehpur Sikri on 29 December 1618, having spent four months in travelling from Ahmadabad, almost five and a half years since leaving for Ajmer. Jahangir had planned to continue on to Agra but the city was still reporting cases of bubonic plague, so it was quickly decided that the emperor would remain in Sikri. It had been many years since Jahangir had lived in the former imperial capital, built by his father in 1571 to commemorate the influential Chishti Shaykh Salim and the birth of his three sons. Having remained in the newly built city for less than fifteen years, Akbar left it in 1585 to more closely pursue a campaign against his half-brother Muhammad Hakim, who had seized imperial territory around Kabul. The royal court never returned – Akbar revisited Fatehpur only once, in 1601– and the former imperial capital fell into disuse. William Finch visited the area in 1606 and described it as 'all ruinate', although some Mughal family members remained and it had not been completely deserted.[4]

While waiting for the most propitious day to enter the city, Jahangir's royal camp was temporarily established beside the lake, which the emperor busily ordered measured. Finally, the imperial banners made a ceremonious entrance into Sikri on 6 January 1619. Jahangir waited almost three weeks before making a pilgrimage to the shrine of Salim Chishti, where he recited the *Fatiha*.[5] Recalling the miracle of Salim Chishti's foretelling of his birth, Jahangir went on to offer another story of his divine connection to the Chishti shaykh. When he was a child, Jahangir explained, Shaykh Salim told Akbar that he would die when the prince had memorized and recited a line. Two years later a woman unaware of the prediction taught the child a verse. The news reached the king just as a fever began in the shaykh. Akbar's court singer, the famed Tan Sen, was called to sing the shaykh into death. According to Jahangir, at the moment before his passing, Shaykh Salim placed his own turban on the head of the prince, naming him his own successor and entrusting him to God.[6] The emperor's point was clear: that he had been divinely chosen to rule over the material world and that inheritance was matched by an even earlier appointment to leadership on a spiritual plane.

Having freshly reasserted his ruling authority in the place of his birth, Jahangir's attention shifted to the mundane, as he went on to measure every aspect of the mosque – its gates and chambers, domes and arches – built by Akbar for Salim Chishti's tomb. He would spend the next three months at Fatehpur Sikri, visiting nearby imperial gardens in the company of his intimate companions and his mother, who had ridden out from Agra to visit her son. While in his father's former capital, Jahangir acted as tour guide for his third and favourite son, showing off Akbar's palace to Khurram and pointing out a massive tank built there by the emperor, which he claimed had been filled with coins for the poor to take as needed.[7] Much of his time was spent in visiting the local estates of his noblemen and Sikri's suburban pleasure gardens – the Nur Mahal, the Bustan Sara and the Nur Manzil – where he oversaw the work he had ordered, adding additional pools, jets and water chutes, and an avenue planted with trees. When finally the outbreak of plague had passed and the astrologers determined the auspicious day and hour, Jahangir finally entered Agra in April of 1619. Mounted on a royal elephant, he scattered coins to the crowds of onlookers who filled the streets and the doorways and the rooftops all the way to the palace. He had been away from the city for more than five and a half years.

Even at the moment of his return to the capital of his empire, Jahangir determined on another journey, to Kashmir, which he declared 'the garden of perennial spring'. Having already experienced the difficulties of the mountain passages that lay ahead, Jahangir immediately set in motion preparations for this journey, ordering Nuruddin Quli to go ahead with masons and stone cutters to ready the path for the court progress. His work would represent an expansion of earlier infrastructure projects, designed for the support of merchants and itinerants. Having already had rows of shade trees planted on either side of the roadways from Agra to the river at Attock and to Bengal, Jahangir now ordered that distance markers be erected at every *kos* along the road from Agra to Lahore and a well dug every three *kos*, for the ease and comfort of travellers.

Jahangir began the journey with an evening boat ride to the imperial encampment erected just outside of Agra, where they remained for eight days while final arrangements were made for the massive court progress. From there he made a brief visit to Akbar's tomb at Sikandra, finished in 1612–13 and now a showcase for displays of filial pride and piety. From his father's tomb, Jahangir made a series of visits to the ascetic Jadrup Gosain, who since the emperor's last visit had left Ujjain and was now residing near the temple complex at Mathura, on the banks of the Yamuna River. The hermit profoundly affected Jahangir, who expressed an overwhelming desire to visit with him to discuss 'lofty things'. Shortly afterwards, perhaps influenced by his conversation with Gosain, Jahangir ordered his son Khusraw released from prison, attempting once again to return his eldest to court and the service of the empire.

In a series of slow marches, Jahangir reached Delhi on 11 November, where he met with local dignitaries and visited the tombs of his grandfather Humayun and the Sufi shaykh Nizamuddin Chishti. Travelling by boat, Jahangir made his way up the river to Akbarpur, from which point the court steadily continued north. As he had on his earlier trip to Kashmir, as they reached the more isolated northern reaches of the empire, Jahangir began sending many of his noblemen to their own estates, sensitive to the vast size of the company which strained food supplies and drove up local prices. As a more streamlined court progress continued, a letter arrived from Punch warning that the roads had suffered from heavy rains and the mountain passes had become clogged with snow, and advising the emperor that a month-long wait for the weather to improve would make the passage easier. Jahangir shrugged off these concerns. The very point of the journey to Kashmir, he declared, was to see the spring flowers; to wait a month would be to miss their peak season. 'There was nothing to do but set out.'[8]

The roads proved to be as difficult as predicted. After fording the fast-flowing Bahat River, the progress followed the same route as the previous journey to Kabul, reaching Hasan Abdul in mid-February. Once again it was decided that the emperor's procession was too large for the difficult mountain passages they would face and arrangements were made to break into groups, with I'timaduddawla leading the first company, which included artisans of the imperial workshops, while a second group was to travel via Punch. It was decided that the women of the harem would remain for a few days to rest before proceeding, while the restless and undaunted emperor went on ahead with a much smaller assembly.

Crossing the mountains on the road to Kashmir, Jahangir rhapsodically described fields of bright yellow mustard flower and red blossoms that grew so close together that it seemed they had merged into a single flower. Wild fruit trees produced inedible peaches, apricots and pears but Jahangir admired the beauty of their blossoms. Jahangir also experimented with the local *buza*, brewed from bread and rice, and aged for years and at times drunk with *bhang*. The local ruler brought him a cup and Jahangir claimed to find it stimulating, although the effects soon wore off, putting the user to sleep. 'If there is no wine available', the emperor mused, 'this would do for a replacement'.[9]

Still the rain and snow continued and, as most of the roadway led along a cliff side, twenty-five elephants fell from their slippery path and were killed. The company was forced to make camp for two days to recover. It was not a significant loss, however, for there still remained a great many elephants in the progress. As they entered Ladakh, and were again required to split into smaller groups with Jahangir in the forward camp, it was decided that he should be accompanied by seven hundred of the remaining elephants, the minimum number he considered necessary to carry his provisions. Jahangir remained enthusiastic about the journey, and when preparations were made for a Nowruz celebration on a lovely hillside along the Kishen Ganga River, he claimed that 'the workmen of destiny had prepared it for just such a day of celebration'.[10]

After another treacherous march through continued snowfall, the royal court crossed the Kuwarmat Pass and the mountain paths were finally behind them. Perhaps relief over their successful passage enhanced the emperor's pleasure, as he remarked on a series of highland meadows that stretched before them, filled with blooming flowers and aromatic herbs. The flowers of Kashmir, he wrote in his memoir, were so many that the number was impossible to count or describe.[11] Once again, Jahangir's notes became a travelogue, with detailed lists of the various species of animals, birds and flowers, their names in Hindi and local languages as well as in the emperor's native Persian. The overarching theme of his writing was the beauty of the landscape and Jahangir's own great joy in his travels.

As summer faded the royal court was forced to abandon the flowers and waterfalls of Kashmir. They seem to have lingered overlong, for once again the mountain crossing proved a treacherous journey. By early October, snow was falling in the passes. Planning for greater comfort on his return, Jahangir had earlier ordered the construction of permanent way stations in the snowy mountain passes. The buildings were still too new, however, to be of use – they were damp and smelled of lime plaster – so the royal camp was forced to continue to rely on their tents. The passes and roadways were slippery and difficult and the Mughal camp again divided into smaller contingents. Jahangir's horses struggled to maintain their footing on the ice, but he expressed gratitude that they did not have to make their way through snowfall as had the groups starting immediately before and after his own. For ten days, the royal court wound its way through the mountains, finally reaching the plains of Hindustan on 20 October, Jahangir noting the abrupt change in air, language, flora and fauna. Once again travelling in comfortable conditions, the court progress slowed to a crawl while the emperor organized a series of *qamargha* hunts and visited local natural wonders. It would be another month before they reached Lahore. Although the emperor praised the beauty of the northern capital, he would remain in Lahore for only little more than a week. By 3 December the forward camp had begun the journey to Agra, with the emperor and the imperial army following two weeks later. By the beginning of February, they had reached Delhi. Boating and camping along the banks of the Yamuna River they waited for three days at the Nur Afshan garden before entering Agra at an auspicious hour on 24 February 1621.

Poetry at the Mughal court

It was while travelling along the road to Lahore in January 1620 that Jahangir had appointed his first official poet laureate, Talib Amuli, whom he entitled the King of Poets (Malik al-Shu'ara). The Mughals had only inconsistently identified a chief court poet, Akbar first appointing the Iranian poet Ghazali of Mashhad and eventually replacing him with Faizi, the brother of Abu'l Fazl. The Iranian Talib Amuli was the first so honoured since Faizi's death, in 1595.[12] Yet poetry was woven into the fabric of Mughal court life, a legacy of the earliest Timurid emigres. Timur's descendants in fifteenth-century Mawarannahr had evolved an elaborate court culture around intimate and generous artistic patronage. Their cultural authority affirmed their power as the 'ultimate arbiters of sophistication and taste' throughout much of the Islamic world.[13] Notably, poetry, dominated by the refinement and sophistication of Persian forms, was a skill highly prized at the various Timurid princely courts. Professional poets were forced to compete for attention with aspiring intellectuals, for 'ambitious Turco-Mongol aristocrats were expected to be able to compose verse'.[14] All vied for a place in the salons of the Timurid aristocracy, where they displayed their varying degrees of literary talent. A renowned poet complained, 'What a sad state this is that in Herat one cannot stretch out one's foot without poking a poet in the ass.'[15] The Timurid prince Babur, who would establish the Mughal Empire as a neo-Timurid state in India, was himself a somewhat successful poet and the author of a *masnavi*. His literary reputation was perhaps as important to him as his political success, and he shared his poetry among his companions 'seeking, presumably, literary immortality'.[16]

Although Babur often chose to compose in Chaghatay Turkish, Mughal court poetry would be dominated by Persian literary forms and speakers, and even more so in the latter half of the sixteenth century as large numbers of professional poets made their way from Iran in hopes of the famously generous patronage of the Mughal kings.[17] Among the reasons for the intellectual exodus, the Iranian court was more conservative and less generous than that of the much wealthier Mughals, an Iranian poet writing: 'There is no buyer of poetry in this land… my life has become intolerable in Iran; I should go to India. All the poets like sweet parrots have made India their home.'[18] Encouraging this literary/intellectual immigration, Akbar actively recruited men of letters from Iran, sending invitations directly and at times paying the expense of their move to his court.

The literary culture at Jahangir's court was less productive or far reaching than had been the case with Akbar, in one of the very few marked discontinuities between the reigns of father and son. Jahangir preferred a more intimate setting in which the dominant literary force was poetry. In the tradition of his forebears, Jahangir composed verses himself, claiming that his poetic nature meant that lines of poetry would occur to him spontaneously, at times with little provocation.[19] Among the entertainments at his gatherings, he encouraged the kind of competitive versifying for which the Timurid princely courts had been known. When a verse was recited before him, he countered with a verse of his own, inviting those present to compose a line in the same mode. Gathered at the *majalis* with his intimate companions in 1609, he challenged them with the distich: 'What shall I do? The grief of distance from you [O Lord] is like arrows shot into my heart faster than the blink of an eye.' Having heard their suggestions, Jahangir added, 'You made me love you as the whole world is in love with you. I pray that I will be safe from evil eye,' ending with: 'I hope that my worship before the dawn lightens up my dark grave when I need help.'[20] When the Naqshbandi shaykh, Khwaja Hashem Dahbedi, sent Jahangir the gift of a line of poetry composed by Babur, Jahangir responded with his own verses, a personal letter and a thousand mohurs. He then challenged his companions to compose a similar quatrain, and the author of their most successful effort was awarded another thousand mohurs.

Jahangir regularly expressed confidence in his own skills and the discernment of his taste, asserting his preference for the classical *ghazal* and *ruba'i* forms and highly critical of *marsiyas*, laments, and the panegyric genre known as *qasidas*.[21] While he was able to make 'technical comments as well as emit sharp judgements', he could be defensive.[22] Visiting Jahangir's court late in his reign, the poet Mutribi attended the *majalis* where he was challenged to participate in one of the emperor's spontaneous versifying competitions. Mutribi claimed to have acquitted himself well, silencing a critic who suggested that his verses were not original. When another criticized a couplet he had quoted, originally by the late Uzbek ruler Abdullah Khan, Jahangir stepped in to defend the verse, insinuating that a king's poetry should be above reproach.[23] Jahangir sprinkled his memoir with verse, usually quoting the great Persian poets of the age – Jami and Sa'di, most commonly, along with the beloved Hafez, Amir Khusraw and Fighani. He enjoyed demonstrating his knowledge of the canon, but he occasionally included a verse of his own creation. Jahangir was a competent, sometimes even gifted, poet. Celebrating the beauty of spring, he composed the verse, 'Once again, there came from the Supreme Commander an order for nonexistence to give back what it had devoured.'[24] A full ghazal occurred to him, modelled on the Persian Sufi poetry so beloved by the Mughals: 'I am drunk in union with the Beloved and disconsolate in separation. Alas for such grief that torments me. It is time to admit helplessness, Jahangir. Offer your head in hopes that a spark of light may come to help.'[25] Similarly, one of the verses Jahangir most admired from Talib Amuli employed the Sufi trope of drunkenness to describe an ecstatic state, 'I have two lips, one devoted to wine and the other apologizing for drunkenness.'[26] It is not difficult to imagine that the heavy drinking emperor enjoyed both the metaphorical and literal meaning in these references.

Poetry gave Jahangir a vehicle to express strong emotion. His delight in viewing the Gul Afshan garden after heavy rain inspired a quote from Anvari, 'It is a day for enjoyment and revelry in the garden; it is a day for a market of flowers and herbs. The earth gives off an odor of ambergris; rose water drips from the breeze's skirt.'[27] Poetry could also be deployed as support for decisions or conflicts. Khurram went into revolt in 1623; Jahangir used an original verse to explain away his own son's disloyalty: 'A tree whose nature is bitter may be planted in paradise / Even if you pour pure honey from the stream of heaven on its roots / In the end its essence will produce the same bitter fruit.'[28] Jahangir also used poetry as a vehicle for communication with favoured shaykhs and heads of state. His letters to Shah Abbas were composed in consultation with his poets.[29] Letters to Adil Shah included poetry.[30] Sending a returning courtier a gift of attar of roses, Jahangir included a line of verse: 'I have sent my own scent in your direction to bring you to me more quickly.'[31]

While Persian was the Mughal court language, Jahangir patronized and rewarded poets who composed in Hindi. When Man Singh's brother, Raja Suraj Singh, visited the royal court, his poet praised Jahangir in a series of witty word plays, writing:

> If the sun had a son, it would always be day and never night because after sunset the son would take the sun's place and keep the world bright. Thanks be to God that He granted your father such a son so that after his death the people should not have to wear mourning, which is like the night. The sun itself is jealous, and says, 'Would that I too had a son to take my place and not allow night to come into the world.' By your rightness and brilliance despite such a catastrophe, the world is so illuminated that it us as though night had neither name nor trace.[32]

A delighted Jahangir gifted the poet an elephant. Other Hindi language poets wrote panegyrics that powerfully reinforce our awareness of the extraordinary Mughal cultural and spiritual synchronicity:

> See how the emperor Jahangir is astonishing as the lord Indra.
> In his court are poets and generals, skilled artists and deserving scholars,
> Warriors, officers, stable masters, shaykhs, masterminds,
> A range of entertainers and their companions.
> There are beautiful songs, haunting to the soul.
> Keshavdas says, Jahangir is a capable ruler in every respect –
> He is kind to the deserving and
> Harsh to those who break the law.
>   (From the *Jahangirjaschandrika* of Keshavdas)

Nur Jahan, Padshah Begim

Having once again returned to Agra in 1621, Jahangir and his intimate companions spent their days visiting the suburban garden complexes, boating to Nur Jahan's properties at Nur Afshan for the regular Thursday drinking party and hunting at Samugarh. By late summer the heat of the plains began to exacerbate the emperor's now chronic illness, however, and in mid-October the emperor made plans for a return to the north. Jahangir's health had become a real concern. An earlier protracted illness had been so fierce that his Persian doctor refused to treat him, claiming to lack sufficient knowledge or skill. The remaining doctors at the court also refused, terrified of being held responsible for the death of the emperor. Jahangir was resigned to treating himself with cups of wine and faith in 'the Absolute Physician', but as the weather became warmer, he continued weakening. The only member of the court with seemingly enough courage to intervene was Nur Jahan, who reduced his wine drinking and treated him with her own remedies. Jahangir claimed that her treatment worked especially well because of the kind sympathy with which she treated him. 'I trusted in her affection,' he would later write.[33]

But even as Jahangir recovered to lead his court progress north, Nur Jahan's mother became ill and almost immediately passed away. Jahangir was upset by the loss, having had a close attachment to her, and was sympathetic to the bereavement of her husband and children. In particular, I'timaduddawla, Jahangir's vizier and father-in-law, seemed unable to recover from the loss. Four months later, early in 1622, while on the road to Kangra, I'timaduddawla himself became ill. On learning of his worsening condition, Jahangir, who had pushed on with a forward camp, rushed back to the Mughal base. Reaching his father-in-law's bedside, Jahangir found him to be on the verge of death. Jahangir claimed that Nur Jahan asked her hallucinating father if he recognized Jahangir and was answered with a quote from the poet Anvari, 'It is he on whose world-adorning forehead a man blind from birth could see greatness,' affirming the dying man's recognition and taking the opportunity to reassert his own claim of divine appointment.[34] The empire's vizier, I'timaduddawla, died on 27 January 1622.

After only a day of condolences and mourning, the royal court turned once again to the Kangra fortress. Marking the unprecedented nature of Jahangir's success in the region, the raja of neighbouring Chamba, the most powerful zamindar of the hill country, made his way to the Mughal court progress to make his first homage to a foreign king. On arriving at the newly conquered fortress, a swaggering Jahangir made a show of the victory of Islam over a Hindu bastion, not only ordering the call to prayer and having the *khutba* read in his name, but even slaughtering a cow and ordering the construction of a mosque – startling gestures given his usual sensitivity to the religious diversity of his subjects.[35] Jahangir immediately reverted to type thereafter, however, by turning to the measurement of the inside perimeter and the height of the fortress, listing the number of towers and gates, and finishing his analysis with the size of the two pools inside. Jahangir then visited a nearby Durga temple, expressing disgust that devotees of all faiths, including Islam, made pilgrimages to the black stone, which he claimed had been put there fraudulently by a fake Brahmin. He left it in place, however, and moved on to admire and even make an imperial claim to the landscape, ordering 'well-proportioned buildings' to be erected at the site of two lovely waterfalls. To mark the conquest of Kangra, and the construction of the mosque he had ordered, a chronogram was composed, which Jahangir quoted in full, describing the emperor as not only 'world seizer', but also 'world giver, world holder, world adorner'.[36]

Within a few days of the visit to Kangra, Jahangir had arranged the deposition of his former vizier's property. It was not the I'timaduddawla's sons but his powerful daughter, the emperor's favourite wife, to whom Jahangir would assign the inheritance. Incredibly, this included not only her father's lands, but also his household, his titles, and his affiliated rights 'as chieftain and amir'.[37] Having formally placed her in the ranks of the highest noblemen of the empire, Jahangir ordered that drums be sounded for her at her advance, just after his own imperial drums were beaten. Shortly afterwards the royal court would celebrate her new title, *Nur Jahan*.

Already recognized for her exceptional political and administrative acumen, after 1622 Nur Jahan's personal political power would be even more publicly, and controversially, wielded. The degree of power accrued by her family had already become the subject of harsh criticism. Although Nur Jahan's father was already one of the most powerful men at Jahangir's court at the time of her marriage to the emperor, his fortunes had continued to rise with hers. Nur Jahan's brother, Asaf Khan, would come to be one of Jahangir's closest intimates, although he was the focus of much gossip and mistrust. The families became even more closely tied when just a year after her own marriage to Jahangir, Nur Jahan's niece, her brother Asaf Khan's daughter Arjumand Banu Begim, had been married to Khurram, from whom she would receive the title Mumtaz Mahal. Nur Jahan's servants, slaves and eunuchs were given household positions, and her wet nurse was named *Sadranath*, the head of the royal harem. At the end of 1620, a marriage between Nur Jahan's daughter Ladli Begim and the youngest of Jahangir's sons, Prince Shahryar, was arranged, ostensibly by her grandfather, the I'timaduddawla. The creation of a potential new locus of political power at a time of apprehension over the emperor's health was of real concern to many, in particular to Khurram, it seems, and resentment against the queen's growing influence and power was openly expressed. After watching her two brothers receive promotions, a disapproving Mu'tamid Khan would claim that Hindustan itself was little more than a *jagir* for her relatives.[38]

As the emperor's favourite, Nur Jahan already regularly participated in the complex ritual of gift exchange at the royal court. She publicly acted as the primary wife in honouring Khurram after he had won a notable military victory, by personally offering him an elaborate robe of honour, a jewelled sword, a horse and saddle and a royal elephant with golden trappings, as well as gifts for his sons, the women of his harem, and his most important followers.[39] On his reassignment to the Deccan, Nur Jahan gifted the prince with an elephant again.[40] She even participated in ritual gift exchange with noblemen who were not directly related to the family, including the Mewari prince Karan. At his presentation at court, she gave him 'a sumptuous robe of honor' along with a sword, a horse, and a royal elephant.[41] When Jahangir's disciple Mirza Nathan was promoted to Amir in 1621, his orders were signed by both the emperor and Nur Jahan, the latter personally sending him a robe of honour. She was in return gifted forty-two thousand rupees by the nobleman.[42] Other young noblemen would benefit from the patronage of the queen. After briefly joining Khurram in rebellion, and watching his younger brother receive rewards from the emperor in his place, a regretful Jagat Singh turned to the most powerful woman of the royal court. 'Having no other recourse, he used his influence to apply to Nur Jahan Begim to express his repentance and shame. Through her intercession on his behalf, and in order to please her, his rebellious crimes were pardoned.'[43]

Among the rare mentions of Nur Jahan in the *Jahangirnama*, Jahangir describes her as hosting several of his court parties. It seems unlikely that this represented a norm among dynastic women but on several occasions Nur Jahan arranged mixed gatherings, where alcohol was served, on her own properties. Her delighted husband, as well as '*amirs* and intimates', attended by formal invitation of the queen. Jahangir mentioned one such event in 1617, another in 1620, when she arranged a banquet to celebrate the creation of a private garden-palace, the Nur Sarai, and again in 1622, on an occasion when the royal party boated to her Nur Afshan garden.[44] The nobility and members of the royal family made ritual offerings to the emperor and, in the evening, illuminations 'the like of which had never before been seen' surrounded the nearby lake. The alcohol flowed, as the emperor generously supplied the attendees with all of the wine and intoxicants they could wish. Jahangir later declared it a very good party.[45]

She had been issuing edicts for some years, as was not uncommon among other powerful women of the Mughal royal family, but from 1622, at the time of her inheritance, they were signed not as the wife of the emperor but in her own name, as Nur Jahan *Padshah Begim*, Empress.[46] Taking on some of the jealously guarded attributes of kingship, 'sometimes she would sit in the balcony of her palace [*jharoka*], while the nobles would present themselves and listen to her dictates'.[47] Ceremonial coins were struck bearing the inscription, 'By order of the King Jahangir, gold has a hundred splendors added to it by receiving the impression of the name of Nur Jahan, the Queen Begim'.[48] So powerful had she become that she was the recipient of her own panegyric, written by a poet under her patronage, and would be the only woman included in a catalogue of 370 biographies of Mughal imperial elites.[49] Those close to the throne were outraged when the emperor Jahangir blithely commented that he was ready to retire and planned to retreat to a quiet life of devotion, leaving the talented Nur Jahan to reign in his place, although it was surely meant as an affectionate jest. He made no gesture or sign that he actually intended handing over the reins of governance to his wife and not even her enemies claimed that the *khutba*, the ultimate affirmation of sovereignty, was ever read in her name.

In the latter years of her husband's reign, Nur Jahan had become not only powerful but an independently wealthy woman. A part of her wealth came from her income producing properties, those given to her by Jahangir and others inherited from her father, but in addition Nur Jahan participated in international trade. Mughal royal women had done so for generations, operating through agents, who were sent to negotiate with Europeans at court.[50] Nur Jahan not only maintained a number of ships but also received revenue from the customs dues exacted on travellers and merchants who passed through her lands.[51] She dealt regularly with the English merchants, protecting their trade, likely in the expectation that her goods, primarily indigo and embroidered cloth, might be carried on their ships.[52] The Mughal court was often on bad terms with the Portuguese, but Nur Jahan maintained trade with the merchants of Daman and Diu from whom she hoped to acquire rare and unusual goods from countries to the east.[53]

It is fitting that, as much of the queen's personal wealth was acquired in international trade, in turn she used it to pay for a series of caravanserais which housed and protected merchants. Francisco Palsaert, a senior factor for the Dutch East India Company, described the variety of merchandise moving across the Yamuna River at Agra, on which Nur Jahan's agents collected duties:

> On the other side of the river is a city named Sikandra, well-built and populated, but chiefly by banian merchants, for through it must pass all the merchandise brought from Porop [the east], and Bengal and the Bhutan mountains, namely, cotton goods from Bengal, raw silk from Patna, spikenard, borax, verdigris, ginger, fennel, and thousands of sorts of drugs, too numerous to detail in this place. Here the officers of Nur Jahan Begam [*sic*], who built their sarai there, collect duties on all these goods before they can be shipped across the river;

and also on innumerable kinds of grain, butter, and other provisions, which are produced in the Eastern provinces, and imported thence.[54]

Peter Mundy wrote in 1632 that Nur Jahan's large stone caravanserai at Sikandra was so large that 'there may stand 500 horses and there might conveniently lye 2 or 3000 people'.[55]

Another caravanserai built by Nur Jahan between Agra and Lahore reinforces our understanding of her active presence as both patron and participant in an international merchant community. Notably, the structure was named for the queen who built it, the inscription on the west gate reading: 'During the just rule of Jahangir, son of Akbar Shah whose like neither Heaven nor Earth remembers, the Nur Serai was founded in the district of Phillaur by command of the angel-like Nur Jahan Begim'.[56] It has been described as perhaps the most magnificent caravanserai in India, built of red sandstone that had been brought from a quarry at Fatehpur Sikri over 300 miles away and highly decorated with low relief carvings of animals and designs. Including a serai of over 550 square feet, it boasted an arcaded enclosure wall that contained more than 124 chambers facing an internal courtyard. A modest fee was charged for rooms but most travellers slept in the courtyard for free, a policy confirmed by the inscription on the west gateway and reinforced by later imperial edicts. In all, over two thousand travellers might fit into the caravanserai, along with their camels and horses. The chronogram on its face dates to 1619, indicating that the queen may have commissioned this in support of a larger imperial infrastructure project, for this was the year that Jahangir had ordered the installation of *kos minars* (mileage markers) along the Agra-Lahore road, with a well installed every third *kos* for the benefit of travellers.[57] Finished in 1621, the building included royal apartments built into the south wall. Jahangir reported staying there with his entourage, and participating in a lavish feast, in the year it was built.[58] Although not related to mercantile activity, Nur Jahan commissioned other architectural masterpieces including the small Patthar mosque in Srinagar, Kashmir, built in 1620. Two years later she began the construction of her parents' tomb. Known as the *I'timaddudawlah*, it is set in a classic Persian chahar bagh, on the banks of the Yamuna River in Agra. It was finished within six years, by 1628, long pre-dating the Taj Mahal to which it is at times compared: a delicate white marble jewel box, decorated with pietra dura flowers of lapis, onyx, jasper and cornelian. It remains among the loveliest of Mughal monuments.

Foreign merchants resented the power of the queen in matters of trade. While most caravanserais were built 'at the cost of princes or rich and powerful men, who erect them in order to keep their memory green or to satisfy their consciences' and were therefore accepted as 'works of piety and acceptable to God', the queen's patronage was described as entirely self-serving. While confirming that 'she [Nur Jahan] erects very expensive buildings in all directions – *sarais*, or halting-places for travelers and merchants, and pleasure-gardens and palaces such as no one has ever made before', the resentful and critical Pelsaert claimed that Nur Jahan's caravanserais were indications of an overweening vanity rather than piety and were intended 'to establish an enduring reputation'.[59]

Nur Jahan's open displays of power were also met with resentment among members of the Mughal nobility. It is true that, compared to their contemporaries in east and west, 'Mughal dynastic histories ... readily acknowledged that women were capable of governing'.[60] In the generations of Mughal rule, only one woman received reproach for her behaviour at the centre of power: Nur Jahan. Accused of supplanting the power of the emperor, she was a talented and ambitious woman who had real interest in a political role and demonstrated complete loyalty to her husband. It is impossible to know just how much control Jahangir surrendered to her – likely less than he is accused of yielding, although his own political interests had always been limited. While he took seriously the task of balancing the loyalties and ambitions of the nobility and his political rivals, Jahangir's enthusiasms were engaged by the attributes of the mobile Mughal camp, as he rhapsodized over the ever-changing landscape of his imperial territories and enjoyed convivial late-night conversations fuelled by his evening ration of six cups of wine. Yet while he surely passed a degree of power to his wife, there is simply no evidence that he grew physically and intellectually incompetent, retreating, as has been claimed by others, from imperial responsibilities and relinquishing rule. Observers of his royal court, even to the last year of his reign, describe an active and involved ruler who continued to daily meet with his noblemen and visitors and who led an active court progress.[61]

Nur Jahan's seeming menace perhaps lay not in any actual seizure of control but, more directly, in the lack of subtlety she and her husband displayed. As queen, she publicly seized the visual attributes of kingship – drums and coins and appearances in council – and participated in the grand theatre of court power almost as if she were a man, just as Jahangir had invited her to do when he ceded her father's lands and rights to her. It is evident that the criticisms brought against the queen may have had less to do with her committing transgressions than in the conditions of her position within the dynasty, as an ambitious outsider with complicated familial baggage. The ascendancy of Nur Jahan's relatives – specifically, the degree of power accrued by her ambitious father and brother – could well have been perceived or portrayed as predatory in the context of her husband's known addictions.[62] It served the purposes of her rivals at court, foreign and domestic, to frame the queen and her family as inherently self-interested and corrupt. The reputations of her brother and father for bribe-taking may well have been accurate, but rumours of a 'junta' are simply not believable. While it is true that members of Nur Jahan's family did see a rapid rise in power and wealth, their ascendancy was not unique; other powerful families, such as that of Abdur Rahim Khankhanan, held similarly advantageous positions.[63] Modern scholars have been unable to identify any single dominant cohort at Jahangir's court, such as the queen's family is reputed to have been. Perhaps most tellingly, at no time did Nur Jahan, Khurram, Asaf Khan and I'timaduddawla operate strategically as a single block; their political interests were not, it seems, generally aligned. All evidence shows that the queen herself was, at least until a few years before Jahangir's death, in complete accord with her husband and did not use her influence 'for factional ends'.[64]

12

Rising crises

Threats to power and kingship

In 1620, when Jahangir's court was still in Lahore, the Ethiopian general of the Deccan, Malik Ambar, began reasserting his power, recapturing much of his original territory and pushing the Mughal imperial armies all the way back to Burhanpur and the fort of Ahmednagar. As recently as 1616, Khurram had been sent to replace his ineffectual brother Parvez as leader of the imperial forces in the Deccan. Once there, he personally reached out to the rulers of Bijapur and Golconda for assistance in the campaign against Malik Ambar. Under pressure, with Khurram's forces in Burhanpur and Jahangir camped in Mandu, the two Deccani rulers acknowledged Mughal suzerainty. Ambar, lacking local support, had been forced to settle again with the Mughals, handing over Ahmednagar in 1617, although retaining the city of Daulatabad. Jahangir, clearly impressed by the quality of Ambar's fighters, and hoping to stave off renewed efforts at local independence, began a policy of drawing Maratha warriors into the Mughal imperial army, rewarding their leaders with *mansab* and *jagir*. Mughal attention having moved away from the Deccan, however, within just a few years Ambar had again taken up arms.

Jahangir had come to rely heavily on the military prowess of Prince Khurram. In the face of Ambar's newly aggressive actions, he ordered his son to lead the imperial armies south yet again. Having finished a Deccani campaign only three years earlier, however, Khurram was not inclined to return. Among Khurram's concerns must have been Jahangir's increasingly regular bouts of ill health. Should his father die suddenly while he himself was in the Deccan, his distance from the throne would offer one of his brothers an opportunity to seize power. It was perhaps for this reason that when Khurram finally did agree to lead the Mughal armies south, he requested that his older brother Khusraw accompany him, under his guardianship. The request was quickly granted.

On arriving again at the Deccani front, Khurram led his armies in pursuit of Adil Shah, the ruler of Bijapur, who managed to flee to Khirki. His refuge was only temporary however, as the Mughal armies seized the city and burned it to the ground. Their real target, Ambar, had remained safely out of the fray in Dawlatabad, however. Once again, he deftly treated with the Mughals, trading off portions of his kingdom in exchange for peace. In addition, he agreed to pay a joint Deccani indemnity of fifty lakhs of rupees, of which twelve lakhs would be contributed by Ahmednagar, eighteen by Bijapur and twenty by Golconda.[1] Khurram accepted the terms in 1621, lingering with his armies in the south.

In August of that year, Jahangir once again fell ill and although he eventually recovered, he remained frail. At his weighing ceremony in September, the emperor himself noted that the resulting charitable contribution would be less than in previous years because of his drastic weight loss.[2] Prince Parvez was so concerned about his father that he attempted to circumambulate the emperor's sickbed three times, seemingly in an effort to draw his father's illness into himself, before his father stopped him.[3] It was only a few weeks later that Nur Jahan's mother died, and a month after that, in January 1622, the family suffered yet another death, that of Jahangir's eldest son, Khusraw.

The cause of Khusraw's death was ostensibly a bout of colic, although that it happened while in the care and keeping of his ambitious younger brother caused a great deal of suspicion. His own contemporaries and modern historians alike have suggested that Khurram must have poisoned his brother.[4] At the time of his death, however, Khusraw had already spent thirteen years in confinement; his allies were dead or dispersed, his fortune and his retinue gone.[5] It is hard to imagine that he posed a credible threat to his ambitious younger brother, himself a powerful and successful general, the chosen successor of their doting father and to whom he had given the title *Shah Jahan*. As we have already seen, while eldest sons were often preferred successors, in the absence of a system of primogeniture a younger son could (and often did) succeed his father. What lends the rumour of Khusraw's murder real credibility is the behaviour of Khurram when he finally did achieve the throne only five years later. Among his first acts was to order his remaining brothers and nephews killed, even those who were too young to offer an immediate threat. While succession conflicts regularly resulted in the deaths of Mughal princes, it was highly unusual that accessional murders would be committed off the battlefield and with no special effort made to establish a juridical justification.

The gossip among the foreigners in India, at the time and after, suggests that Khusraw was seen by many both at court and among the general public as a sympathetic character – if only because his long absence from public view had made of him a blank slate upon which any number of mutually competing values and aspirations might be attached. By the time of his death, however, there were few in the family who mourned him. Jahangir commented only briefly on the loss of his eldest son. Khurram immediately returned to his Deccani campaign.

A new crisis emerged in March 1622, as rumours began to reach the court that Shah Abbas was marching with a Safavid army on the disputed territories of Qandahar. Jahangir initially expressed disbelief; the relationship between the kings had remained amicable and the Mughal forces protecting Qandahar were known to be well armed and well prepared. All the same, Jahangir immediately called for Khurram to make his Deccani forces and himself available in the north, to demonstrate for Abbas the result of a broken oath.[6] Having so ordered, Jahangir continued his progress towards Kashmir. He arranged a *qamargha*, continued meeting with the continual stream of noblemen and local elites who came to pay homage, beneficently cancelled Kashmir's payment of a 'garrison tax,' and underwent treatment with a new doctor brought to him by his nobleman Mahabat Khan, who had recently returned from assignment in Kabul. The grateful Jahangir gave Mahabat Khan a new title: *Ruknussaltana*, the Pillar of the State.

Within just a few days, however, confirmation of Safavid aggression in Qandahar arrived from multiple sources. Jahangir immediately began preparations for war, calling on his generals to prepare their armies and their treasuries and arranging for local grain merchants to accompany the troops as they marched through regions with scant agriculture. Jahangir abruptly turned his own court progress from Kashmir towards Lahore which, as the northern capital, would serve as the gathering point for imperial troops, already arriving from the Deccan, Gujarat, Bengal and Bihar.

In the midst of his arrangements, Jahangir received a surprising letter from Khurram, who answered his father's call to arms by declaring that he had chosen to remain in Mandu in order to wait out the monsoon. Incensed by the delay, Jahangir yet responded cautiously. He declared that if his son chose to remain in the south, he must at least send all of his auxiliary amirs and court servants to join the gathering forces in Lahore, deliberately enumerating the Barha and Bukhari sayyids, the shaykhzades, the Afghans and the Rajputs.[7] Rather than respond directly, Khurram's next move would be an act of territorial theft. Soon after the marriage of her daughter to Jahangir's youngest son, Shahryar, Nur Jahan assigned a few of her own *jagirs* to her new son-in-law, an act which had boosted his wealth and position. Shahryar's agent was sent to take possession of the new properties but when he arrived, he was met with the agents of Khurram, who claimed the lands for himself.[8] A violent confrontation broke out between the factions, resulting in deaths on both sides. Prince Khurram had moved into open revolt.

Jahangir's third son had long been his favourite and presumed successor. Khurram had remained at court until the age of twenty-two. When he was finally appointed to lead a military expedition to Ajmer, his father had expressed concern, describing it as the first time he had allowed his son to leave his side. Khurram's competence as a military leader, evident in campaigns in the Deccan and Gujarat, led his doting father to honour him with new titles, Shah Sultan Khurram in 1609, and in 1617, Shah Jahan, and a special seat near his father's throne. In contrast, his brothers had proven to be relative nonentities. The defeated rebel Khusraw, now deceased, had spent his adult years under house arrest. Parvez, Jahangir's second son, had taken charge of the Deccani campaign twice but on neither occasion had he been able to distinguish himself. Currently governor of Bihar, Parvez was known to have gradually slipped into alcoholism. The youngest prince, Shahryar, born in 1605, was still too young to have had an opportunity to prove himself a capable leader, although as the husband of Nur Jahan's daughter he was beginning to establish a base of power. Only Khurram, the commander of Mughal forces, who had most successfully cultivated political influence and authority, was seen as a viable successor. Like his father before him, he had grown restless waiting for real authority.

Khurram wrote a second letter to his father, criticizing what he described as the unfair division of Mughal territories. Mu'tamid Khan would later point the finger of blame at the queen, whom he accused of having used all her wiles on a weak emperor to promote the young Shahryar, but it is hard to imagine that Jahangir had an alternative. With Khuram demonstrating a threatening personal ambition and Parvez becoming known as a drunkard, the promotion of the youngest prince had become a necessity.[9] In response to Khurram's acts of insubordination, Nur Jahan encouraged her husband to call in the experienced general Mahabat Khan, an old enemy of the prince.[10] The cautious Mahabat stalled, hoping to remain neutral in what looked to be an increasingly explosive family conflict.

Furious over his son's insubordination, Jahangir saw Khurram's letters as statements of outright rebellion – the result, he claimed, of Khurram having been given more patronage and favour than he deserved or could successfully manage. He responded to Khurram's justifications of the land grab with a list of conditions, demanding that the prince pay homage and accept imperial authority, and perhaps most importantly, that he immediately send to Lahore the personnel considered necessary for the Qandahar campaign. Jahangir made the announcement that Shahryar would take command of the imperial armies in place of his delinquent older brother. He reinforced the insult by immediately and unceremoniously reassigning the princely holding of Hisar, historically the *jagir* of the chosen successor, from Khurram, who had held it for years, to Shahryar, ordering Khurram to accept new *jagirs* in the Deccan, Gujarat and Malwa, where he was directed to stay. These last directives were made in an effort to position the rebel prince, and the threat he now embodied, far from his father and the imperial centre.

Khurram refused. The affronted emperor found other ways to vent his anger and frustration. 'Until this time,' he wrote, 'because of the favor and love I had for Khurram and his sons, when his son fell critically ill I vowed that if God spared his life I would never hunt with a gun again and never harm an animal with my own hand. Despite all of the pleasure I derived from hunting, particularly with guns, I didn't do it for five years. Now I am so irked by Khurram's behavior that I began hunting with guns again, and ordered that no one be allowed in the palace without a gun!'[11]

In the midst of this family crises, Jahangir received Safavid emissaries carrying a personal letter from Shah Abbas. The Iranians were graciously awarded robes and allowed to depart. Quoting the letter fully in his memoir, Jahangir interpreted it as an apology and excuse for the recent Safavid acts of aggression in Qandahar. In it, the Shah explained that he had been on a simple hunting trip in the region but when met with rude and unwelcoming local governors, he had been forced to respond in kind. No one had been hurt, the Shah assured Jahangir; surely the friendship between the two kings could withstand such trivial concerns. Jahangir wrote a civil response, describing his surprise on learning of the Safavid aggression and pointing out to Abbas that waiting for a Mughal emissary to resolve the conflict would have been far more appropriate than an attack on Qandahar. Having acted so hastily, Jahangir asserted, it was the Shah who would ultimately be blamed for destroying the unity and loyalty inherent in their relationship, for breaking oaths and destroying norms of virtuous behaviour.[12] For all of their polite mutual protestations, there was no illusion on either side that the letters were entirely sincere or that words alone would resolve the crises. Ordering his generals to him from across the expanse of his empire, from Agra and the Deccan, and calling for 'my favourite son' Parvez to bring his armies from Bihar, Jahangir prepared for war.

Notably, it was in this period that Shah Abbas made a rare intervention on behalf of the Deccani sultanates. Although they had exchanged ambassadors, it is likely that the Shah intended this to irritate his Mughal rival rather than make any imperial claims to Deccani territories. In 1620, however, his ambition rising, he had petitioned Jahangir to allow the Safavid ambassador Qasim Beg to pass through Mughal territory to visit the Deccani courts of the south. When Abbas seized Qandahar in 1622, the envoy of Nizam Shah happened to be in Iran with the Shah, although once Qandahar was taken Abbas would make no further effort to maintain close ties with the Deccani states. Their rhetoric of submission to the Shah aside, neither he nor the Deccani sultans seriously claimed that they were the lieges of Iran.

A secretary's tale of filial revolt

In the seventeenth year of his reign, struggling with filial rebellion and threats to Mughal territory in the north, Jahangir stopped writing his *Jahangirnama*. He explained the abrupt conclusion of his labours by complaining of illness, which took away his interest. By chance, his former *munshi* Mu'tamid Khan had arrived in Lahore from a period of service in the Deccan. As Jahangir would explain, Mu'tamid Khan understood the emperor's character and interests, wrote well and had already been charged with recording events. It would be a simple matter for him to write for the emperor. In any case, the emperor wrote, the work would be a collaboration, Jahangir regularly checking Mu'tamid Khan's notes before allowing him to copy the entries into the *Jahangirnama*.[13]

Beginning in January 1623 and continuing for almost two years more, Mu'tamid Khan took on the authorship of the *Nama*, but we cannot doubt that Jahangir was in constant communication with him as co-author and editor. The *Jahangirnama* retains the familiar quality of the emperor's voice; the narrative not only continues in the first person but the vocabulary and rhythm of the writing is unchanged. A confident and self-aware author claims to elaborate with rich details 'for the sake of enlivening the narrative'. The record remains focused on Jahangir's interests: detailing his interactions with daily visitors to the court, proudly confirming the success of his lion hunts, offering descriptions of strange beasts, detailed reviews of the climate and landscape, and carefully recording the measurement and weight of odd features of the landscape, rivers and monuments. It is as if our emperor had never set down his pen. Yet Jahangir would never reassume sole authorship of the memoir, and the underlying theme of the Mu'tamid Khan years would be one of filial revolt.

The relationship between father and son continued to deteriorate. Reports arrived from Agra confirming that Khurram had left Mandu with an army that Jahangir dismissed as jinxed but which was later described by Mu'tamid Khan as formidable, and was marching on the capital, in hopes of intercepting the transfer of the imperial treasury.[14] Copying a strategy deployed often by his father, Jahangir decided to lead his armies as if he were on the hunt, ready to respond with force if the rebel prince did not back down. As his son's rebellion continued, Jahangir led continuous marches against him. In his rage, he ordered that his son be given a new title, that of *bidawlat*, the unfortunate or wretched, writing, 'And every place in this *Iqbalnama* that "bidawlat" is mentioned, it will mean him.'[15] The emperor added, 'Of the patronage and favors I have showered upon him I can say that until now no monarch has ever showered upon any son. The favors my exalted father showed my brothers I showed his liege men and gave them titles, banners, and drums.' Pointing to his own memoir as evidence of the degree of his paternal affections, Jahangir wrote that his readers would surely recognize the history of favour he had shown the prince. He complained bitterly about his own pursuit of Khurram: 'Of which of my pains should I write? Is it really necessary for me, with my illness and weakness, to get on a horse and gallop around in such hot weather, which is extremely disagreeable to me, running off after an undutiful son?'[16]

Jahangir had left Lahore with a small army but his soldiers rushed to join him from across the region and by the time he reached Delhi his forces had arrived. Jahangir placed the redoubtable Mahabat Khan in command, seemingly on the advice of Nur Jahan. The emperor and his retinue marched near to the armies. Although Khurram was prevented from entering Fatehpur Sikri, his troops had moved into Agra, looting from house to house. Jahangir's outrage was only increased when he learned that with his rebellious son were many of the Mughal elite who had been stationed in the Deccan, including the seventy-year old Abdur Rahim Khankhanan, the son of Bairam Khan, Akbar's mentor. Abdur Rahim had for decades been a popular statesman and military general and an important patron of poets and artists, his household boasting an atelier that was second in size and importance only to the royal workshops. There is even some speculation that his extraordinary talent and success, and the cultural influence he wielded through his patronage, positioned Abdur Rahim as a competitor, perhaps nearly a sibling rival, of the younger Mughal emperor, who had grown up in his shadow.[17] Jahangir seems to have coped with this formidable personality by keeping him at a distance, assigning him duty in the Deccan where his regional expertise, as well as the intellectual, spiritual and artistic milieu he established there, only added to his lustre. His brief disgrace in the failed campaigns of 1612–16, at which time he had been accused of treating with Malik Ambar, had ended with his complete vindication, but now Jahangir fumed over this latest betrayal. 'In the end,' he wrote, 'a wolf cub becomes a wolf, even if it has grown up among humans.'[18]

That the disruption brought on by Khurram's revolt would prevent the Mughals from regaining Qandahar was clearly frustrating to Jahangir, but his greatest expression of regret and sorrow was the loss of his son's supporters, former imperial servants who were now made the emperor's enemies.[19] Jahangir had throughout his reign established a generous patrimonial relationship with the young men who came into the orbit of the Mughal court, on his own behalf or that of his sons. This network of patronage was the core of Mughal stability and power, and Jahangir fumed over the ruined and wasted relationships. Jahangir wrote,

> On account of his [Khurram's] miscreancy, I must requite and kill with my own hands so many servants I have patronized for long year and raised to the rank of Amir, who should today be doing battle [among Jahangir's imperial forces] with the Uzbeks and Qizilbash... What burdens my heart and galls me is that at a time when my sons and loyal Amirs should be endeavoring without partisanship to further the campaign in Qandahar and Khurasan, in which lies the honor of the realm, this unhappy wretch is chopping away at the roots of his own fortune and... complicating matters.[20]

He brooded over the loss of those he considered loyal retainers, who had become a part of Khurram's insurgency, those Mughal amirs and their liege men led by Sundar Das, now camped on the banks of the Yamuna and facing the imperial armies.

At the end of March 1623, battle was joined but almost immediately Jahangir's general Abdullah Khan, leading ten thousand men, deserted the imperial forces and joined with Khurram. Some Mughal soldiers followed Abdullah Khan but others stood their ground; the remaining generals held their troops together and stayed with the emperor. Ultimately, even with the dramatic defection of Abdullah Khan, Jahangir's imperial troops were victorious. The body of Khurram's general Sundar was found by a local village headman. Khan Azam brought his head to Jahangir, who noted that his earlobes had been cut off for the sake of the pearl earrings he had worn.

The surviving insurgents fled the battlefield. Khurram was forced to forsake his march on Delhi and retreat through Ajmer, plundering the city as he fled, while Jahangir followed behind the imperial armies. A second major pitched battle was joined in outside of Mahmudabad, in Gujarat, and again Khurram's forces were defeated. The remaining troops and their general, Abdullah Khan, now named by an outraged Jahangir *La'natullah*, 'God's Curse,' made their way to join the rebel prince at his former base in Burhanpur. A short time later, a third major battle was joined outside of Mandu, when Khurram emerged at the head of twenty thousand cavalrymen. In the meantime, however, Jahangir's general Mahabat Khan had been busily sending word to former colleagues, suggesting their return to the imperial fold. Even as the fight was joined, defections from Khurram's forces began as a trickle and became a flood. Even Abdur Rahim Khankhanan managed to send word that he would return to the imperial armies were he able. Khurram learned of his communique and immediately put the entire family under close watch.

Khurram and his surviving band, including the Khankhanan, headed to the fortress of Asir. Nur Jahan herself had written to the commander, her cousin, advising him to resist its takeover by the rebels. The fortress's defences were expanded and made nearly impregnable, but on the prince's arrival the commander immediately surrendered the fortress to him. Stopping only to drop off the women and goods he could not carry with him, Khurram fled to Burhanpur.

By mid-1624, it had become clear that the prince's rebellion could not be won. Khurram attempted to arrange an honourable peace, sending the Khankhanan to treat with Mahabat Khan. Although the original strategy had been to only allow message to pass between the forces, those accompanying the Khankhanan were quickly frightened off and he was left alone, to be brought before Parvez to pay homage.[21] As the imperial troops began to enter Burhanpur, his generals defeated, and his supporters defecting, Khurram crossed the Tapti River and fled, with his children and dependents, first into the Deccan and then east to Orissa. Parvez, whom Jahangir now referred to as 'my felicitous son', and the old general Mahabat Khan followed in close pursuit, reassuring the emperor that the Deccani states were compliant and the rebel safely contained.

With victory, Jahangir's early outrage and panic began to subside. As deserters from Khurram's rebel army began to flow into the imperial camp, he returned to his favourite pastime, hunting nilgai. He celebrated the beginning of his fifty-fifth year with the usual solar weighing ceremony.[22] Increasingly confident that

Khurram's rebellion had been damaged beyond repair, he left Ajmer in mid-November 1624 to avoid the heat of the Gangetic plain and to enjoy another visit to 'the happy vale' of Kashmir.[23] He reported regular hunts, including that of a lion that Jahangir proudly announced he was able to kill with a single shot. He also recorded an amusing tale of a servant having dropped a tray of refreshment, with golden cups, into a flowing irrigation stream. Boatmen and servants were ordered to thoroughly search, and the tray was found where it had been dropped, right side up and the cups still quite dry. Passing through the mountains, the emperor recorded the visits of local elites, who took advantage of the proximity of the emperor to pay homage. A steady stream of defectors from Khurram's army arrived, to be forgiven and made much of. Although attentive to reports of Khurram's movements, having sent Parvez to Bihar to gather the allied forces in an effort to flush out his rebellious brother, Jahangir returned to the life of the peripatetic camp.

Muhammad Hadi

With that, in April of 1624, Mu'tamid Khan's work on the *Jahangirnama* ends. There is no explanation or note to excuse the abrupt conclusion, three years before the end of a twenty-two-year reign. Many years later Muhammad Hadi, who was probably a secretary working in the Mughal library, chose to use the material from other imperial manuscripts to fill in the gaps and to finish the story of Jahangir. One of those manuscripts must have been the *Iqbalnama*, written by Mu'tamid Khan, the very secretary who had aided Jahangir in writing his final entries in the *Jahangirnama*. Muhammad Hadi seems to have relied heavily on Mu'tamid Khan's eyewitness narrative, at times duplicating his phrasing exactly in what is described by its author as a full account of the contentious and trouble-filled final years of the Emperor Jahangir.

The writing of this last portion of the *Nama* is very different from that of the earlier authors. With the advent of Muhammad Hadi's chapters, the comfortable and informal prose of the emperor was replaced by a more complex and ornate courtier's style. Yet the difference is not only stylistic. Confronted by his son's rebellion, Jahangir had been highly critical of Khurram. The previous chapters, clearly composed by Jahangir and dictated to Mu'tamid Khan, were filled with expressions of rage and frustration in equal measure, referring continually to the emperor's former favourite as *bidawlat*, the wretched and unfortunate. Yet this same son would ultimately succeed Jahangir, becoming the next Mughal emperor,

Shah Jahan. It is probable that Muhammad Hadi, serving at the royal court of the descendants of Jahangir and Shah Jahan, chose to cautiously tread a narrow path in order to narrate the events of the rebellion without insulting the memory of either emperor. When Khurram lost a major battle against imperial troops in 1624 his commander, Abdullah Khan, advised that they flee. In an obvious effort to protect Khurram's reputation, Hadi offered a most exquisite justification for this failure: 'At the beginning of their struggles, such things often happened to rulers of the part – like Amir Timur and Babur... in such case they... retreated, giving no satisfaction to the enemy and by doing so they attained fortune.'[24] His delicate touch was further extended to courtiers who allied with Khurram and survived to serve him as emperor – even the nobleman Mahabat Khan who, as we shall see, would commit the greatest of crimes against Jahangir, received cautious treatment from Muhammad Hadi, including an understanding discussion of his motives. For Hadi, a consummate courtier at the Mughal court, the only rebels deserving of scorn were those proved disloyal to both emperors, father and son, Jahangir and Shah Jahan—a notable exception being the unreliable Asaf Khan.

Although Khurram's insurgency would ultimately prove unsuccessful, in the long months of his rebellion, the Mughal imperial armies had been stretched almost to the breaking point, responding to a series of threats that arose across the subcontinent. Just as the Safavid shah had seized upon perceived Mughal weakness to lay claim to Qandahar, other regional rivals threatened vulnerable Mughal territories. Only a few years earlier, the Mughal and Uzbek states, which had had very little diplomatic contact for a decade, had begun to reconnect. Obvious signs of Safavid ambition had convinced them both of the value in an alliance against Iran. In 1621, with the Safavids preparing for a campaign on the Uzbek borders, the rapprochement was affected by powerful women of the two families, when the mother of Imam Quli Khan sent a letter of friendship and gifts to Nur Jahan. This small gesture was followed up by an envoy sent to India, after which a Mughal embassy made its way to Quli Khan's court. The effort had waited overlong, however. By the time of their arrival, the Safavid seizure of Qandahar had commenced. With the Safavids seeming in the ascendant in the region, the over-extended Mughal armies defending Qandahar from the Safavids were challenged by a newly empowered Uzbek confederation. Aware that the Mughal emperor was distracted and perhaps weakened by internal rebellion, the Uzbeks, pivoting to a new alliance with Iran, began to threaten Mughal Ghazni. As the Uzbeks advanced, the Hazara Afghan tribes living in Ghazni asked the Mughal governor for protection. He responded with alacrity; the imperial armies mobilized and quickly drove the Uzbeks out, destroying their newly built fortress, annihilating their army and sending the head of the Uzbek commander to the Mughal emperor. According to Muhammad Hadi's sources, the Mughals were suspicious that it was the Safavids who had meddled in Uzbek affairs and encouraged the attempted land grab. The leader of the Uzbek forces, Yalangtosh Hasti, 'used to live mostly between Qandahar and Ghazni. Since he repeatedly went to Khurasan, undertaking military actions there, one can assume', comments Hadi, 'that Shah Abbas took some account of him'.

Although low-grade unrest would continue in the region for a few years more, by 1626, Nazr Muhammad had sent a new Uzbek embassy to Jahangir's court, quickly followed by another from Imam Quli Khan, led by the Jubayri Naqshbandi shaykh Khwaja Abdur Rahim. The variety and value of their gifts for the emperor indicate the significance of the embassy, including "'all the best examples of every type of Central Asian specialty which had never before been seen or heard of in India," including horses, mules, furs, camels, expensive books, and pieces of calligraphy, in addition to cash gifts from each of the two rulers, Abdur Rahim and Imam Quli'.[25] Jahangir delayed his departure for Kashmir that spring so as to greet the embassy and he ordered all of the noblemen at his court to gather in their honour. The Naqshbandi shaykh was first greeted by Nur Jahan, a confirmation of her very central role in court functions at the time, then her brother Asaf Khan, and finally, the emperor, who rose from his throne in order to give the shaykh a warm embrace. The shaykh would remain with Jahangir in Kashmir through the summer of 1627.[26]

At the same time, their imperial forces distracted by the Safavid threat and princely rebellion, the Mughals were made vulnerable in the Deccan. Seeking supporters, financing and a safe refuge, Khurram had found only a lukewarm reception in the south and had led his army northeast to Orissa and Bengal and then Benares. Confronted by the imperial armies led by Parvez and Mahabat Khan, Khurram was 'too zealous and too much of a warrior' to listen to a close companion's advice to flee, although by this time his forces numbered only seven thousand cavalry troops against an imperial army of forty thousand. Once again, the battle was a complete rout, with Khurram's armies destroyed. Only a tiny band of supporters remained with the prince in his continued flight.

In the meantime, aware of the many distractions faced by the Mughals, Malik Ambar had begun a new campaign to harass and plunder the imperial armies in Bijapur. Losing the early skirmishes, and with most of their soldiery engaged in the pursuit of Khurram, Jahangir's Deccani units could do little more than remain safely within their fortress until support arrived from Burhanpur. When those forces did at last appear, Ambar was forced temporarily back but then unexpectedly attacked and again defeated the local Mughal troops. The Mughals remained trapped within the fortresses of Ahmednagar and Bijapur while Malik Ambar moved at will between them, free to besiege and conquer smaller and less well-manned fortresses in the region. Obviously, the chaos in the Deccan demanded an imperial response. The decision was made to split the armies then pursuing Khurram, with Mahabat Khan following on the prince's heels while Parvez was sent to the relief of the Deccan.

In an act that must have infuriated Jahangir, the rebel Khurram fled Bihar and Bengal, once again returning to the Deccan and sending an ally, Afzal Khan, to request the help and support of both Malik Ambar and Adil Shah. When Khurram first rebelled, he had attempted an alliance with Ambar and the ruler of Bijapur. Ambar had diplomatically refused to become involved but Adil Shah adroitly accepted the prince's gifts and then reneged on the promise of help. When in 1625 the desperate prince again returned to the Deccan, Ambar at last agreed to support him. The alliance would prove short-lived. Khurram's revolt was in collapse. His health failing, his troops destroyed, his supporters either dead or in flight, Khurram surrendered, writing a letter of apology and regret to his father and begging the emperor's forgiveness. Jahangir, by then once again hunting in the mountains of Kashmir, accepted his son's surrender, demanding that Khurram hand over the fortress of Rohtas and deliver up his two eldest sons to the royal court as surety against their father's loyalty. Khurram complied, although he himself remained away from his father's court. Malik Ambar took full advantage of Mughal disorder and diversion to reconquer most of the Nizam Shahi territories. He would die in May of 1626.[27]

The rebellion of Mahabat Khan

His son's rebellion successfully managed, Jahangir wintered in Lahore, returning to Kashmir in the spring of 1625. Although complaining of continued bad health, the emperor found much to enjoy in his beloved mountain territories. Hunting at Mount Bhaner, the company took 151 mountain rams. On a previous tour, Jahangir had ordered rest houses built on the shores of the Bahat River, so there was no need for the imperial retinue to stay in tents as they had previously. It was early spring, however, and the snow, rain and cold made conditions difficult. Undeterred by the weather, when arriving before a beautiful waterfall Jahangir ordered a fine platform built as a perch for the king, to gaze at the view and drink his wine. As was his habit, he had the date carved onto a stone tablet to mark the occasion. Tulips, lilies and blue jasmine flower were brought to Jahangir from Kashmir, and the local people came to pay homage. With his usual unquenchable curiosity about the natural world, Jahangir investigated an interesting local bird and observed the affectionate relationship between a lion and a goat, the odd couple having been gifts from a nephew. Meanwhile, Khurram's eldest two sons, Dara Shikoh and Aurangzeb, had arrived at their grandfather's court. They brought rich gifts and confirmation that Khurram had as promised given up control over the fortresses of Asir and Rohtas.

The end of Khurram's rebellion would bring Jahangir only a temporary respite, however. With the prince's surrender, Mahabat Khan, who had led the victorious imperial armies against Khurram, had been outraged to find himself assigned the governorship of Bengal. There is some suggestion that because his collaboration with Parvez against Khurram had been so successful, Mahabat Khan had begun to be seen as a threat to other ambitious noblemen, who then managed to have him separated from Parvez and politically marginalized. Some sources accuse Nur Jahan of having arranged his transfer in order to enhance the profile of her new son-in-law Shahryar, although she and Mahabat Khan had long been allies. The Afghan Khan Jahan Lodi was assigned to replace Mahabat Khan as Parvez's *ataliq* in the Deccan. He and Asaf Khan, the brother of Nur Jahan and an intimate of the emperor but also the devoted father-in-law of the failed rebel prince, already openly at odds with Mahabat Khan, would be the primary beneficiaries of the assignment of the powerful general so far from the imperial centre. Once Mahabat Khan was safely in Bengal, Asaf Khan further precipitated a crisis by accusing the old general of misappropriating revenue and withholding imperial elephants in Bengal.

An indignant Mahabat Khan immediately turned back towards the imperial court in Lahore to defend his reputation. Collecting supporters in Ranthampore as he passed, he eventually led a cohort of six thousand soldiers: four thousand 'devoted' Rajputs and the remaining two thousand mostly Afghans. On reaching the city, then governed by Asaf Khan, he was told that he must clear his name of charges before being allowed to join the emperor, who was then on his way to Kabul. A second point of contention arose when Jahangir was informed that Mahabat Khan had recently made his own arrangements for the marriage of his daughter to Khwaja Barkhurdar, a scion of the Naqshbandis, without having first applied for the emperor's approval. The furious Jahangir imprisoned the new husband, had Mahabat Khan's daughter brought to court and readied himself to confront the general.

It seemed to Mahabat Khan that an effort was afoot to completely undermine the general's credibility with the emperor and perhaps ruin his family as well. Muhammad Hadi, writing with the benefit of hindsight, and in the knowledge that Mahabat Khan would later serve as Emperor Shah Jahan's most powerful and trusted general, offered a sympathetic explanation of his rebellious actions. 'The summons had been issued at Asaf Khan's instigation and through his machinations', he explained, 'and now Asaf Khan had made it his single-minded purpose to humiliate Mahabat Khan, strip him of his honor, ravage his women, and deprive him of life and property'.[28] Determined to destroy his rival, an overconfident Asaf Khan became careless. Although the outraged Mahabat Khan was known to be arriving in the company of several thousand loyal Rajput and Afghan warriors, Asaf Khan heedlessly proceeded to lead most of the imperial household across the river, leaving only the emperor and a small number of attendants to spend the night on the opposite bank. Summoned to the imperial camp, on the banks of the Bahat (Jhelum) River, Mahabat Khan, finding the emperor without substantial retinue or guard, impulsively burst into his pavilion and seized him.

Immediately mounting Jahangir on an elephant, 'in the guise of touring and hunting', Mahabat Khan first brought the emperor to his own camp. Quickly realizing his error in leaving Nur Jahan behind, he turned back for the queen. Before he could reach her, however, she had fled to her brother and the imperial forces on the other side of the river, intent on organizing the relief of her husband. Her fame as a hunter caused some fear in the ranks of the rebels, but by the time her rescue was organized Mahabat Khan had already burned the only bridge and Nur Jahan's hastily arranged party was forced to ford the Bahat.[29] Chaos ensued, for 'during the crossing the order of troops was lost, every troop falling in a different direction... cavalry and foot soldiers, horses and camels, plunged into the water, jostling one another and trying to get across'. Realizing that the effort had failed, Nur Jahan made her own way across the river mounted on an elephant and deliberately joined her husband in captivity. Her brother, Asaf Khan, whom Muhammad Hadi had identified as the instigator of the entire affair, took to his heels and 'as badly as those who were present wanted a sign from him by eye or word, there was no trace of which direction he had gone'.[30]

Although they were hostages, Jahangir, Nur Jahan, and their attendants continued on their original path, making their way 'station by station, enjoying hunting' to Kabul. There they camped in the lovely Shahr Ara garden, where twenty years earlier the newly enthroned Jahangir had written of organizing parties for students of the local *madrasa* and sharing bowls of wine with his boon companions. The royal court kept up a pretence of normalcy, continuing to host embassies, including that of Shah Khwaja, who arrived from Balkh bearing gifts of horses and Turkish slave boys. Over the weeks that followed, a further tragedy occurred: the emperor's second son, Parvez, who had spent the last many months chasing after his rebellious brother, sickened and died within a few days, his final illness blamed on alcohol, the family scourge. Faced with so many political and personal crisis, the imperial response to Parvez's loss was muted.[31]

Jahangir and Nur Jahan remained deliberately and strategically complacent, seeming to accept captivity with unconcern, although Mu'tamid Khan would later claim that Nur Jahan was vigilant, always watching for an opportunity to escape. The old general Mahabat Khan, having broken into rebellion spontaneously, now found himself in a state of limbo, unable to act on his own unexpected success. His refusal to take full imperial power, or even seize property or wealth, prevented him from rewarding his Rajput allies and they slowly began to slip out of his control, violently skirmishing with local forces. Their restless aggression and the mounting numbers of casualties distressed and preoccupied Mahabat Khan, who finally let down his guard. At last, again passing over the Bahat River, given an opportunity to escape, the emperor and his queen managed to separate from their captor and flee, taking the road to Lahore.[32] Realizing that he had irretrievably lost control, Mahabat Khan turned and fled through Jaisalmer to the Deccan with the two thousand Rajput troops remaining loyal to him. With Parvez dead and no other options for alliance before him, Mahabat Khan eventually joined forces with Khurram, whose own rebellion, though in abeyance, remained unresolved.

The death of the king

Once again in control of his court progress, the emperor turned towards Kashmir. The trip was of necessity, not by choice, confirmed Mu'tamid Khan, as the heat of the plains adversely affected Jahangir's health.[33] After years of excessive drug and alcohol abuse, and exhausted from the successful effort to crush yet another filial revolt, as well as the rebellion of a formerly trusted courtier, by the fall of 1627 Jahangir had become an invalid. No longer comfortable riding, he was carried in a palanquin. Visibly failing, his condition caused anxiety in his followers, especially among the women of the harem. Jahangir became too frail to eat or even take opium, which he had used daily for forty years, managing only to drink a few bowls of wine. Returning to Lahore, the emperor paused at Bahramgala to hunt. Chasing an antelope into a better position for the emperor's guns, a foot soldier fell from a cliff to his death. The emperor was very deeply affected: 'It was as though the angel of death had appeared in this guise to the emperor,' Muhammad Hadi would later write. The emperor fell into a decline, and although he managed to speak a few words to his companions, Jahangir died shortly thereafter at the age of fifty-eight, having reigned for twenty-two years.[34]

Muhammad Hadi closed his appendix to the *Jahangirnama*, appropriately, with the accession of the new Mughal emperor. The inheritance was not uncontested, as Nur Jahan made a brief effort to put her own son-in-law Shahryar on the throne. As the father-in-law of Khurram, her brother Asaf Khan had very different loyalties.[35] In a strikingly unpredictable alliance, he and Mahabat Khan, who had joined the prince in the previous year on the heels of his own failed revolt, worked at Khurram's side to assure him the throne. Waiting for Khurram to arrive and seize control, Asaf Khan was instrumental in placing Khusraw's eldest son, Dawarbaksh, on the Mughal throne. The young prince was intended as a temporary placeholder however, and when Khurram reached the city, Dawarbaksh was easily forced out. In January 1628, immediately after his formal enthronement as Shah Jahan, in an extraordinary act of accessional familicide, the new emperor would command the execution of his nephews, the briefly enthroned Dawarbaksh and his brother Garshasp, as well as Khurram's own younger brother Shahryar, along with his cousins, Tahmuras and Hoshang, sons of Jahangir's brother Daniyal.[36] All who were seen as potential rivals were destroyed as Shah Jahan and his supporters worked to make his succession secure.

As for Nur Jahan, immediately after the ascension of the new emperor the queen quietly retired to her family's centre of power in Lahore. Asaf Khan would remain the governor of the province for another five years, and although having proven himself an unreliable political ally in the recent past, he would be in a position to protect her should she need his help. It seems that she did not. She lived quietly in Lahore with her daughter, widow of the murdered prince Shahryar, until her death in 1645, remaining completely detached from dynastic politics and busying herself with the construction of Jahangir's tomb in the suburban city of Shahdara. The building would be relatively modest, with no great dome, the tomb humbly seated on a low platform of marble. Asaf Khan would spend the remainder of his career as an intimate of the new emperor, but both he and Nur Jahan would choose to have their own tombs built adjacent to that of Jahangir.

The new emperor took the Mughal throne on 3 February 1628, marking his ascension with a pilgrimage to the Ajmer shrine of the Chishti Sufi saints. He scattered coins to the population, offered gifts and robes to his supporters, and was ceremoniously weighed in celebration of his thirty-seventh birthday. 'The ancient world turned new again', Muhammad Hadi wrote, 'and the world received peace and security'.[37]

Conclusion

Remembering Jahangir

The reputations of Jahangir and Nur Jahan suffered badly in the hands of his successor's courtiers. In an effort to justify Shah Jahan's rebellion, they condemned his predecessor as weakened by a lifetime addiction to alcohol, frail and inept, and willing to allow the ambitious queen and her family to seize control of the functions of government. When several years after Jahangir's death Mu'tamid Khan composed the *Iqbalnama*, he described Nur Jahan as narrowly partisan, lacking in sufficient loyalty to the greater Mughal dynasty and rallying her ambition and talents in support only of her husband and her own male relatives. Her own biographer, Shaikh Farid Bhakkari, who saw fit in 1649–50 to include Nur Jahan among biographies of the Mughal nobility, claimed that eventually 'disposal of the affairs of the kingdom were in her hands', although hastily admitting that 'her good outweighed her evil'.[1]

Foreign merchants had been quick to complain of her power, their writings adding to the narrative of a 'crafty' Nur Jahan.[2] In particular Roe had famously accused the queen of being in the centre of a web of intrigue which, it was claimed, successfully controlled a benevolent but befuddled Jahangir. It was, of course, to Roe's benefit to justify his own failures at the Mughal court by identifying as the victim of a powerful enemy and presenting the king as a hapless ally. While complimenting himself on his relationship with an affable Jahangir, writing that 'Hee is good to me', Roe portrayed both the king and himself as pawns of Nur Jahan's network of corrupt and manipulative court favourites, Jahangir as 'a Patient king whose hart is not understood by any of all these'.[3] The Dutchman Pelsaert too would accuse an ambitious Nur Jahan of having usurped royal power and wealth to the point that her approval was required before even Jahangir's own orders could be implemented.[4] Identifying the source of their diplomatic failures as an ambitious and powerful woman, these merchants and adventurers found excuses in a popular European trope, that of an untrustworthy and manipulative femininity that undermined male power at the royal courts of the Islamic world.

Their narrative of Jahangir's weakness and passivity became widely disseminated and so entrenched in the scholarship that a twentieth-century biographer would describe Jahangir's reputation as that of 'a hard-hearted fickle minded tyrant, soaked in wine and sunk in debauch'.[5] In the face of contradictory evidence, scholars have continued to repeat the claim that Nur Jahan had seized control of Mughal governance by 1622, when Mu'tamid Khan took on the authorship of the *Jahangirnama*, or even as early as 1619, at the time of Jahangir's return to Agra.[6] It has proven hard to dislodge the popular narrative of a weak and undisciplined emperor having fallen under the control of a manipulative and ambitious queen, in part because Orientalist themes of eastern decadence and wily harem women still carry some power, even in the academic world. In addition, while Jahangir was public about both his addictions and the power he granted to his wife, his openness seen by many to confirm the scuttlebutt of rivals and foreign gossip of a failing king.

On the contrary, however, records contemporary to the emperor's reign confirm that Jahangir remained politically engaged and physically active nearly to the time of his death in October 1627. While suffering from occasional bouts of ill health, the emperor was by no means frail and incapacitated. Confronted by his son's revolt, Jahangir's response was not to withdraw but to issue a resounding repudiation of his personal ban on hunting and immediately call for a campaign against the rebellious prince. Over the next several months Jahangir joined a series of continuous marches to the battle front. For as long as Khurram represented a threat to the empire, Jahangir stationed himself on the changing lines of the campaign against his son, only returning to the north when the power of the prince was broken. In fact, beginning even before Khurram's rebellion, from 1619 the court progress had remained constant and even intrepid, from Agra to Delhi, then Lahore and Kashmir, south to Gujarat and Ajmer and then north to Lahore and Kashmir again, where the king was described as hunting daily. In 1627, a member of the emperor's retinue sent a letter to his superiors to complain of the emperor's still relentlessly mobile court. 'The King goes running about his kingdoms', he wrote bitterly, echoing of the criticism levied at Jahangir by Sir Thomas Roe many years earlier, on the journey to Mandu, 'and in those journeys one suffers so much that one cannot imagine it ... extreme privations, discomforts, and a continual agitation bodily and mentally'.[7]

As for the affairs of the royal court, while all sources confirm that the queen was a powerful political actor, there is no contemporary evidence that Jahangir had become marginalized by his favourite wife. To whatever degree Nur Jahan had taken on the running of the empire in the five or more years before Jahangir's death, the era was notable for its continued competent adherence to Jahangir's administrative style and political values. Mughal state politics remained utterly consistent throughout: there were no discernible shifts in diplomatic or economic policy nor sudden changes in the make-up of the imperial nobility. Even in the final year of Jahangir's life, visitors confirm that the emperor held court daily and maintained the evening *majalis*, described so many years earlier by his devoted courtier, Abdus Sattar.[8] A Jesuit in Jahangir's retinue in 1626–27, the last year of the emperor's life, described nightly 'discussions, and very stubborn ones, before the King about our Holy law ... for he too likes to hear them and express his doubts', confirming that Jahangir had remained to the end an active and engaged ruler, fascinated by the intricacies of religious and spiritual details and practices, still willing to track the lineages of intellectual debate.[9]

Although intended to uphold his sovereignty, the *Jahangirnama* itself seems to have damaged its author's reputation. That Jahangir's reign is not remembered as a success is not only a reflection of the record created by his rivals and successors, but a result of his own telling. As the most complete and detailed historical record of the period, the *Jahangirnama* suffices as an extraordinary imperial legacy, but of course it was much more than a simple chronicle. Like Babur's *Vaqa'i*, the *Jahangirnama* was a personal justification for rule and a defence of his patrimonial prerogatives. In addition, in cohering with the larger canon of dynastic histories, the *Jahangirnama* affirmed and defended the power of its author's exemplars and models, adding another chapter to the intergenerational mediation on power, kingship and dynasty, identity and self, which encompassed and represented the Mughal collective memory. Yet even as he confirmed his adherence to dynastic precedence, unequivocally claimed divine appointment and committed himself to the Persio-Islamic archetype of just kingship, in public gestures that were described by contemporaries as prodigious and self-sacrificing, Jahangir conceded personal flaws and failings. In his memoir, the emperor publicly acknowledged his addictions in excruciating detail. He lamented his own occasional misjudgement and even exposed the inconsistency of his flirtation with Akbar's flamboyant claims of divinity, his pose as Authority of the Age undermined by the emperor's own sceptical rationality and public admission of his flawed humanity.

In this, he followed the model of his great-grandfather, whose own powerful writings had established the political and personal rewards of public self-examination. Babur, the poet-warrior, would be celebrated for his particularities rather than an adherence to medieval standards of leadership, his memoir heightening recognition of the individual personality and both emphasizing and reinforcing the value of self-representation in constructing what would become a canonical historical telling. One hundred years later, Jahangir used his memoir to claim legitimate rule and defend his power. Like Babur, he too would emerge from the pages as charming and drunken, highly sensitive, occasionally cruel, loyal, proud of a charismatic lineage and completely confident in his right to rule – acknowledging his personal failings even as he made the case for power and kingship.

Native son

The Mughal chronicles make clear that Akbar's personality and reputation had both awed and intimidated his three sons. Raised to assume the mantle of kingship yet tightly controlled by their powerful father, the princes had struggled to keep rising ambition in check. In adulthood, all three would find refuge in alcohol, among other acts of opposition. The eldest was the only one of the brothers to break into open revolt. His rebellion was costly and damaging, but there is perhaps a grain of truth in Muhammad Hadi's later assertion that Jahangir's effort to seize an independent state was evidence of his 'bravery and manliness'. In any case, his reconciliation with Akbar, coming as it did just before his father's death, allowed Jahangir to claim not only the imperial throne but also his father's powerful legacy. Once enthroned, the competitive rivalry that had undermined his adult relationship with Akbar may have worked in his favour. Aspiring to fully assume his father's mantle, Jahangir charted a public course of filial loyalty and admiration, committing his reign to the emulation, reinforcement and protection of the best of his father's policy positions.[10] His cautious management of the empire and protection of dynastic values, and his adept handling of noblemen, diplomats and rivals, kept the empire stable and solvent throughout his reign, the only real threats to his power coming from his own sons, just as Jahangir as a restless prince had threatened Akbar.

The *Jahangirnama* makes clear, however, that the Mughal emperor cherished nothing more than to ramble across the landscape of his beloved South Asian territories. His was a restless reign. To be sure, the massive court progress could be justified as a projection of imperial Mughal kingship and power, the king's mobility marking him as a *chakravartan*, a wheel-turning ruler, but in fact the journeys on which he led his court were most profoundly influenced by the changing seasons and the beauty of the landscape. The first of the Mughals to have been born in the Gangetic plain of Hindustan, Jahangir found his greatest pleasure in journeying across the empire, attentive to the beauty of his surroundings and relishing the intimacy and informality of the imperial camp. Jahangir had both a sensory and an intellectual relationship with South Asia – its people and creatures, its flowers and fruits, its waterfalls, rivers, mountains and jungles. Perhaps even more than his immediate Mughal predecessors, he was drawn to analysis and inquiry – measuring and weighing, testing and experimenting, he 'assess[ed] his dominions scientifically'.[11] Yet his compulsive collecting of artefacts and oddities, of maps and data, in no way lessened the power of his emotional and aesthetic response to the landscape. So affected was he by the scenic beauty around him that even the tribulations of the journey could not slow his constant touring. While the summer heat on the Gangetic plain compelled him to head north, it was the promise of spring in Kashmir that inspired his dangerous late winter journeys through mountain passes blocked by ice, so that Jahangir might be on hand to witness the very first wild blossoms emerge from the snow. He would write, 'All over, everywhere I look, a blandishment catches my heart by the skirt saying, "this is the place!"'[12] Neither a warrior nor an exile, as his predecessors Akbar, Humayun and Babur had been, the peripatetic Emperor Jahangir was a native son who viewed Hindustan as a paradisiacal land of marvels and wonders.

As for his successor, the Emperor Shah Jahan chose a very different model of kingship. Cautious and deliberate in his presentation of sovereignty, self-consciously concerned for an unblemished record of his regnal history, he employed a series of professional court historians to tightly craft a seamlessly perfect imperial image. His first historian, Qazvini, described the emperor as deeply involved in the process.

> Sometimes, the writer of these pages enters the assembly by imperial command and reports on the content of each and every narrative that has been written. If a slip in the contents or an error in the expression has occurred, His Majesty corrects it and guides this worthless speck of dust to the exalted words and pleasing turns of phrase that occur to the royal mind and the inclusion of which in this history would occasion felicity of expression, indeed which are necessary concomitants to this art.[13]

It is not difficult to imagine how, under the pressure of such intense scrutiny, the charm of the earlier court writings was lost. While the importance of dynastic history continued to be recognized and imperial courtiers would continue to compose detailed and formal court chronicles, in the long years of Mughal rule after Jahangir's death, the members of the royal family of India would never again return to the intimacy and spontaneity of personal memoir and of Jahangir's peripatetic royal court.

Notes

Epigraph

1 Henry Beveridge, review of Beni Prasad's *History of Jahangir*, London: Oxford University Press, 1922, published in the *Journal of the Royal Asiatic Society*, Vol. 55, No. 3 (July 1923), pp. 483–484.
2 Barbara Metcalf, 'Narrating Lives', review, *The Journal of Asian Studies*, Vol. 54, No. 2 (May 1995), pp. 474–480.

Introduction

1 Among those redressing the lack of sound scholarship on Jahangir, very fine work is being done by Corinne LeFevre, most recently: *Pouvoir impérial et élites dans l'Inde moghole de Jahāngīr (1605-1627)*, Les Indes savants, 2018. Recent popular histories include that of Parvati Sharma, *Jahangir: An Intimate Portrait of a Great Mughal*, New Delhi: Juggernaut Books, 2018 and Ruby Lal's *Empress: The Astonishing Reign of Nur Jahan*, New York and London: W. W. Norton & Company, 2018.
2 Beni Prasad, *History of Jahangir*, London: Oxford University Press, 1922, p. 25.
3 Manuscripts used for this study include: Nuruddin Muhammad Jahangir, *Jahangirnama*, British Library MS OR 1644; *Jahangirnama (Tuzuk-i Jahangiri)*, Tehran: Buny adi Farhangi Iran, 1359 (1980); *The Jahangirnama, Memoirs of Jahangir, Emperor of India*, Wheeler M. Thackston, tr., New York: Oxford University Press, in association with the Freer Gallery of Art and the Arthur Sackler Gallery, Smithsonian Institution, Washington, DC, 1999.
4 Among them, the *Zafarnama* (Book of Conquests) of Nizamuddin Ali Shami, written in 1404, which served as the basis of other surviving histories of Timur, including the *Zafarnama* of Sharaf al-Din Ali Yazdi, completed in 1425 for Ibrahim Sultan ibn Shahrukh, then governor of Shiraz. Over the next eighty years, Yazdi's manuscript would be copied and illustrated thirty times.
5 Zahiruddin Muhammad Babur, *Baburnama (Vekayi), Critical Edition Based on Four Chaghatay Texts*, Eiji Mano, ed., Japanese and Chaghatay, 4 vols., Kyoto: Syokado, 1995. Also see *Baburnama*, Wheeler M. Thackston, tr., text in Chaghatay, Persian and English, 3 vols., Cambridge, MA: Harvard University Department

of Near Eastern Languages and Civilizations, 1993. See also Taymiya R. Zaman, 'Instructive Memory: An Analysis of Auto/Biographical Writings in Early Mughal India', *Journal of the Economic and Social History of the Orient*, Vol. 54, No. 5 (2011), pp. 677–700, who uses the term 'auto/biography' in order to emphasize the 'overlap between writing one's life, composing a history of one's time (which often included biographies of eminent men of letters) and locating one's authorial self within social, political, familial and literary circles'. I of course agree that both *Jahangirnama* and the *Vaqa'i* were, as Zaman asserts, 'a manifestation of the writing of lives in Mughal India'. However, while recognizing the deep connections between these genres, and that there were historical writings that offered what Zaman might consider an auto/biographical precedent, Babur's memoir is exceptional not only for the motives that produced it but for the unprecedented depth of his individual and idiosyncratic self-exposure. Zaman's discomfort with the term 'autobiography' is explained by the assertion that, 'biographical writing has been traditionally viewed in terms of eighteenth century notions of self-consciousness as expressed within the psyche of the male enlightenment individual' (Zaman, pp. 678–680). While I agree that the term is heavily weighted by early modern Western forms of knowledge and modernity, Dale has shown that we can claim those notions for the East as well. As this book will argue (in particular, see Section 4), Jahangir and his Mughal predecessors participated in discourses that the West would describe as 'Enlightenment', just as Babur's Central Asian ancestors participated in what has been called 'a Timurid renaissance'. See Stephen Frederic Dale, 'Steppe Humanism: The Autobiographical Writings of Zahir al-Din Muhammad Babur, 1483–1530', *International Journal of Middle East Studies*, Vol. 22, No. 1 (February 1990), pp. 37–58.

6   Mirza Haydar Dughlat, *Tarikh-i Rashidi: A History of the Khans of Moghulistan*, W.M. Thackston, tr./Persian and English texts, 2 vols., Cambridge, MA: Harvard University Department of Near Eastern Languages and Civilizations, 1996.

7   There is only a single extant manuscript of the *Humayunnama*, and it is sadly incomplete: Gulbadan Begim, *Humayunnama*, British Library Or. 166. Two translations are available in English, the earliest by Annette S. Beveridge (tr. and ed./English and Persian texts), Delhi: Idarah-i Adabiyat-i Delli, 1972 and more recently in *Three Memoirs of Homayun*, Wheeler M. Thackston, tr./English and Persian texts, Costa Mesa, CA: Mazda Publishers, 2009, pp. 1–68.

8   Jauhar Aftabchi, 'Tadhkiratu'l-vaqa'i', and Bayazid Bayat, 'Tarikh-i-Humayun', along with Gulbadan Begim, 'Humayunnama', have been edited and translated in one volume as *Three Memoirs of Homayun*, Wheeler Thackston, ed. and tr., Costa Mesa, CA: Mazda Publishers, 2009.

9   Ghiyas al-Din Khwandamir, *Qanun-i Humayuni* (*Humayunnama of Khwandamir*), M. Hidayat Hosain, ed., Calcutta: Royal Asiatic Society of Bengal, 1940.

10 Abu'l Fazl Allami, *A'in (Ayn)-i Akbari*, Vol. 1, H. Blochmann, tr., 2nd ed., Lieut Colonel D.C. Phillott, ed., New Delhi: Munshiran Manoharlal Pub. Pvt. Ltd.,

3rd ed., 1977, vols. 2 and 3, Colonel H.S. Jarrett, tr. and ed., 2nd ed., Sir Jadunath Sarkar, ed., 3rd ed., 1977, and *Akbarnama*, H. Beveridge, tr., 3 vols., Delhi: Manmohan Satish Kumar, Rare Books, 1st Indian edition, 1972. Respectively cited as *AA* and *AN* throughout.

11 Muhammad Sharif Mu'tamid Khan, *Iqbalnama-i Jahangiri*, British Library Add 2621; OR 14342; Add 26612, William Erskine, tr; Khwaja Kamgar Husaini, *Ma'asir-i Jahangiri (A Contemporary Account of Jahangir)*, Azra Alavi, ed. (Persian text with English introduction), New York: Asia Publishing House, Inc., 1978.

12 Barbara Metcalf, 'Narrating Lives', pp. 477–478.

13 The most thorough and thoughtful analysis being that of Stephen Dale, *Garden of the Eight Paradises*, Leiden: Brill, 2004. See also Dale, 'Autobiography and Memoir: The Turco-Mongol Case: Babur, Haydar Mirza, Gulbadan Begim and Jahangir', *The Rhetoric of Biography; Narrating Lives in Persianate Society*, L. Marlow, ed., Cambridge, MA: Harvard University Press, 2011, pp. 89–105.

14 Maria Szuppe, 'A Glorious Past and an Outstanding Present: Writing a Collection of Biographies in Late Persianate Central Asia', *The Rhetoric of Biography: Narrating Lives in Persianate Societies*, Cambridge, MA: Harvard University Press, 2011, pp. 41–88, 45.

15 Gulru Necipoglu, 'Word and Image: The Serial Portraits of Ottoman Sultans in Comparative Perspective', *The Sultan's Portrait: Picturing the House of Osman*, Istanbul: Is Bank, 2000, pp. 22–61, 28.

16 Richard Foltz, 'Two Seventeenth-Century Central Asian Travelers to Mughal India', *Journal of the Royal Asiatic Society*, Third Series, Vol. 6, No. 3 (November 1996), pp. 367–377, 367.

17 See Stephen F. Dale, 'The Poetry and Autobiography of the Bâbur-nâma', *The Journal of Asian Studies*, Vol. 55, No. 3 (August 1996), pp. 635–664.

18 Zahir al-Din Muhammad Babur, *Baburnama (Vekayi)*, p. 659.

19 For example, E.M. Forster, 'The Emperor Babur', in *Abinger Harvest*, Boston, MA: Houghton Mifflin, 1950. More recently, Amitav Ghosh writes that 'The British had a particular affection for Babur in whom they imagined themselves to have discovered a precursor for their hard-drinking, free-living imperialist pioneers'. See Ghosh, 'The Man behind the Mosque', *The Little Magazine*, Vol. 1, No. 2 (2000).

20 Writing in Chaghatay Turkish also allowed Babur to avoid the allusive and metaphorical language of early modern Persian court writers. Although writing in Persian, Jahangir too would manage to emulate this simpler, though sophisticated, voice.

21 Ali Anooshahr has suggested that Babur hoped to move beyond the limitations of his own Turco-Mongol audience, once he had become established in India, by commissioning an early translation of the *Vaqa'i* into Persian. Anooshahr argues that the Persian translation was part of a deliberate campaign to speak in local idioms of power, thereby broadening Babur's readership to include Hindustan's

pre-Mughal local Muslim powers. It is unclear just who in the region of his latest conquests would have benefitted from this translation however. Muzaffar Alam has pointed out that Persian was not a dominant language in Hindustan at that time, as Babur himself confirmed, and argues instead that the new translation into Persian may have been driven by 'a convergence of factors within the Mughal regime', rather than the Indo-Persian heritage of their predecessors. In any case, Zayn's early translation was considered a failure. It would not be replaced until the Emperor Akbar's reign, when the *Vaqa'i* was translated into Persian by Abdur Rahim Khankhanan. See Ali Anooshahr, *The Ghazi Sultans and the Frontiers of Islam*, London and New York: Routledge, 2009; Muzaffar Alam, *The Languages of Political Islam, India 1200–1800*, Chicago: University of Chicago Press, 2004.

22 Jahangir, fs. 84b–85a.
23 For example, Milo Cleveland Beach describes a set of *Jahangirnama* illustrations in Iran, which were probably taken there by Nadir Shah after his looting of Mughal Delhi in 1739. See in Beach, 'Jahangir's Jahangir-Nama', *Powers of Art*, Barbara Stoler Miller, ed., Delhi: Oxford University Press, 1992, pp. 224–234.
24 Wheeler Thackston describes the *Jahangirnama* as 'really *the* history of his reign'. See *Jahangirnama*, 1999, translator's preface, p. xxi.
25 Mu'tamid Khan and Khwaja Kamgar Husaini previously cited; Abdus Sattar Lahauri, *Majalis-i Jahangiri*, Arif Naushahi and Mu'in Nizami, eds., Tehran: Miras-i Maktub, 2006. My thanks to Narjes Khademi for her help with Sattar.

Chapter 1

1 see Zahir al-Din Muhammad Babur, Baburnama (Vekayi).
2 Ibid., f. 30b.
3 Abu'l Fazl, *AN*, II, p. 503.
4 Ibid., p. 237.
5 Khwaja Moin married Humayun's daughter, while a second daughter, Bakshi Banu Begim, married the grandson of Khwaja Khwand, Mirza Sharif al-Din, in 1560 or 1561 in Agra. During the reign of Akbar, another of Humayun's daughters, Fakhr al-Nisa Begim, was married to a KAbu al-i Ahrari known as Hasan Naqshbandi, who later allied himself with the rebellion of Akbar's half-brother, Mirza Muhammad Hakim, and was forced to flee Kabul for Balkh a year later. His son, Mirza Wali, who despite his father's disgrace had been welcomed with an imperial appointment at Akbar's court, later married the niece of the emperor Jahangir, Bulaqi Begim, daughter of his brother Danyal. The Ahraris had been the most powerful Naqshbandi lineage in the late Timurid period. See JoAnn Gross, 'Khoja

Ahrar: A Study in Perceptions of Power and Prestige in the Late Timurid Period', unpublished PhD dissertation, New York University, 1982.
6 Muzaffar Alam, 'The Mughals, the Sufi Shaikhs and the Formation of the Akbari Dispensation', *Modern Asian Studies*, Vol. 43, No. 1 (January 2009), pp. 135–174, 161.
7 Abu'l Fazl, *AN*, II, p. 504.
8 Ibid., p. 507.
9 It is telling that Akbar took the opportunity of his pilgrimage to assert imperial control over the Chishti shrine at this time. He demanded an investigation which, unsurprisingly, indicated that the shaykhs who managed the shrine were making false genealogical claims. Akbar replaced them with Shaikh Muhammad Bukhari, 'a sayyid of Hindustan'. The emperor established rules for treatment of pilgrims and ordered mosques and *khangahs* to be built in the area. He then led the court progress to Delhi, where he visited shrines and administered justice. Ibid., p. 351.
10 Jahangir, f. 2a. The shaykh's naming of Salim has an interesting dynastic precedent, in that the great Naqshbandi Khwaja Ahrar in late Timurid Mawarannahr was believed to have selected the name for Zahiruddin Muhammad Babur, the Mughal dynastic funder. See Babur, *The Baburnama*, Beveridge, tr., p. xxviii.
11 Akbar's own mother was given the title *Maryam al-Makani*, 'In the Place of Mary', in a deliberate enhancement of his own claims of divinity – for himself but also for his direct line of succession.
12 Ibid., p. 516.
13 Munis Faruqui, *The Princes of the Mughal Empire*, New York: Cambridge University Press, 2012, p. 73.
14 Abu'l Fazl, *AN*, III, p. 106.
15 Ibid., pp. 106–107.
16 Abu'l Fazl, *AA*, I, p. 289.
17 Abu'l Fazl, *AN*, III, p. 43.
18 Abdur Rahim spoke Arabic, Persian, Turkish and Hindi, later learning Sanskrit and Portuguese on the order of Akbar.
19 John Seyller, *Workshop and Patron in Mughal India*, Zurich: Artibus Asiae Publishers in association with the Freer Gallery of Art, Smithsonian Institution, 1999.
20 Abu'l Fazl describes near simultaneous marriages in 1587, when Salim married a daughter of Rai Rai Singh, while 'at about that time' the daughter of Said K. Gakkar 'entered the service of that nursling of the Caliphate and thereby conferred greatness on her family'. Abu'l Fazl, *AN*, III, p. 749.
21 At one point, Akbar suggested that his eldest son might marry the daughter of his half-brother, Muhammad Hakim, who had gone into rebellion in Kabul. It had

required a mix of military threat and family diplomacy to bring him firmly under Akbar's control. In fact, cousin marriage was very common amongst the Timurid-Mughals but in this case, Abu'l Fazl declared this close family relationship to be generally unacceptable, forgiven in this case only as a slight evil could be forgiven for a greater good. In any case, the marriage did not take place. See Abu'l Fazl, *AN*, III, p. 353.

22 Marriage as a Timurid-Mughal institution is explored in more detail in Part 3 of this study. A side note: during the celebration of the beginning of the twenty-seventh year of his reign, Akbar called a massive assembly, during which he called on the nobility to submit a suggestion or make an argument for change. In his turn, Prince Salim called for an end to child marriages, saying that all marriages before the age of twelve accrued 'much harm and little advantage'. He was at the time thirteen and as yet unmarried. See Abu'l Fazl, *AN*, III, p. 559.

23 Ibid., p. 105.

24 Ibid., p. 308. The ranking system of the Mughal nobility was called *mansab* (an Arabic word meaning rank or position). These were meritorious, not hereditary positions. Appointed personally by the emperor, the holder of a mansab (called *mansabdar*) was given financial support in the form of a *jagir*, a revenue assignment tied to the income drawn from a property, although not ownership of the property itself, which remained state held land. The income of an individual mansabdar was determined by how many armed cavalrymen (along with horses, elephants, weapons and supplies) he was expected to support and supply to the imperial armies. Mansab assignments were made without distinction between military and civil positions.

25 Ibid., pp. 463–464.

26 Sir Edward Maclagan, *The Jesuits and the Great Mogul*, London: Bruns, Oates and Washburn, Ltd., 1931, pp. 68–69.

27 Construction began in 1569, and the completed city served as the Mughal capital from 1571 to 1585.

28 Among the Nine Jewels, Mullah Do Piaza left no contemporary historical record and is considered by some modern scholars to have been a later invention. The identities of the so-called Nine Jewels are uncertain in a few cases, reflecting a fluid membership and changes in personnel over time, as well as fictionalization.

Chapter 2

1 Faruqui, p. 194.

2 Fr. Monserrate, *The Commentary of Father Monserrate, S.J., On His Journey to the Court of Akbar*, J.S. Hoyland, tr., Oxford, 1922, p. 5.

3   It is worth remembering that Mirza Muhammad Hakim died only a few years earlier, in 1585, of alcohol poisoning.
4   Jahangir, f. 118b.
5   Prasad, p. 39, quoting Peruschi, Monserrate and Aquaviva.
6   Faruqui, p. 156.
7   The animosity between the factions fuelled conspiracy theories and rumour. Long after Urfi's death in 1591, it was rumoured he'd been poisoned by Abu'l Fazl and Faizi; see Khafi Khan, *Muntakhab al-Labab*, Kabir al-Din Ahmad, ed., Vol. 1, Calcutta, 1869, p. 241.
8   Abu'l Fazl, *AN*, III, p. 1132.
9   Ibid., p. 1140.
10 Muhammad Hadi, 'Preface [and conclusion] to the Jahangirnama', *The Jahangirnama, Memoirs of Jahangir, Emperor of India*, Wheeler M. Thackston, tr., New York: Oxford University Press, in association with the Freer Gallery of Art and the Arthur Sackler Gallery, Smithsonian Institution, Washington, DC, 1999, p. 11.
11 Muhammad Sharif's father, Khwaja Abdus Samad, had long been a valued calligrapher/painter in the Mughal royal ateliers, having been given the title *Shirin Qalam*, Sweet Pen, by the Emperor Humayun. As emperor, Jahangir would write that Muhammad 'had grown up with me from childhood' (Jahangir, f. 5b). The relationship of the prince and the painter's son is a clear indication of the high position given favoured artists within the royal court. See Khwaja Kamgar Husaini, *Maasir-i Jahangiri*, Azra Alavi, ed., New Delhi: Asia Publishing House, 1978, pp. 22–23. In 1589, Muhammad Sharif Khan was found to be connected to a plot to 'dishonour a peasant's daughter'. For his complicity, Akbar had ordered him beaten and imprisoned. Abu'l Fazl, *AN*, p. 861.
12 The two acts of minting coins and having the khutba read in the rulers name were the principal prerogatives of those claiming legitimate sovereign rule.
13 Incidentally, in 1607 while serving as governor of Bengal province, Qutbuddin Khan was killed by the rebellious Afghan nobleman Sher Afghan, who was himself struck down immediately afterwards, thereby making a widow of his wife, Mihrunnisa. She would later marry the emperor Jahangir, becoming known to posterity by her later title, Nur Jahan.
14 Shahnawaz Khan and Abdul Hai, *Maasir-ul-Umara*, Calcutta: Bibliotheca Indica, 1887–96; H. Beveridge and B. Prasad (tr.), Maasir-ul-Umara of Shahnawaz Khan and Abdul Hai, Calcutta, I, 1941, II, 1952.
15 For a thoughtful discussion of this phenomenon, see Faruqui, pp. 158–162.
16 Ibid., pp. 161–162.
17 Abu'l Fazl, *AN*, III, p. 1104.
18 Jahangir, f. 9b. Khwaja Kamgar Husaini, author of the *Maasir-i Jahangiri*, blamed Abu'l Fazl for undermining Salim's relationship with his father. Any court history of the period of Jahangir (or in this case, Shah Jahan) would have an interest in

supporting the narrative of the eventual successor to the throne and his line of descent.
19 Abu'l Fazl, *AN*, III, p. 1230.
20 Ibid. The Akbarnama claims that 'the fawning of the prince did not remedy the inward dissatisfaction of the sovereign'. The clearly disapproving author adds that putting his turban on the prince's head was an omen of Salim's eventual succession, but insists that Akbar as yet disapproved of Salim and had only 'involuntarily put the crown of dominion on the head' of a prince unworthy to rule.
21 Ibid., pp. 1242–1243. It is possible that the men were attempting to make their way to the court of Prince Danyal which, if true, might better explain Salim's violent reaction.
22 Hamida Banu Begim had met Humayun when she was only thirteen, the daughter of a Persian immigrant who had joined the court of Babur. She was living in the household of his brother Hindal, and some suggest that Hindal had hoped to marry her himself, but after some initial resistance, she was married to Humayun in 1541 – although he had already lost his throne to the Afghan Sher Khan and was in the midst of a brutal battle over sovereignty with his brothers. She gave birth to their son Akbar in Rajput Umerkot, and only two years later was forced to flee Kamran's army, leaving the child behind to be raised in the household of his seditious uncle. She and Humayun went into exile in Safavid Iran. She was reunited with her son a few years later, during Humayun's lengthy but ultimately successful campaign to regain his patrimony. She would be a universally respected and powerful figure in her son's royal household, advising Akbar on politics and family – concerns that were inseparable in the pre-modern royal court.
23 Ibid., p. 1248.

Chapter 3

1 Jahangir, f. 5b.
2 While loyalty could at any time be unreliable, an added complexity was the Mughal dynasty's intermarriage into families of the elite, which further muddied the lines of allegiance. Raja Man Singh, for example, was the brother of Jahangir's wife, and hence his own brother-in-law, which also made him Khusraw's uncle, but of course he also served as Khusraw's ateke.
3 Quote from *Tarikh-i Khan Jahani*, in Afzal Husain, 'Afghan Nobility under Akbar and Jahangir – The Family of Daulat Khan Lodi', *Proceedings of the Indian History Congress*, Vol. 48 (1987), pp. 187–196, 191. Khan Jahan's continued influence at Jahangir's court was due to much more than his Afghan identity. The story of an alliance between his Lodi ancestors and Babur may have been apocryphal but was

in common currency in the seventeenth century, and his promotion would have been in keeping with Jahangir's strategy of loyalty to the traditional elites, those he would refer to as 'ancient families'. Until his death, Jahangir would refer to him as *farzand* (son), claiming that he would forgive even the most enormous crimes if the request came from Khan Jahan.

4   Jahangir, f. 7b. Thackston, tr., p. 30.
5   Ibid., 11a.
6   Azfar Moin, *The Millenial Sovereign: Sacred Kingship and Sainthood in Islam*, New York: Columbia University Press, 2012, p. 174.
7   Jahangir, f. 2a.
8   Ibid., f. 5a. Thackston, tr., p. 27.
9   The phrase 'the sun of the kingdom' is a chronogram, its numerical value being equal to the year of Jahangir's accession, 1014, of the lunar calendar. See Susan Stronge, 'By the Light of the Sun of Jahangir', *God Is the Light of the Heavens and the Earth: Light in Islamic Art and Culture*, Jonathan Bloom and Sheila Blair, eds., New Haven, CT: Yale University Press, 2015, pp. 256–281, 259.
10 'Murtib' al-Assam Samarqandi, *Conversations with Emperor Jahangir*, Richard C. Foltz, tr., Costa Mesa, CA: Mazda Publishers, 1998, p. 30. As explained in Thackston, *Jahangirnama*: 'The letters in the words *Sahib qiran-i sani* (second Sahib Qiran) yield 1013. To this is added the first letter of *iqbal* (fortune's head) which has a numerical value of one, for the Hegira date of 1014', (1605), p. 28.
11 Jahangir, f. 12a. Thackton, tr., p. 36.
12 Ibid., f. 9b.
13 The *qibla* is the point towards which Muslims turn to pray, specifically, in the direction of the Ka'ba, or House of God, at Mecca.
14 M. Athar Ali, *Mughal India: Studies in Polity, Ideas, Society and Culture*, New York: Oxford University Press, 2003, pp. 184–185.
15 Fernao Guerreiro [Relations of], tr. C.H. Payne, *Jahangir and the Jesuits*, London: George Routledge & Sons, 1930, p. 3. On the other hand, Father du Jarric claimed that Jahangir had communicated with the Jesuits even while in rebellion, writing letters professing his love for them, sending gifts and even requesting a Jesuit presence at his own princely court. See Fr. Pierre du Jarric, *Akbar and the Jesuits*, C.H. Payne, tr. and ed., London: George Routledge and Sons, 1906, pp. 182–187.
16 I use the terms 'Hindu' and 'Hinduism' here with some reluctance. The non-Muslim/non-Christian religions of South Asia are best described collectively as *brahmana/shramana*, which, as Romila Thapar writes, expresses 'not rigid religious identities but cover[ing] a range of sects in varying stages of agreement and disagreement'. *Brahmana* refers to a broad group led by a priestly class who follow the scripture/divine revelation of the Vedas, as well as the collection

of writings known as the Brahmanas and Upanishads. The *Shramana*, while sharing with brahmanas the core understanding of *samsara*, the cycle of death and rebirth, rejects the authority of the Brahman priests and the Vedas. This category includes not only Buddhism and Jainism but also Yoga, and other forms of religion now commonly described under the umbrella of 'Hinduism'. For this reason, the term 'Brahmana' alone is not adequate to replace 'Hindu'. Historically, the terms 'Hindu' and 'Hindustan' (the land of the Hindus) were used by Muslim rulers to describe non-Muslims in North India from about the fourteenth century. This usage was reinforced and broadened in the colonial period by the British, who deliberately cultivated distinct and hardened religious identities as a means of organizing and controlling their subject populations. While using the term 'Hindu' to describe the entire breadth of non-Muslim and non-Christian religious identities is therefore inadequate and ahistorical, there exists no other popularly understood terminology that describes 'brahmana/shramana'. Therefore, for the sake of clarity, I use the term 'Hindu/Hinduism' here, but advisedly and as rarely as possible. See Romila Thapar, *The Past as Present: Forging Contemporary Identities through History*, New Delhi: Aleph Book Company, 2014.

17   Jahangir, f. 13b.
18   Ibid., f. 23a.
19   Father Fernao Guerreiro, C.H. Payne, tr., *Jahangir and the Jesuits*, From the 'Relations' of Father Fernao Guerreiro, S.J., New York: Robert M. McBride & Co., 1930, pp. xviii–xix.
20   Edward Terry, *Early Travels in India, 1583–1619*, Sir William Foster, ed., 1st ed. London: Humphrey Milford, OUP, 1921; reprinted Delhi: LPP, 2007, pp. 288–332, 331. Terry was in India from 1616 to 1619.
21   Thomas Coryat, *Early Travels in India, 1583–1619*, Foster, Sir William, ed., 1st ed. Humphrey Milford, London: Oxford University Press, 1921; reprint Delhi: LPP, 2007, pp. 234–287, 247. Coryat was also in Ajmer at time of the British ambassador Sir Thomas Roe, and came to share a house with him there and later in Mandu. Coryat did visit the imperial court of Jahangir and was among the few European travellers who learned Persian, along with some Arabic and Turkish. He died in Surat of dysentery in 1617.
22   Guerreiro, p. 314, footnote 2.
23   Sir Thomas Roe, *The Embassy of Sir Thomas Roe to the Court of the Great Mogul, 1615–1619*, William Foster ed., London: Hakluyt Society, 1899, Kraus reprint, 1967, p. 367.
24   Ibid., p. 366.
25   Jahangir, fs. 3b–4a.
26   Ibid., f. 5a; Thackston, tr., p. 28.
27   See in particular, Muhammad Baqr Najm-i-Sani, *Art of Governance: An Indo-Islamic Mirror for Princes (Mauizah-i Jahangiri)*, Sajida S. Alvi, tr., Albany, NY: State University of NY Press, 1989.

28 Jahangir, f. 3b.
29 Lefevre describes the bells as solely symbolic. I do not argue with her point that the apparatus was not expected to be 'an effective administrative instrument'. Premodern kingship was, however, as Jahangir continually demonstrated, largely made up of symbolic gestures. The deployment of these markers in pursuit of charisma and authority not only made them effective administrative tools but formed the core of ruling legitimacy. Corinne Lefevre, 'Recovering a Missing Voice from Mughal India: The Imperial Discourse of Jahāngīr (r. 1605–1627) in His Memoirs', *Journal of the Economic and Social History of the Orient*, Vol. 50, No. 4 (2007), pp. 452–489, 470.
30 William Hawkins, an Englishman in India and at the royal court of Jahangir from 1608 to 1613, described the chain. For his comments, see William Foster, ed., *Early Travels in India, 1583–1619*, Delhi: LP Publications, 1999, p. 113. The chain is also described in Jesuit documents; see *Jahangir and the Jesuits*, p. 13. In his recent work, Michael Fisher suggests that the chain was mere legend and that there is no proof of its actual installation. While it is possible that these European based their accounts on gossip, they and the inclusion of the chain in paintings of his own and his successor's ateliers should be seen as strong evidence for its existence. See Michael Fisher, *The Mughal Empire*, London and New York: I.B. Tauris, 2016, p. 151. That Jahangir did make himself habitually accessible to the public is not only confirmed by his own writings, but also by those of contemporaries, as this study shows.
31 Roe, p. 108.
32 Ibid., p. 110.
33 Guerreiro, p. 36.

Chapter 4

1 Ram Prasad Khosla, *Mughal Kingship and Nobility*, Delhi: Idarah-i Adabiyat-i Delli, 1976, p. 100.
2 Faruqui, p. 204.
3 Jahangir, f. 20b.
4 Ibid., f.24b; Thackston, tr., p. 55. Among the pre-Islamic kings of Iran, Jamshid's reputation for justice made him an imperial icon across the Persianspeaking world. The imagery of his cup has generally been interpreted as "an emblem of mystical gnosis and divine love," and a signifier of "the transience of kingly power and glory." See Julie Scott Meisami, *Medieval Persian Court Poetry*, Princeton, NJ: Princeton University Press, 1987, p. 288.
5 See Inayat Ali Zaidi, 'The Political Role of Kachawaha Nobles during Jahangir's Reign', *Proceedings of the Indian History Congress*, Vol. 36 (1975), pp. 180–197.

At the end of his reign, in the face of Khurram's rebellion and Mahabat Khan's insurgency, the Kachawaha would indeed remain loyal, only switching loyalties to the new emperor after Jahangir's death.

6   For a concise examination of the changing narrative surrounding the death of Guru Arjun, see Louise E. Fenech, 'Martyrdom and the Execution of Guru Arjan in Early Sikh Sources', *Journal of the American Oriental Society*, Vol. 121, No. 1 (January–March 2001), pp. 20–31.

7   At the early modern Islamic courts, the blinding of unsuccessful aspirants to the throne had become the traditional method of destroying their claims and ambitions without killing them – it was understood that a blind king could not rule. The Mughals proved very resistant to the practice and it was done only rarely and after the most serious infractions. Khusraw's great uncle Kamran had been blinded, after years of armed revolt against his brother, with a hot lancet and lemon juice, on the orders of the Mughal Emperor Humayun.

8   Jahangir, f. 70b.

9   Mu'tamid Khan claimed that the women of the harem begged that Khusraw be allowed to make the ritual obeisance before the king, but he confirmed that the prince's melancholy led the emperor to confine his son again. See *Iqbalnama*, Erskine, tr., f. 38.

10 See Chapter 12 of this book.

11 Jahangir, f. 19b. Thackston, tr., p. 48. Here Jahangir uses the term *khil'at* in order to describe a robe of honour that monarchs of the Islamic/Asian world regularly conferred upon favoured dignitaries and nobles. In this case, he evokes the imagery of a powerful ruler (god) rewarding an honoured subject (himself, as king). See Section 3 for details on the use of khilat at the Mughal royal court.

12 Ibid., fs. 40a and b.

13 Ibid., f. 43a.

14 For a detailed discussion of Babur's complex relationship with the late Timuird milieu of Herat, see Stephen Dale, *Eight Paradises*, Leiden: Brill, 2004 and Lisa Balabanlilar, *Imperial Identity in Mughal India*, London and New York: I.B. Tauris, 2012.

15 Jahangir described it as holding nearly two Hindustani *maunds*, which could range from 27 to 86 pounds or more.

16 Jahangir, f. 44a. Jahangir's ability to communicate in Turkish is confirmed by the English visitor to his court in 1615, William Hawkins, who had learned the language while a merchant in the Ottoman territories and conversed with the Mughal emperor in Turkish. The court language of the Mughals was Persian, however. See Muzaffar Alam, 'The Pursuit of Persian: Language in Mughal Politics', *Modern Asian Studies*, Vol. 32, No. 2 (May 1998), pp. 317–349.

17 Jahangir, fs. 49a and b.

Chapter 5

1. J.F. Richards, 'The Formulation of Imperial Authority under Akbar and Jahangir', *The Mughal State 1526–1750*, J.F. Richards, ed., Delhi: Oxford University Press, 1998, pp. 126–167, 127.
2. For a thorough discussion of these relationships, see LeFevre, *Pouvoir impérial et élites (1605–1627)*.
3. Jahangir, f. 55a. Thackston, tr., p. 91.
4. The Tora, or Yasa, was the law code that was believed to have been created by Chingis Khan. It was likely a reference to customary law in the Mongol territories, but Jahangir (and others) would call on it regularly in order to justify imperial decisions. As David Morgan has written, it was supremely useful to Chingis Khan's descendants to be able to cite an authoritative ancestral law code of which no record in fact existed. See David Morgan, 'The "Great 'yasa' of Chingiz Khan" and Mongol Law in the Ilkhanate', *Bulletin of Oriental and African Studies, in Honor of Ann Lambton*, Vol. 49, No. 1 (1986), pp. 163–176.
5. Because blinding a prince was traditionally understood to make him ineligible for kingship, this act would be seen as an effort to meddle in inheritance, succession and imperial politics.
6. Jahangir, f. 173a. Writing in his memoir, Jahangir claimed that Akbar, in contrast, had never allowed banners and drums to his sons' followers.
7. Ibid., f. 146b.
8. Ibid., f. 18b; Thackston, tr., p. 46.
9. Hafez, Divan 6:10, quoted in *Jahangrinama*, f. 18b; Thackston, tr, p. 46.
10. Dispatch of Yadgar Ali Shah Talish, in *Alamara-i-Abbasi*, 2:782f, quoted in Jahangir, Thackston, ed. and tr., p. 122.
11. Roe, p. 119. See Chapter 6 of this book for a discussion of Jahangir and royal painting/portraiture.
12. Jahangir, fs. 77a–78b. Thackston, tr. and marginalia, pp. 121–122.
13. Roe, pp. 296–297.
14. Abu'l Fazl, *AN*, III, p. 207.
15. Ibid., pp. 322–323.
16. Jahangir, f. 93b.
17. Ibid., f. 130a.
18. Jorge Flores, *The Mughal Padshah: A Jesuit Treatise on Emperor Jahangir's Court and Household*, Leiden: Brill, 2015, p. 17.
19. Jorge Flores, 'The Sea and the World of the Mutasaddi: A Profile of Port Officials from Mughal Gujarat (*c.* 1600–1650)', *Journal of the Royal Asiatic Society*, Vol. 21, No. 1 (2011), p. 60. Muqarrab Khan was not solely the king's agent for goods, of course, but served as an important political actor, a liaison between the foreigners who populated the port and the central Mughal government. When the Franks of

Goa plundered foreign ships and took Muslim hostages, Muqarrab Khan was sent 'to set things right'. See Jahangir, f. 100a.
20 Jahangir, f. 84b. Thackston, tr., p. 133. The turkey was not the only North American product which made its way to Jahangir's court. Jahangir also mentions tobacco, of which he disapproved, illustrating the increasingly interconnected globe of the seventeenth century.
21 Sattar, p. 122.
22 Jahangir, f. 264a.
23 Ibid., Thackston sidenotes, p. 149.
24 As previously stated, *khilat* is an Arabic term, meaning 'robe of honour'. The Persian term is *sir-o-pa*, meaning literally 'head and foot', in the context of honorary dress.
25 Balkrishan Shivram, 'Court Dress and Robing Ceremony in Mughal India', *Proceedings of the Indian History Congress*, Vol. 66 (2005–06), pp. 404–422, 407.
26 Ibid., p. 413.
27 Abu'l Fazl, *AA*, p. 96. Also, Shivram, p. 412. Shah Jahan would carry several thousand khilat to hand out on the field during the Mughal campaign in Balkh, 1640–47. See Inayet Khan, *Shajahannama*, W.E. Begley and Z.A. Desai, eds., Delhi: Oxford University Press, 1990, p. 355.
28 Jahangir, f. 149a.
29 Ibid., f. 90a.
30 Ibid., f. 58a.
31 Ibid., f. 267a.
32 Ibid., f. 148b.
33 Ibid., fs. 190b–191a.
34 Ibid., f. 148b.
35 Diane Eck, *Darsan: Seeing the Divine Image in India*, New York: Columbia University Press, 2nd ed., 1996, p. 3.
36 Ibid., p. 7.
37 Flores, *Mughal Padshah*, p. 93.
38 Coryat claimed the elephant fights took place twice a week, See Coryat, p. 247. See also William Hawkins, *Early Travels in India, 1583–1619*, 1st ed., London: Humphrey Milford, OUP, 1921; reprint Delhi: LPP, 2007, pp. 60–121, 108.
39 Roe wrote that Jahangir as 'sometimes see[ing] with too much delight the execution done by his Eliphants'. Roe, p. 108.
40 Flores, *Mughal Padshah*, p. 92. This Jesuit treatise was composed by a priest at Jahangir's court in Agra, from 1610 to 1611.
41 Roe, p. 87.
42 Abu'l Fazl, *AA*, I, p. 165.
43 The princes too held regular viewings, and even offered justice to those who came as supplicants. See Faruqui, p. 119.
44 Roe, pp. 107–108.
45 Hawkins, p. 116.

46 Flores, *Mughal Padshah*, p. 94 and Roe, p. 108.
47 Roe, p. 108.
48 Ibid., p. 363.
49 Ibid., pp. 257–258 and 276.
50 Balabanlilar, *Imperial Identity*, pp. 89–94.
51 Jahangir, fs. 118b–119b.
52 The *surkh*, also known as *ratti*, is a small seed which represented a common measurement.
53 Roe, p. 304.
54 Jahangir, f. 273b.
55 Ibid., f. 251b.
56 Ibid., f. 60a.
57 Ibid., f. 53b.
58 Ibid., f. 118b. It does seem that Khurram would continue to use alcohol from this time. Jahangir referred to his son having 'his mind loosened by wine' some years later (see Jahangir, f. 220b), and Thomas Roe asserted that Khurram asked him directly for cases of wine.
59 Ibid., p. 93. Mu'tamid Khan would also confirm Parvez's alcoholism in his *Iqbalnama*.
60 Roe, p. 119.
61 Ibid., p. 227.
62 Jahangir, f. 40a.
63 Ibid. f. 277b.
64 Ibid., f. 66a.
65 Ibid., f. 171b.
66 Abu'l Fazl, *AN*, II, p. 156.
67 Quoted in Flores, *Mughal Padshah*, opening page.
68 Ibid.
69 Jahangir, f. 66a.
70 Ibid., f. 111b.
71 Ibid., fs. 190a and b.
72 Ibid., fs. 270b–271a. Although he obviously felt some guilt over the response to his careless joke, his addition of the story in his own memoir not only confirms a willingness to admit mistakes, but also illustrates the degree to which he made himself accessible to his subjects in the most mundane ways.
73 Ibid., fs. 75a and b.

Chapter 6

1 Moin, p. 152.
2 Ibid., p. 146.

3   Ibid., pp. 154–155. Aquiviva and Monstserrat, respectively.
4   Audrey Truschke, 'Cosmopolitan Encounters: Sanskrit and Persian at the Mughal Court', unpublished PhD dissertation, Columbia University, 2012, p. 105.
5   Years after leaving the Mughal court, Monserrate admitted that Akbar's interest in Christianity was likely less motivated by sincere interest in doctrine, but rather 'by a certain curiosity and excessive eagerness to hear some new thing'. See Monserrate, p. 126. [Correia-Afonso, Letters]
6   Henri Hosten, 'Three letters of Fr. Joseph de Castro, S.J., and the Last Year of Jahangir', *Mughal India According to European Travel Accounts; Texts and Studies*, Vol. 1 (1998), pp. 243–268, 248.
7   Terry, p. 315.
8   Although Sattar recorded 124 accounts, there are only 113 extant.
9   Sattar, p. 1.
10 Ibid., pp. 34 and 201, for example.
11 Ibid., pp. 5–6.
12 Ibid., p. 13.
13 Ibid., p. 58. For a rich treatment of Sattar's work and larger discussion of intellectual debate at Jahangir's court, see Corinne LeFevre, 'Messianism, Rationalism and Inter-Asian Connections: The *Majalis-i Jahangiri* (1608–11) and the Socio-intellectual History of the Mughal ulama', *The Indian Economic and Social History Review*, Vol. 54, No. 3 (2017), pp. 1–22, 5.
14 Babur, Mano, ed., p. 559. Thackston, ed. and tr., p. 742. Complaining of Humayun's reported solitude, Babur wrote to him, 'For kings, it is a mistake to desire solitude … If you feel chained, resign yourself.'
15 Richards, 'The Formulation of Imperial Authority', pp. 268–269.
16 Badauni, *Tawarikh*, II, pp. 349 and 336.
17 Jahangir, f. 23a.
18 Ibid.
19 Mirza Nathan was the author of a history of the Mughal wars of Bengal and Orissa. See Mirza Nathan ('Alau'd- Din Isfahani), *Baharistan-i Ghaybi*, M.I. Borah, tr., Gauhati, Assam: Narayani Handiqui Historical Institute, 1936.
20 Ibid., I, p. 17.
21 Ibid.
22 This sharp separation between the two manuscripts has been pointed out by others. See Muzaffar Alam and Sanjay Subramanyam, 'Frank Disputations', *The Indian Economic Social History Review*, Vol. 46, No. 4 (2009), pp. 457–511, 488.
23 Ibid., p. 487.
24 Roe and Hawkins both confirm their own attendance in these sessions. Hawkins also confirms that Jahangir had someone present to keep notes, 'who by turns set downe everything in writing which he doth, so that there is nothing that passeth in his lifetimes which is not noted'. It is possible that the person Hawkins is describing

was Sattar, as their presence in the majalis did overlap. See Hawkins, p. 116. According to Sattar, these outsiders were invited for the most mundane of reasons: it was hoped that they would be encouraged to praise Jahangir on returning to their homelands.

25 Roe, p. 117.
26 Sattar, p. 9.
27 Ibid., p. 11.
28 Ibid., p. 8.
29 Ibid., p. 210.
30 Roe, p. 244.
31 Shireen Moosvi, 'The Conversations of Jahangir 1608–11: Table Talk on Religion', *Proceedings of the India History Congress*, Vol. 68, No. 1 (2007), pp. 326–331, 329.
32 Sattar, pp. 220 and 206.
33 LeFevre, 'Messianism, Rationalism and Inter-Asian connections', pp. 1–22, 3.
34 Responding to Moin, p. 177.
35 Ibid., p. 209. See Elaine Julia Wright and Susan Stronge, eds., *Muraqqa: Imperial Mughal Albums from the Chester Beatty Library*, Dublin Alexandria, VA: Art Services International, 2008, pp. 288, 344.
36 Moin, p. 189. For a detailed and thoughtful discussion of the allegorial paintings of Jahangir in the context of dynastic messianic claims, see Moin, pp. 170–210.
37 Abu'l Fazl, *AN*, p. 115.
38 There is an important exception to this, however, in Mughal portraits of women. While women are often present in Jahangir-era paintings of the royal court, for the most part they were painted to represent an ideal of womanhood and little effort was made to differentiate between them and assign specific identity. There are a few Mughal portraits that scholars tentatively identify as portrayals of Nur Jahan, but the effort at identification remains highly speculative.
39 Milo Cleveland Beach, 'The Mughal Painter Abu'l Hasan and Some English Sources for His Style', *The Journal of the Walters Art Gallery*, Vol. 38 (1980), pp. 6–33. Abu'l Hasan signed his work, unusual in Mughal painting to the time of Jahangir, as opposed to inscriptions added by a clerk. It is not only a clear indication of his stature at the royal court but affirms the increasing recognition of individuals in Mughal culture.
40 Jahangir, f. 194a; Thackston, tr., p. 276.
41 Richard C. Foltz, 'Two Seventeenth-Century Central Asian Travelers to Mughal India', *Journal of the Royal Asiatic Society*, Third Series, Vol. 6, No. 3 (November 1996), pp. 367–377, 374. While the artist is not named in the *Nama*, he has been identified as Abu'l Hasan. See Susan Stronge, *Painting for the Mughal Emperor: The Art of the Book, 1560–1660*, London: Victoria & Albert Museum, 2002, p. 133.

42 Jahangir, f. 29b.
43 Ibid., f. 62a.
44 Ibid., Thackston, tr., p. 319.
45 'Jahangir Shooting the Head of Malik Ambar', Freer Gallery of Art, F1948.19a.
46 'Jahangir Embraces Shah Abbas', Freer Gallery of Art, F1945.9.
47 Ebba Koch, 'Jahangir as Francis Bacon's Ideal of the King as an Observer and Investigator of Nature', *Journal of the Royal Asiatic Society*, Third Series, Vol. 19, No. 3 (July 2009), pp. 293–338, 335.
48 'The Princes of the House of Timur', The British Museum, No. 1913,0208,0.1. See Sheila Canby, ed., *Humayun's Garden Party: Princes of the House of Timur*, Bombay: Marg Publications, 1994.
49 Stronge, p. 138. Regarding the profound influence of European painting on the Mughal ateliers, Ebba Koch has commented, 'In the area of naturalistic representation and allegorical symbolic construction in the arts, Europe for them [the Mughals] had to offer the best solutions. They did not realize (and in any case, would not have been bothered) to what extent they were to irritate modern Indian art historians who out of post-colonial resentment often try to ignore of explain away this interest.' See Koch, 'Jahangir as Francis Bacon's Ideal', p. 332.
50 Roe, p. 119.
51 Ibid., pp. 253–256.
52 Fr. Pierre du Jarric.
53 Revd Samuel Purchas, *Hakluytus Postumus: or, Purchas his Pilgrims*, 4 vols., London: William Stansby for Henrie Fetherstone, 1625–26, Vol. 4, p. 52. In Paula Henderson, '"Elysian Fields such as the Poets Dreamed of"': The Mughal Garden in the Early Stuart Mind', *The British Art Journal*, Vol. 10, No. 3 (Winter/Spring 2009/2010), pp. 35–45, 38.
54 Ebba Koch, 'Mughal Palace Gardens from Babur to Shah Jahan (1526–1648)', *Muqarnas*, Vol. 14 (1997), pp. 143–165, 147.
55 They were his uncle, Muhammad Hakim, and his great-uncle Kamran – interesting choices, as both had led disastrous rebellions!
56 Roe, p. 143, and seen again in 1617, p. 394.
57 Corinne LeFevre, 'Curiosité et pouvoir: les collections de l'empereur moghol Jahāngīr (r. 1605–1627)', *Études Épistémè*, Vol. 26 (2014), p. 5.

Chapter 7

1. This in stark contrast to the Ottoman Turks who, like the Mughals, had their origins in land-locked Central Asia. On conquering territories in the Western Anatolian coast, however, they built a powerful naval force that would eventually turn the entire Mediterranean into what contemporaries referred to as an 'Ottoman lake'.
2. Guerriero, p. 36.
3. Ibid., p. 45.
4. Sattar, p. 216.
5. Hosten, p. 254.
6. Ibid. See also Alam and Subramanyam, p. 481. The Jesuits blamed the Christian requirement of monogamy for their inability to convert the king.
7. The EIC had been founded only eight years previously, in 1600.
8. Central Asian Turkish continued to be taught to Mughal princes at least through the reign of Jahangir's grandson, the Mughal emperor Aurangzeb (1618–1707). Jahangir confirmed his own knowledge of it when he described reading his great-grandfather's memoir, the Baburnama, in the original Turkish during his first trip to Kabul in 1607. Mughal attachment to the language of their ancestors was an act of dynastic nostalgia, for they had little opportunity to actually use it. Their court language was Persian, the language most commonly spoken by educated elites across much of west and south Asia.
9. Roe confirms Jahangir's disapproval of those who drank to excess. 'This king's disposition seems composed of extremes … often overcome with wine but severely punishing that fault in others'. See Roe, pp. 330–331.
10. The virginal is an instrument of the harpsichord family, the cornet is similar to a trumpet.
11. Nicholas Withington, *Early Travels in India, 1583–1619*, Sir William Foster, ed., 1st ed., Humphrey Milford: Oxford University Press, 1921; Delhi: LPP, 2007, pp. 188–233, 200–201.
12. Ibid., p. 190.
13. Richmond Barbour, *Before Orientalism: London's Theatre of the East 1576–1626*, Cambridge: Cambridge University Press, 2003, p. 150.
14. Roe, p. 46. Participating were four English ships anchored off the port of Surat: the Dragon, Lion, Expedition and Peppercorn.
15. Ibid.
16. Barbour, p. 154.
17. Roe, pp. 79 and 310.
18. Ibid., p. 97.
19. Ibid., pp. 118–119.

20 Roe and Terry, 322n–323n. See Barbour, p. 169.
21 Roe, p. 119.
22 Colin Paul Mitchell, *Sir Thomas Roe and the Mughal Empire*, Karachi, Pakistan: Oxford University Press, 2000, p. 112.
23 Sattar, p. 122.
24 Jahangir, f. 34b; Thackston, tr., p. 66.
25 Ibid., fs. 77a–78b; Thackston, tr. and editor's notes, p. 122.
26 Ibid.
27 Once again we see political power built on a broad and diverse array of elite lineages – Turkic, Persian and Byzantine, spiritual and military – and cultural references that would be understood regionally as legitimizing.
28 Moin, p. 129.
29 Rather than interpret this as a conversion to Shi'ism, as it has been traditionally framed, it may instead have been acceptance of discipleship to a Sufi pir. The spiritual beliefs of the Safavids of this period cannot be described as Shi'ism in the juridical sense, and will not be for some generations, but instead may be understood as devout adherence to a saintly sufi lineage. Ibid., pp. 128–129.
30 Riazul Islam, *A Calendar of Documents on Indo-Persian Relations*, Tehran: Iranian Culture Foundation and Karachi: Institute of Central and West Asian Studies, 1982, 2:294.
31 One such being Akbar II, who proved to be yet another Timurid-Mughal supplicant. The son of Aurangzeb, he fled to the Safavid court in Iran in 1688 after a failed rebellion against his father.
32 Abu'l Fazl, AN, p. 1112.
33 Riazul Isam, *Indo-Persian Relations: A Study of the Political and Diplomatic Relations between the Mughal Empire and Iran*, Tehran: Iranian Culture Foundation, 1970, p. 207.
34 Jahangir, f. 27b.
35 Purchas, IV, pp. 272–273.
36 Jahangir, f. 114a.
37 Mirza Nathan took part in these campaigns and described them in the *Baharistan-i-Ghaybi*.
38 See Chapter 9 for details about the campaign against Mewar and Chapter 11 for the Kangra conquest.
39 Richard Eaton, *A Social History of the Deccan*, Cambridge, UK: Cambridge University Press, 2005, p. 108.
40 Ibid., p. 111.
41 Jahangir, f. 86b.
42 M. Siraj Anwar, 'The Safavids and Mughal Relations with the Deccani States', *Proceedings of the Indian History Congress*, Vol. 52 (1991), pp. 255–262, 259.

43   Ibid., p. 258.
44   Jahangir, f. 120b.
45   Ibid.
46   Eaton, p. 121.
47   *Iqbalnama*, f. 106.
48   'Jahangir Shoots Malik Ambar', painting by Abu'l Hasan, *c.* 1616, Chester Beatty Library Archives, AB 58.
49   K.N. Hasan and Mansura Haidar, 'Letters of Aziz Koka to Ibrahim Adil Shah II', *Proceedings of the Indian History Congress*, Vol. 27 (1965), pp. 161–167.

Chapter 8

1   'Marry women of your choice, two or three or four; but if ye fear that ye shall not be able to deal justly (with them), then only one, or (a captive) that your right hands possess, that will be more suitable, to prevent you from doing injustice'. Qur'an, Sura 4 (An-Nisa), Ayah 3.
2   The belief that these women were entirely without ties to family and homeland has been at least in part proven inaccurate. See Leslie Pierce, *The Imperial Harem: Women and Sovereignty in the Ottoman Empire*, New York: Oxford University Press, 1993. The larger argument remains, however, that the families of the women at the sultan's court played little to no role in dynastic politics.
3   It is reputed to have been Bibi Mubaraika who famously remained to guard and protect Babur's tomb when the Mughals were driven out of India by Sher Shah Suri in 1540. Impressed by her courage and loyalty, the Suri king allowed her to accompany the body north, where it was reinterred in the dynastic capital of Kabul, at the time under the control of Babur's rebellious son, Kamran.
4   Those marriages that resulted in children who survived to adulthood were to Dildar Begim, the mother of Gulbadan Begim (1523–1603) and Hindal Mirza (1518–51), and Gulrukh Begim, the mother of Askari Mirza (1516–58) and Kamran Mirza (1509–57).
5   Stephen Dale, 'The Legacy of the Timurids', *Journal of the Royal Asiatic Society*, Third Series, Vol. 8, No. 1 (April 1998), pp. 43–58, 47.
6   We have already met this son, Abdur Rahim, who became one of Akbar's premier military leaders better known by his father's title of *Khankhanan*, Nobleman among Noblemen, and would serve as *ateke* and ally to Jahangir.
7   Abu'l Fazl, *AN*, II, p. 242.
8   James Tod, *Annals and Antiquities of Rajasthan or the Central and Western Rajput States of India*, 3 vols. (London, New York: H. Milford, Oxford University Press, 1920), Vol. III, p. 1482.

9   Ruby Lal, 'Settled, Sacred and All-Powerful: Making of New Genealogies and Traditions of Empire under Akbar', *Economic and Political Weekly*, Vol. 36, No. 11 (17–23 March 2001), pp. 941–958, 954.

10 Badauni, Abd al-Qadir Ibn Muluk Shah, *Muntakabu-t-Tawarikh*, W.H. Lowe, tr., 3 vols., Patna, India: Academica Asiatica, 1973, II, p. 211: Badauni has Akbar saying 'in early youth he had not regarded the question and had married whatever number of women he pleased, both freeborn and slaves, [but] he now wanted to know what remedy the law provided for his case'. These conversations seem to have occurred in about 1578, in the middle of Akbar's reign, as Badauni seems to confirm that Akbar's aunt Gulbadan Begim left for Mecca later in the same year (Ibid., p. 216).

11 Ibid., pp. 211–213. *Mut'ah* marriages are often described as temporary marriages, as they are privately arranged by contract, requiring that the length of the marriage – the minimum length is debated and could be as little as three days – and the amount of dowry paid to the woman are arranged beforehand. It is not universally accepted within Islamic law. In fact, according to *al-Muwatta*, the juridical opinions of Malik ibn Anas, and contrary to the determination of the Akbari court, *mut'ah* is not accepted.

12 Antonio Monserrate, *The Commentary of Father Monserrate, S.J., on His Journey to the Court of Akbar*, S.N. Bannerjee, ed., Oxford, 1922, p. 202.

13 Barbara Watson Andaya, 'Women and the Performance of Power in Early Modern Southeast Asia', *Servants of the Dynasty: Palace Women in World History*, Anne Walthall, ed., Berkeley, CA: University of California Press, 2008, pp. 22–44, 26–27.

14 William Finch, *Early Travels in India, 1583–1619*, Foster, Sir William, ed., 1st ed., London: Humphrey Milford, Oxford University Press, 1921; reprint Delhi: LPP, 2007, pp. 122–187, 166. The European merchants shared gossip between themselves. Roe also discussed the rumour of Anarkali. See Roe, p. 330.

15 The legend inspired a film called *Mughal-e-Azam*, starring Dilip Kumar and Madhubala. Released in 1960 to critical acclaim, it became the highest-grossing Bollywood film, a record it held at least until 1975.

16 In March of 1611, just a few months before his daughter's marriage to the emperor, he would be made vizier over the entire empire.

17 *Iqbalnama*, f. 29.

18 For example Mu'tamid Khan confirms that they met at 'a Nowruz entertainment'. Ibid.

19 For the sake of simplicity, she will be referred to as Nur Jahan throughout.

20 For example, the recent article by Shivangini Tandon, 'Negotiating Political Spaces and Contested Identities: Representation of Nur Jahan and her Family in Mughal Tazkiras', *The Delhi University Journal of the Humanities and Social Sciences*, 2, 2015, pp. 41–50, discusses in detail the rumours of a love match, but the author dismisses the possibility as unlikely.

21 Jahangir, f. 104a; Thackston, tr., p. 161.
22 Ibid., f. 271b.
23 Terry, p. 329.

Chapter 9

1 Jahangir, f. 98b.
2 Ibid., f. 98a.
3 Ibid., f. 99b.
4 Ibid., f. 98b.
5 Ibid., f. 100b.
6 Ibid., fs. 106b–107a; Thackston, tr., pp. 164–165.
7 Abu'l Fazl, *AA*, p. 173.
8 Shaha Parpia, 'Reordering Nature: Power Politics in the Mughal *Shikargah*', *International Journal of Islamic Architecture*, Vol. 7, No. 1 (2018), pp. 39–66, 50.
9 Between 1556 and 1739, it is estimated that the Mughal court remained on tour 40 per cent of the time. See Stephen P. Blake, *Shahjahanabad: The Sovereign City in Mughal India, 1639–1739*, Cambridge: Cambridge University Press, 1991, p. 97.
10 Hamid ud-Din Bahadur, *Ahkam-i Alamgir*, trans. by Jadunath Sarkar as *Anecdotes of Aurangzeb*, London: Sangam Books Limited, 1988 (1st and 2nd ed. 1925; 3rd 1949), pp. 37 and 41.
11 For a more complete discussion of this cultural comparison, see Balabanlilar, 'The Emperor Jahangir and the Pursuit of Pleasure', *Journal of the Royal Asiatic Society*, Series 3, Vol. 19, No. 2 (2009), pp. 1–14.
12 Francois Bernier, *Travel in the Mogul Empire, AD 1656–1668*, tr., Archibald Constable, London: Cambridge University Press, 1934; New Delhi: Munshiram Manoharlal Publishers Pvt, Ltd., Oriental Reprint, 1983, p. 358.
13 Terry, p. 404.
14 Ibid., p. 399.
15 Ibid., p. 400.
16 Finch, p. 146.
17 Roe, pp. 326 and 363.
18 Hawkins, pp. 60–121, 106.
19 Terry, p. 398.
20 James L. Westcoat. Jr., 'Gardens, Urbanization, and Urbanism in Mughal Lahore', *Mughal Gardens: Sources, Places, Representations, and Prospects*, James L. Westcoat and Joachim Wolschke-Bulmahn, eds., Washington, DC: Dumbarton Oaks, 1996, pp. 139–170, 158–159.
21 The Seljuk king, Malek Shah Alp Arslan (1055–92), famously advised by the famed politician Nizam al-Mulk, built four pleasure gardens in Isfahan. Each boasted

fruit trees, roses and cypress trees lining the banks of the streams, with pavilions placed so as to command views of the gardens. The Ilkhanid Mongol ruler, Ghazan Khan (1271–1304), who converted to Islam in 1295 when taking the throne, built a 'Garden of Justice' (bagh-i-adalat) near Tabriz, in a square, walled enclosure, housing a golden platform and a golden pavilion, towers, baths and streams fed by tanks and cisterns, 'to provide a pleasant and agreeable meadow for the sojourn of the emperor'.

22   Although Babur would make the outrageous claim that there were no gardens in India, he saw many that he refused to acknowledge for reasons both political and personal. See Anthony Welch, 'Gardens That Babur Did Not Like: Landscape, Water and Architecture for the Sultans of Delhi', *Mughal Gardens: Sources, Places, Representations, and Prospects*, James L. Westcoat and Joachim Wolschke-Bulmahn, eds., Washington, DC: Dumbarton Oaks Research Library and Collection, 1996.
23   Dale, *Garden of the Eight Paradises*, p. 186.
24   Jahangir, f. 105a. Emphasis mine.
25   Finch, p. 166.
26   Jahangir, fs. 105a–b.
27   Roe, p. 138.
28   Most famously, the garden of Shalimar, also a favourite of his successor, Shah Jahan.
29   John Richards, 'The Historiography of Mughal Gardens', *Mughal Gardens: Sources, Places, Representations, and Prospects*, James L. Westcoat and Joachim Wolschke-Bulmahn, eds., Washington, DC: Dumbarton Oaks, 1996, pp. 259–266, 263.
30   Monserrate, in Koch, 'Mughal Palace Gardens', p. 163, f. 4.
31   Jahangir, fs. 191a–b.
32   Babur, Mano, ed., p. 607.
33   Jahangir, f. 43a.
34   Ibid., f. 249a.
35   Ibid. The dynastic passion for gardens did not end with Jahangir. We have the lovely story of Khurram arriving at the Nur Afza, disappointed that storms had blown away the cherry blossoms he'd hoped to see, but declared himself compensated for the loss with the discovery of blooming irises. He claimed to have counted 212 flowers, opened or budding. See Koch, 'Mughal Palace Gardens', p. 147. As Koch comments, on the previous day Khurram had visited the magnificent gardens of Shalimar in Lahore, where he saw no less than 4,500 flowers and buds!

Chapter 10

1   Jahangir, f. 143a.
2   Ibid., f. 159b.
3   Ibid., f. 143a.

4   Ibid., f. 39b.
5   Ibid., f. 202a.
6   Ibid., f. 199a.
7   Ibid., f. 142a.
8   Roe, p. 276.
9   Ibid., p. 375.
10 Ibid., pp. 446 and 484.
11 Terry, p. 404.
12 Shaha Parpia, 'Mughal Hunting Grounds: Landscape Manipulation and "Garden" Association', *Garden History: Journal of the Gardens Trust*, Vol. 44, No. 2 (2016), pp. 171–190, 179.
13 Terry, p. 402.
14 Ibid., p. 403.
15 Ibid.
16 Jahangir, fs. 145a–b.
17 Terry, p. 404.
18 Jahangir, fs. 81a–b.
19 Abu'l Fazl, *AA*, I, p. 299.
20 Ibid., pp. 298–299.
21 Jahangir, f. 76a.
22 Abu'l-Fazl described the *shikar-i ahu ba ahu* (hunting antelope with antelope) and other Mughal hunting techniques in the *A'in-i Akbari*, I, pp. 302–303.
23 Jahangir, fs. 36b and 37a; Thackston, tr., p. 69.
24 Ibid., f. 74b.
25 Ibid., f. 76a.
26 Ibid., f. 148a.
27 Ibid., f. 224b.
28 Ibid., f. 198a.
29 Ibid., f. 193b.
30 Ibid. f. 214a.
31 Roe, p. 303.
32 Allsen, *The Hunt in Eurasian History*, Philadelphia, PA: University of Pennsylvania Press, 2006, p. 181.
33 Jahangir., f. 54b.
34 Ibid., f. 146b.
35 Roe, p. 365.
36 Jahangir, f. 195b. This was in September of 1618, at the end of his fiftieth year, only days after affirming his personal vow to no longer hunt.
37 Ibid., f. 299a.
38 Hunts in 1610 and 1616 were organized in response to specific lion and tiger threats, and while both fell on non-hunting days, the emperor's enthusiasm in the

case of these two exceptions illustrates his willingness to carry the (pleasurable) burden of these particular responsibilities of kingship.
39 Ibid., f. 164b.
40 Ibid., fs. 166 a–b.
41 Ibid., f. 175a.
42 Ibid., fs. 183 a–b.
43 Ibid., f. 184a. Thackston, tr., p. 265.
44 Ibid., f. 192b.
45 Ibid., f. 187b. His use of the term 'dervish' (*darwishan*) is notable, as he was of course referring to a non-Muslim mystic.
46 Ibid., fs. 200b–201a.
47 Jahangir has been previously recognized by modern scholars as a talented naturalist. See M.A. Alvi and A. Rahman, *Jahangir the Naturalist*, New Delhi: Lakherwal Press, 1968.
48 Jahangir, f. 231a. The woman in question was a gardener's daughter who lived near Daulatabad and noted for her full moustache and heavy beard. The sceptical emperor thought she might be a hermaphrodite, ordering the women in his household to confirm her gender. She was found to be no different from any other woman.
49 Ibid., f. 281b.
50 Ibid., f. 309b.
51 Ibid., f. 139 a.
52 Koch, 'Jahangir as Francis Bacon's Ideal', p. 299.
53 Jahangir, f. 93b.
54 Ibid., f. 138a.
55 Sarus cranes are native to South Asia. The tallest of flying birds, they can reach almost 6 feet in height. Like all cranes, they mate for life. Jahangir clearly saw them as romantic figures, writing of a crane starving to death over the body of her dead mate.
56 LeFevre, 'Messianism, Rationalism, and Inter-Asian connections', p. 2.
57 As noted by Koch, 'Sir Francis Bacon's Ideal', p. 299.
58 See Dale, *Eight Paradises*, for a full discussion of Babur's observations.
59 The Jesuits posited their own explanation for Akbar's experiment. Claiming that Akbar was 'in a state of irresolution' regarding his own religious identity, du Jarric wrote that Akbar had planned to convert to the religion of the people whose language these children spoke. See du Jarric, p. 84.
60 Jahangir, fs. 213b–214a.
61 Pramod K. Nayar, 'Marvelous Excesses: English Travel Writing and India, 1608–1727', *Journal of British Studies*, Vol. 44, No. 2 (April 2005), pp. 213–238, 235.
62 Jahangir, f. 186b.

63 Alvi and Rahman, p. 17.
64 Koch, 'Jahangir as Francis Bacon's Ideal', p. 307.
65 Jahangir., f. 186b.
66 Ibid., f. 341b. The sobriquet translates as Master Mansur, Unique of his Era.
67 Ibid., fs. 197a-b. See also Ellen Smart, 'The Death of Inayat Khan by the Mughal Artist Balchand', *Artibus Asiae*, Vol. 58, No. 3/4 (1999), pp. 273–279, 273. As the name Inayat Khan was a title, there are several Mughal courtiers with that appellation. Apart from the emperor's record of an obsession with his emaciated frame, this particular Inayat Khan is unknown.
68 Jahangir, f. 197a. Thackston, tr., p. 280.
69 Ibid.
70 An early twentieth-century observer wrote, 'It was not his own (*Inayat Khan's*) desire but the almost morbid curiosity of his master that caused this wonderful and ghastly little picture to come into existence.' Jarl Charpentier, 'A Note from the Memoirs of Jahangir', *Journal of the Royal Asiatic Society of Great Britain and Ireland*, No. 3 (1 July 1924), pp. 440–442.
71 Jahangir, f. 162b.
72 Ibid., f. 280a.
73 For example, Jahangir recorded a most extravagant year ending in early 1621. Ibid., f. 264b.
74 Ibid., f. 108b.
75 E.A. Morinis, 'Pilgrimage: The Human Quest', *Numen*, Vol. 28, No. 2 (December 1981), pp. 281–285, 282.
76 Jahangir, f. 70b.
77 Terry, pp. 315–316.
78 Terry would praise Akbar's tomb, writing: 'Among many faire piles there dedicated to this use, the most excellent is Secandra.' Ibid.
79 Jahangir, fs. 223a and 226a, respectively.
80 Ibid., 52a.
81 Ibid., f. 54a.
82 Sattar, pp. 16–18.
83 Jahangir, f. 270a.
84 Ibid., f. 218b.
85 Ibid., f. 250a.
86 Ibid., f. 302b.
87 Ibid., f. 117b. See Foltz, 'The Naqshbandi Connections of the Mughal Emperors', *Journal of Islamic Studies*, Vol. 7, No. 2, Islam in Central Asia and the Caucasus (July 1996), pp. 229–239, 233.
88 Samarqandi, p. 40.
89 Foltz, p. 371.

90 Ibid., p. 373.
91 Truschke, p. 102.
92 Ibid., p. 170.
93 Ibid., p. 174. Truschke points out that Sattar too mentions Jahangir's temporary ban on renunciants, affirming that while some of its elements are fanciful, the legend is not entirely apocryphal. See Sattar, p. 272.
94 Among the loveliest of Mughal paintings is that depicting Jahangir celebrating the festival of Holi with the women of his harem. Likely painted by his court artist, Govardin, a few years after the emperor's death, it is currently in the Chester Beatty Library, Minto Collection, in 07A.4a.
95 Jahangir, f. 13b. Thackston, tr., p. 40.
96 Sattar, pp. 72 and 13–14. His refusal to impose a single state religion led some foreigners to mistakenly believe the emperor Jahangir had no strong personal allegiance to Islam. Sir Thomas Roe would claim that 'hee is the moste impossible man in the world to be converted, or the most easy; for he loves to heare and hath so little religion that that he can well abyde to have any decided'. See Roe, p. 316.
97 Jahangir, f. 11b. For his discussion of the castes of India, see Jahangir, fs. 95a–96a. For the celebration of Rakhi, f. 96b.
98 Ibid., f. 273b.
99 *Iqbalnama,* Erskine, tr., f. 47.
100 Jahangir, f. 225a.
101 Ibid., f. 140a. In describing Jadrup Gosain, Jahangir uses the Sanskrit term *sanyasi* rather than the Persian *darwish* and then couples it with the Persian term *murtazi*, stressing ascetic discipline. See Ibid., fs. 139b–140a.
102 Mu'tamid Khan, f. 47. Emphasis mine.
103 Shirin Moosvi, 'The Mughal Encounter with Vedanta, Recovering the Biography of Jadrup', *Social Scientist,* Vol. 30, No. 7/8 (July–August 2002), pp. 13–23, 14–15.
104 Jahangir, f. 140a.
105 Ibid., f. 141a. Baba Fighani, *Divan*, 214, line 2837.
106 Translated by Maaz Bin Bilal. Bulleh Shah was a follower of Shah Inayat Qadiri, of the Qadiri-Shatari silsilla, in Lahore – a Sufi lineage popular with Mughal elites. Its membership included Jahangir's granddaughter, Jahanara, and grandson, Dara Shikoh, whose writings confirm the mystical and pluralistic confluence of Sufism and Vedanta. Most famously the *Majma al-Bahrain* (The Confluence of the Two Oceans) and the *Sirr-i Akbar*, a Persian translation of the Upanishads.
107 Jahangir, f. 187b. For 'type' Jahangir uses the word *taifa*. Within the context of the sentence, in which it explicitly refers to those who detach themselves from material needs, it is clear that the 'type' in question is not Hindu devotees specifically but ascetics more generally.

108 Ibid., fs. 187b–188a.
109 This was of course Varaha, the third incarnation of Vishnu.
110 Ibid., fs. 224a–b. Thackston, tr., p. 311.
111 Sattar, p. 6.
112 Ibid., fs. 41a–b. The *'anga* is also commonly known in Persian literature as the *simurgh*, usually roughly translated as phoenix.
113 Ibid.

Chapter 11

1   For the sake of clarity, I will continue to refer to the prince as Khurram throughout, until his ascension in 1627.
2   Jahangir's use here of the word *ghaza* is interesting, making a claim that this was a holy war against a non-Muslim ruler. The tone is less tolerant than that he would generally use to refer to even the independent kings of South Asia.
3   Jahangir, f. 259a; Thackston, tr., p. 352.
4   It has long been believed that the royal court's desertion of the city may have been due to limited water supplies. Jahangir confirms this in part by describing a cistern for rainwater under the mosque courtyard which had been built to supplement a water supply he describes as 'little, and that is bad'. See Jahangir, f. 209b.
5   This is the first sura in the Quran.
6   Ibid., f. 209a.
7   Ibid., f. 208a.
8   Ibid., f. 231b.
9   Ibid., f. 234a. This is reminiscent of Jahangir's great-grandfather, Babur, who wrote of trying a local date wine on his arrival into Hindustan. He was much more disappointed with his experiment than Jahangir, complaining that the promised effect was 'not obvious'. Babur, Mano, ed., p. 458.
10 Ibid., f. 235a; Thackston, tr., p. 325.
11 Ibid., 236b.
12 Of the four named poet laureates at the Mughal court, three were Persian, including Shah Jahan's favourite poet, Kalim of Hamadan. See Sunil Sharma, *Mughal Arcadia*, Cambridge, MA: Harvard University Press, 2017, p. 23.
13 Ibid., p. 299.
14 Dale, *Garden*, p. 255.
15 Babur, Mano, p. 280. Thackston, tr., p. 375. This comment was made by Ali Shir Nava'i at a chess party in Herat, intended as a jibe against another poet, and rival, Banni'a, who answered him, 'Yes, and if you pull your foot back in, you'll poke another.'

16 Dale, 'Poetry and Autobiography', p. 640.
17 The Mughal court was not the only destination for émigré Iranian poets and literati, many of whom found their way to Deccani royal courts.
18 Sharma, p. 22.
19 Jahangir, f. 89b.
20 Sattar, pp. 9–10.
21 Ibid., pp. 38–42 and p. 199, for example.
22 Alam and Subramanyam, p. 488.
23 Mutribi al-Assam Samarqandi, *Conversations with Emperor Jahangir*, Richard Foltz, tr. Costa Mesa, CA: Mazda Publishers, 1998, p. 62.
24 Jahangir, 55a; Thackston, tr., p. 92.
25 Ibid., f. 64a; Thackston, tr., p. 103.
26 Ibid., f. 230a; Thackston, tr., p. 320.
27 Ibid., f. 22a; Thackston, tr., pp. 306–307. Anvari, Divan 79, lines 1–2.
28 Ibid., f. 289a; Thackston, tr., p. 389.
29 Sattar, for example see both 81st and 83rd assemblies, pp. 198–200 and 203–205.
30 Jahangir, f. 194a.
31 Ibid., f. 229a; Thackston, tr., p. 318.
32 Ibid., f. 56a; Thackston, tr., p. 93.
33 Ibid., f. 271b.
34 Anvari, Divan, 470, line 9, in Jahangir, Thackston, tr., p. 373.
35 Ibid., f. 276a.
36 Ibid., f. 277b.
37 Ibid., f. 278a.
38 *Iqbalnama*, Erskine, tr., f. 38.
39 Jahangir, f. 157a. The act of gifting was not unique to Nur Jahan. Other important dynastic women gifted *khilat* and played the role of patron in the royal court.
40 Ibid., f. 262a.
41 Ibid., f. 108a.
42 Mirza Nathan, II, p. 666.
43 Jahangir, f. 308a; Thackston, tr., pp. 413–414.
44 Ibid., f. 262b. The Nur Serai was a caravanserai but included private royal quarters. For event of 1617, see f. 134 a/b; for 1622 party at the Nur Afshan, see f. 265b.
45 Ibid., f. 152a.
46 Lal, p. 142.
47 *Iqbalnama*, fs. 29–30. We know that as prince Khurram also sat in a darshan regularly.
48 The coins minted in the queen's name do not seem to have been offered for circulation but remained solely commemorative. Their existence has been seen, however, as evidence of inappropriate reach of the queens' ambition, the historian John Richards referring to their production as 'most startling', for example, and

concluding that it confirmed the gossip of the power and authority of 'the Nur Jahan group'. Richards, *Mughal Empire*, p. 103.

49 Kami Shirazi, *Waqa-i-uz-Zaman (Fath Nama-i-Nur Jahan Begam)*, W.H. Siddiqi, ed., Rampar, UP: Rampur Raza Library, 2003; Shaikh Farid Bhakkari, *Dhakiratul Khawanin (Nobility under the Great Mughals)*, Z.A. Desai, tr., New Delhi: Sundeep Prakashan, 2003, pp. 14–20, 14.

50 Roe, pp. 436–437.

51 Miryam Makani, the mother of Akbar, had owned trading ships which plied their trade in the Indian Ocean and Arabian Sea, carrying spices, opium and textiles for export and returning with perfumes, brocade, amber and ivory. The Portuguese capture of her ship, the *Rahimi*, led to collapse in Portuguese-Mughal relations (East India Company, 1968, II, 213). Turco-Mongol women were actively involved in trade: 'Among the Mongols it was customary for important women to be active in commerce, and the same practice may have been true under the Timurids. During a revolt at Yazd, rebels seized three assloads of silk fabrics which had been purchased for Saray-Mulk Khanim and which were being stored along with two years of tax revenues in cash.' See Priscilla P. Soucek, 'Timurid Women: A Cultural Perspective', *Women in the Islamic World*, Gavin Hambly, ed., New York: St. Martin's Press, 1998, 1999, pp. 199–226, 206.

52 William Foster, ed., *The English Factories in India, 1618–1621*, Oxford: Clarendon Press, 1906, p. 148. See also Roe, p. 444.

53 Foster, p. 81.

54 Francisco Pelsaert, *Jahangir's India, The Remonstrantie of Francisco Pelsaert*, W.H. Moreland and P. Geyl, tr., Cambridge: W. Heffer & Sons, Ltd., 1925, p. 4. See also Joannes De Laet, *The Empire of the Great Mogul*, tr. J.S. Hoyland, annotated S.N. Bannerjee, New Delhi: Oriental Books Reprint Corporation, 1974, p. 41. 'Hither are brought all kinds of merchandise from Purob, Bengala, Purbet and Bouten [Bhutan]; these pay dues to the queen before they are taken across the river.'

55 Peter Mundy, *The Travels of Peter Mundy in Europe and Asia*, Cambridge: Hakluyt Society, 1907, Vol. II, pp. 78–79.

56 Wayne E. Begley, 'Four Mughal Caravanserais Built during the Reigns of Jahangir and Khurram', *Muqarnas*, Vol. I (1983), pp. 167–179, 169.

57 A *kos* is a distance of almost 2 miles.

58 The Nur Serai was surveyed by Alexander Cunningham in 1878–79 and described in Archaeological Survey of India Reports, 14:63 (14:62–65).

59 Pelsaert, *Jahangir's India, The Remonstrantie of Francisco Pelsaert*, p. 50. Suspicion of Nur Jahan as a public and politically engaged woman continued well into of the twentieth century, which asserted that unlike the rich men of the empire, the queen's motives were self-aggrandizing, as 'the architectural grandeur and extravagance of her *serai* should perhaps be viewed as expressions of her political aspirations and personal ambition rather than her piety'. See Begley,

'Four Mughal Caravanserais Built during the Reigns of Jahangir and Shah Jahan', pp. 167–179, 170.

60 Gregory Kozlowski, 'Private Lives and Public Piety: Women and the Practice of Islam in Mughal India', Gavin R.G. Hambly, ed., *Women in the Medieval Islamic World*, New York: St. Martin's Press, 1998, 1999, pp. 469–488, 470.

61 For example, see Hosten, for the letters of a Jesuit at the court in 1626–27 and Foltz, 'Naqshbandi Connections', describing visitors from Central Asia in the same years.

62 For example, see Richards, *Mughal Empire*, pp. 102–103.

63 S. Nurul Hasan, 'The Theory of the Nur Jahan "Junta" – a Critical Examination', *Proceedings of the Indian History Congress*, Vol. 21 (1958), pp. 324–335, 335.

64 Ibid.

Chapter 12

1 M. Sirj Anwar, 'Malik Ambar and the Mughals, 1601–26', *Proceedings of the Indian History Congress*, Vol. 55 (1994), pp. 355–367, 360.

2 Jahangir, f. 272a.

3 This evokes the Central Asian Turkic belief that an illness can be transferred into the body of another with a ritual circumambulation, sacrificing a life for a life. The dynastic founder in India, Babur, performed this act in 1530, in an effort to cure his son Humayun, who was believed to be dying of a grave illness. Babur was reported to have sickened immediately after and died within days, leaving Humayun his successor. See Guldadan Begim, fs. 16b–17b.

4 The histories composed in the twentieth century continued to treat this as a murder. For example, see Richards, *Mughal Empire*, p. 114. It is not my claim that Khurram did not murder his brother, only that the evidence is completely circumstantial. The absence of evidence, of course, proves nothing.

5 It is however true that in 1614, when Khurram had been sent to campaign against Mewar, he complained of the attitude of a noblemen who had been assigned with him, claiming that Khan Azam's misbehaviour was due to his close relationship with Khusraw. Khan Azam, who had a long and contentious relationship with the Mughal family, as Akbar's milk brother, was recalled and his household brought to Jahangir in Ajmer. Jahangir, f. 101b.

6 Ibid., f. 278b.

7 Ibid., f. 280b.

8 Mu'tamid Khan, writing during the reign of Khurram, would attempt to justify the seizure in explaining that the prince had sent a letter to his father requesting the lands but had sent his own agent to take possession and begin administering them before the emperor could respond. See *Iqbalnama*, Erskine, tr., f. 91.

9 Ibid., f. 92.
10 Mahabat Khan was also, not incidentally, a rival and enemy of the queen's brother Asaf Khan, whose own loyalties were with Khurram, the prince who had married his daughter.
11 Ibid., f. 281a. Thackston, tr., p. 380.
12 Ibid., 284a–285b. Letters fully translated in Thackston, ed., pp. 383–385.
13 Ibid., f. 286a.
14 *Iqbalnama*, Erskine, f. 94.
15 Jahangir, f. 287a.
16 Ibid.
17 Corinne Lefèvre, 'Pouvoir et noblesse dans l'empire moghol: Perspectives du règne de Jahāngīr (1605–1627)', *Annales. Histoire, Sciences Sociales*, 62e Année, No. 6 (November–December 2007), pp. 1287–1312, 1296.
18 Jahangir, f. 288a; Thackston, tr., p. 388. From Sa'di, *Gulistan* in *Kulliyyat* 42.
19 Khurram, as the Emperor Shah Jahan, would be able to win back Qandahar in 1638. His success was only temporary, however, and the Mughals would lose the region to the Safavids once again in 1649, never to regain it. The reason was Shah Jahan's ill-fated campaign against the Uzbeks, part of his effort to regain the Timurid Central Asian homeland. Taking advantage of that moment of Mughal distraction, the Safavid armies once again took Qandahar. The Mughal-Safavid war over Qandahar would last for several years, but by 1653 the Mughals were forced to retreat. They never returned to Central Asia.
20 Ibid., fs. 2787a–b; Thackston, tr., p. 388.
21 His son remained with Khurram, however, whether by choice or because he was prevented from leaving is unclear. At the imperial camp, Khankhanan would always be considered suspect, remaining under close watch. See *Iqbalnama*, fs. 109–110.
22 This was the occasion on which he gave two thousand rupees of the total to Ahmad Sirhindi.
23 Ibid., f. 106.
24 Hadi, Thackston, tr., p. 426.
25 Foltz, p. 237.
26 The shaykh made his way to Lahore after the emperor's death, where he died in October of the same year.
27 Having been the bane of Jahangir's reign, after his death Ambar would be acclaimed for his administration and judgement even by Jahangir's confidantes and allies. The more direct legacy of his military genius, however, lay in the success of his successors, the Bhonsle clan of the Marathas. The famed Shivaji, who would contest Mughal power in the Deccan against Khurram and his son and successor Aurangzeb, was the son of Ambar's Maratha general.
28 Hadi, Thackston, tr., p. 438.

29 Ibid., fs. 129–130. It would later be claimed that the followers of Mahabat Khan were afraid of the reputed accuracy of the queen's arrows. Her attempt to lead a force against the rebels caused 'disruption and agitation [among her enemies] on account of the fiery shots of the queen's gun, which could overthrow even lions' Shirazi, *Waqa-i-uz-Zaman (Fath Nama-i-Nur Jahan Begam)*, p. 156.
30 Ibid., p. 442.
31 The *Jahangirnama* offers only a bland comment. Mu'tamid Khan would commemorate Parvez by writing that before he began drinking to excess his father had been very fond of him. See *Iqbalnama*, Erskine, f. 132.
32 Ibid.
33 Ibid., f. 138.
34 Ibid., f. 138. Also see Hadi, Thackston, tr., p. 456.
35 Asaf Khan was of course the father of Mumtaz Mahal, who would die giving birth to Khurram's fourteenth child in 1631. Her husband would eventually build the Taj Mahal as a shrine and mausoleum for them both, on the banks of the Yamuna River in Agra.
36 The 1628 executions evoke Ottoman traditions of accessional fratricide but represent the first wholesale execution of male relatives in Mughal history. Rival male members of the family were regularly killed, but only on the battlefield and only after they openly contested the throne. Those who did not offer any threat were allowed to remain to serve as useful members of the nobility.
37 Hadi, Thackston, tr., p. 460.

Conclusion

1 Bhakkari, p. 14.
2 Roe, p. 364.
3 Ibid., pp. 484 and 364.
4 Pelsaert, p. 524.
5 Prasad, p. 405.
6 Richards, *Mughal Empire*, p. 113.
7 Hosten, p. 257.
8 Ibid., p. 247. The Jesuit, Father de Castro, wrote that the gatherings took place 'almost every night, up after midnight *ut plurinum*'.
9 Ibid., p. 253.
10 Jahangir's allegiance to Akbar's liberal and inclusive values would last through the entirety of his reign. For example, his continued embrace of religious debate is confirmed by a Jesuit priest who travelled with the emperor, writing as late as 1627 that representatives of other religions 'take amiss our liberty … [but] out

of fear of the King they dare not make against us any other demonstration; and thus, in the best way we can, before so many lords of divers nations, Gentile and Maumetan ... we preach Christ and Him crucified'. See Hosten, p. 262.
11 Koch, 'Sir Francis Bacon's Ideal', p. 73.
12 Jahangir, f. 258b; Thackston, tr., p. 351. This comment evokes the poem by Amir Khusraw, beloved by Shah Jahan and quoted on the walls of his throne room: 'If there is a paradise on earth, this is it!'
13 Muhammad Amin Kazwini, 'Padshahnama', Elliot & Dowson, VII, pp. 1–3.

Bibliography

Primary sources

Aftabchi, Jauhar, 'Tadhkiratu'l-waqiat', *Three Memoirs of Homayun*, Wheeler Thackston (trans.), Costa Mesa, CA: Mazda Publishers, 2009, Vol. 1, English text, pp. 69–175/ Persian text, pp. 1–214.

Allami, Abu'l Fazl, *A'in (Ayn)-i Akbari*, Vol. 1, H. Blochmann (trans.), 2nd ed., Lieut. Colonel D.C. Phillott (ed.), New Delhi: Munshiran Manoharlal Pub. Pvt. Ltd., 3rd ed., 1977, vols. 2 and 3, Colonel H.S. Jarrett (trans. and ed.), 2nd ed., Sir Jadunath Sarkar (ed.), 3rd ed., 1977.

Allami, Abu'l Fazl, *Akbarnama*, H. Beveridge (trans.), 3 vols., Delhi: Manmohan Satish Kumar, Rare Books, 1st Indian ed., 1972.

Babur, Zahiruddin Muhammad, *Baburnama (Vekayi), Critical Edition Based on Four Chaghatay Texts*, Eiji Mano (ed.), Japanese and Chaghatay, 4 vols., Kyoto: Syokado, 1995.

Babur, Zahiruddin Muhammad, *Baburnama*, Wheeler M. Thackston (trans.), text in Chaghatay, Persian and English, 3 vols., Cambridge, MA: Harvard University Department of Near Eastern Languages and Civilizations, 1993.

Babur, Zahiruddin Muhammad, *The Baburnama in English*, Annette Susannah Beveridge (trans. and ed.), London: Luzac and Company, Ltd., 1969.

al-Badauni (Badaoni), Abd al-Qadir Ibn Muluk Shah, *Muntakhabut al-Tawarikh*, W.H. Lowe (trans.), 3 vols., Patna: Academica Asiatica, 1973.

Bahadur, Hamid ud-Din, *Ahkam-i Alamgir* or *Anecdotes of Aurangzeb*, Jadunath Sarkar (trans.), London: Sangam Books Limited, 1988 (1st and 2nd ed., 1925; 3rd ed., 1949).

Bayat, Bayazid, 'Tarikh-i Humayun', *Three Memoirs of Homayun*, Wheeler M. Thackston (trans./English and Persian texts), Costa Mesa, CA: Mazda Publishers, 2009, II.

Bernier, Francois, *Travel in the Mogul Empire, AD 1656–1668*, Archibald Constable (trans.), London: Cambridge University Press, 1934; New Delhi: Munshiram Manoharlal Publishers Pvt. Ltd., Oriental Reprint, 1983.

Bhakkari, Shaikh Farid, *Dhakiratul Khawanin* (*Nobility under the Great Mughals*), Z.A. Desai (trans.), New Delhi: Sundeep Prakashan, 2003, pp. 14–20.

Clavijo, Ruy Gonzales de, *Embassy to Tamerlane, 1403–1406*, Guy Le Strange (trans.), New York and London: Harper Brothers, 1928.

Coryat, Thomas, *Early Travels in India, 1583–1619*, Foster, Sir William, ed., 1st ed., Humphrey Milford, London: Oxford University Press, 1921; reprint Delhi: LPP, 2007, pp. 234–287, 247.

Coverte, Robert, *A True and Almost Incredible Report of an Englishman*, London, 1612; Amsterdam and New York: Da Capo Press, reprint 1971.

Cunningham, Alexander, Archaeological Survey of India Reports, 1878–79, 14:63 (14:62–65).

Dawlatshah, 'Tadhkirat al-shu'ara', *A Century of Princes: Sources on Timurid History and Art*, Wheeler M. Thackston (trans.), Cambridge, MA: The Aga Khan Program for Islamic Architecture, 1989, pp. 11–62.

de Laet, Joannes, *The Empire of the Great Mogul*, J.S. Hoyland (trans.), annotated S.N. Bannerjee, New Delhi: Oriental Books Reprint Corporation, 1974.

du Jarric, Fr. Pierre, *Akbar and the Jesuits*, C.H. Payne (trans. and ed.), London: George Routledge and Sons, 1906.

East India Company, *Letters Received by the East India Company from Its Servants in the East*, 2 vols., London, 1896; reprint Amsterdam: N. Israel, 1968.

Elliot, Sir H.M. and John Dowson (eds.), *The History of India, as Told by Its Own Historians: The Posthumous Papers of Sir H.M. Elliot*, 8 vols., London: Trubner and Co., 1872, New York: AMS Press, Inc., 1966.

Finch, William, *Early Travels in India, 1583–1619*, Foster, Sir William (ed.), 1st ed., London: Humphrey Milford, Oxford University Press, 1921; reprint Delhi: LPP, 2007, pp. 122–187.

Foster, Sir William (ed.), *Early Travels in India, 1583–1619*, 1st ed., London: Humphrey Milford, Oxford University Press, 1921; reprint Delhi: LPP, 2007.

Foster, Sir William, *The English Factories in India, 1618–1621* (a calendar of documents in the India Office and British Museum), Oxford: Clarendon Press, 1906.

Gulbadan Begim, 'Humayunnama', *Three Memoirs of Homayun*, Wheeler M. Thackston (trans./English and Persian texts), Costa Mesa, CA: Mazda Publishers, 2009, pp. 1–68.

Gulbadan Begim, *Humayunnama (The History of Humayun)*, Annette S. Beveridge (trans. and ed./English and Persian texts), Delhi: Idarah-i Adabiyat-i Delli, 1972.

Gulbadan Begim, *Humayunaama*, British Library Or. 166.

Guerreiro, Father Fernao, C.H. Payne (trans.), *Jahangir and the Jesuits*, From the 'Relations' of Father Fernao Guerreiro, S.J. (New York: Robert M. McBride & Co., 1930), pp. xviii–xix.

Hadi, Muhammad, 'Preface [and Conclusion] to the Jahangirnama', *The Jahangirnama, Memoirs of Jahangir, Emperor of India*. Wheeler M. Thackston (trans.), New York: Oxford University Press, in association with the Freer Gallery of Art and the Arthur Sackler Gallery, Smithsonian Institution, Washington, DC, 1999.

Hawkins, William, *Early Travels in India, 1583–1619*, 1st ed., London: Humphrey Milford, Oxford University Press, 1921; reprint Delhi: LPP, 2007, pp. 60–121.

Hosten, Henri, 'Three Letters of Fr. Joseph de Castro, S.J., and the Last Year of Jahangir', *Mughal India According to European Travel Accounts; Texts and Studies*, Vol. 1 (1998), pp. 243–268.

Ibn Arabshah, Ahmed ibn Muhammad, *Tamerlane, or Timur the Great Amir*, J.H. Sanders (trans.), Lahore: Progressive Books, 1936, reprint 1976.

Inayat Khan, *Shah Jahan Nama*, A.R. Fuller (trans.), W.E. Begley and Z.A. Desai (eds.), Delhi, New York, and London: Oxford University Press, 1990.

Iradat Khan, 'Tarikh-i Iradat Khan', *History of India, as Told by Its Own Historians*, Sir H.M. Elliot and John Dowson (eds.), New York: AMS Press, Inc., 1966, VII, pp. 534–564.

Islam, Riazul, *A Calendar of Documents on Indo-Persian Relations (1500–1700)*, Tehran: Iranian Culture Foundation; Karachi: Institute of Central & West Asian Studies, 1979–1982.

Jahangir, Nuruddin Muhammad, *The Jahangirnama, Memoirs of Jahangir, Emperor of India*, Wheeler M. Thackston (trans.), New York: Oxford University Press, in association with the Freer Gallery of Art and the Arthur Sackler Gallery, Smithsonian Institution, Washington, DC, 1999.

Jahangir, Nuruddin Muhammad, *Jahangirnama*, British Library MS OR 1644.

Jahangir, Nuruddin Muhammad, *Jahangirnama (Tuzuk-i Jahangiri)*, Tehran: Buny adi Farhangi Iran, 1359 (1980).

Kambu (Kambo), Muhammad Salih, 'Amal-i Salih', *History of India, as Told by Its Own Historians*, Sir H.M. Elliot and John Dowson (eds.), New York: AMS Press, Inc., 1966, VII, pp. 123–132.

Kamgar Husaini, Khwaja, *Ma'asir-i Jahangiri (A Contemporary Account of Jahangir)*, Azra Alavi (ed.) (Persian text with English introduction), New York: Asia Publishing House, Inc., 1978.

Kazwini, Muhammad Amin, 'Padshahnama', *History of India, as Told by Its Own Historians*, Sir H.M. Elliot and John Dowson (eds.), New York: AMS Press, Inc., 1966, VII, pp. 1–3.

Khafi Khan, Muhammad Hashim, *Muntakhab al-Labab*, Kabir al-Din Ahmad (ed.), Calcutta: Asia Society of Bengal, 1869.

Khwandemir, Ghiyasuddin, *Qanun-i Humayuni (Humayunnama of Khwandamir)*, M. Hidayat Hosain (ed.), Calcutta: Royal Asiatic Society of Bengal, 1940.

Lahori [Lahauri], Abd al-Hamid and Muhammad Waris, *Padshahnama*, Kabir al Din Ahmad and Abdal Raman (eds.), Calcutta: Royal Asiatic Society of Bengal, 1867; A.R. Fuller (trans.), 1851, reprint. 1990.

Lahori [Lahauri], Abd al-Hamid and Muhammad Waris, 'Badshahnama', *History of India, as Told by Its Own Historians*, Sir H.M. Elliot and John Dowson (eds.), New York: AMS Press, Inc., 1966, VII, pp. 3–72.

Manrique, Fray Sebastien, *Travels of Fray Sebāstien Manrique, 1629–1643: A Translation of the Itinerario de las missiones orientales*, C. Eckford Luard and H. Hosten (ed.), 1927, Nendeln, Liechtenstein, Kraus Reprint, 2 vols., 1967.

Monserrate, Fr., *The Commentary of Father Monserrate, SJ, on His Journey to the Court of Akbar*, J.S. Hoyland (trans.), S.N. Bannerjee (ed.), London and Bombay: Oxford University Press, 1922.

Mundy, Peter, *The Travels of Peter Mundy in Europe and Asia*, Cambridge: Hakluyt Society, 1907.

Mu'tamid Khan, Muhammad Sharif, *Iqbalnama-i Jahangiri*, British Library, Add 26218/ see also OR 14342. See also W. Erskine condensed translation, Add 26612.

Najm-i Sani, Muhammad Baqir, *Art of Governance: An Indo-Islamic Mirror for Princes (Ma'uizah-i Jahangiri)*, Sajida S. Alvi (trans.), State University of New York Press, 1989.

Nathan, Mirza ('Alau'd- Din Isfahani), *Baharistan-i Ghaybi*, M.I. Borah (trans.), 2 vols., Gauhati, Assam: Narayani Handiqui Historical Institute, 1936.

Nawa'i, Mir Ali Sher [Shir], 'Preface to His First Turkish Divan: Gharayib al- Sighar', *A Century of Princes: Sources on Timurid History and Art*, Wheeler Thackston (trans.), Cambridge, MA: The Aga Khan Program for Islamic Architecture, 1989, pp. 363–372.

Nawaz Khan, Shah, *Maasiru-l-Umara*, Ashraf Ali (ed.), Vol. 3, Calcutta: Asia Society of Bengal, 1891.

Pelsaert, Francisco, *Jahangir's India, the Remonstrantie of Francisco Pelsaert*, W.H. Moreland and P. Geyl (trans.), Cambridge: W. Heffer & Sons, Ltd., 1925.

Roe, Sir Thomas, *The Embassy of Sir Thomas Roe to the Court of the Great Mogul, 1615–1619*, William Foster (ed.), London: Hakluyt Society, 1899. Kraus reprint, 1967.

Sa'di Shirazi, *A Thousand Years of Persian Rubaiyat*, Reza Saberi (ed.), Bethesda, Maryland: IBEX Publishers, 2000.

Samarqandi, Mutribi al-Asamm, ['Murtib' al-Assam], *Conversations with Emperor Jahangir*, Richard C. Foltz (trans.), Costa Mesa, CA: Mazda Publishers, 1998.

Sattar, Abdus (ibn Qasim Lahauri), *Majalis-i Jahangiri*, Arif Naushahi and Moin Nizami (eds.), Tehran: Miras-i Maktub, 2006.

Shah Nawaz Khan, Nawab Samsam ud- Daula and Abd al-Hayy, *Maathir (Ma'asir)-ul- Umara: Biographies of the Muhammadan and Hindu Officers of the Timurid Sovereigns of India from 1500 to about 1780 A.D.*, H. Beveridge (trans.), Baini Prashad (ed.), 2 vols., Calcutta: The Asiatic Society, 1952; Delhi: Low Price Publications, 1999.

Shirazi, Kami, *Waqa-i-uz-Zaman (Fath Nama-i-Nur Jahan Begam)*, W.H. Siddiqi (trans.), Rampur: Rampur Raza Library, 2003.

Terry, Edward, *Early Travels in India, 1583–1619*, Sir William Foster (ed.), 1st ed., London: Humphrey Milford, Oxford University Press, 1921; Delhi: LPP, 2007, pp. 288–332.

Tirmizi, S.A.I., *Edicts from the Mughal Harem*, Delhi: Idarah-i Adabiyat-i Delli, 1979.

Withington, Nicholas, *Early Travels in India, 1583–1619*, Sir William Foster (ed.), 1st ed., London: Humphrey Milford, Oxford University Press, 1921; Delhi: LPP, 2007, pp. 188–233.

Secondary Sources

Alam, Muzaffar, 'Guiding the Ruler and Prince', *Islam in South Asia in Practice*, Barbara Metcalf (ed.), Princeton, NJ: Princeton University Press, 2009.

Alam, Muzaffar, *The Languages of Political Islam, India 1200–1800*, Chicago: University of Chicago Press, 2004.

Alam, Muzaffar, 'The Mughals, the Sufi Shaikhs and the Formation of the Akbari Dispensation', *Modern Asian Studies*, Vol. 43, No. 1 (January 2009), pp. 135–174.

Alam, Muzaffar, 'The Pursuit of Persian: Language in Mughal Politics', *Modern Asian Studies*, Vol. 32, No. 2 (1998), pp. 31–49.

Alam, Muzaffar, 'State Building under the Mughals', *L'Heritage Timouride, Iran- Asie Central- Inde, XVe–XVIIIe Siecles, Les Cahiers d'Asie Centrale*, Maria Szuppe (ed.), Tachkent- Aix-en-Provence, 1997, pp. 105–128.

Alam, Muzaffar and Sanjay Subramanyam, 'Frank Disputations', *The Indian Economic Social History Review*, Vol. 46, No. 4 (2009), pp. 457–511.

Alam, Muzaffar and Sanjay Subrahmanyam, *The Mughal State, 1526–1750*, New Delhi: Oxford University Press, 1998.

Algar, Hamid, 'The Naqshbandis and Safavids: A Contribution to the Religious History of Iran and Her Neighbors', *Safavid Iran and Her Neighbors*, Michel Mazzaoui (ed.), Salt Lake City, Utah: The University of Utah Press, 2003, pp. 7–48.

Algar, Hamid, 'Political Aspects of Naqshbandi History', *Naqshbandis: Cheminements et Situation actuelle d'un ordre mystique musulman*. Actes de la Table Ronde de Sèvres, Marc Gaborieau et al. (eds.), Editions Isis: Istanbul, 1985, 1990, pp. 123–152.

Algar, Hamid, 'The Naqshbandi Order: A Preliminary Survey of Its History and Significance', *Studia Islamica*, Vol. 44, No. 136 (1976), pp. 123–152.

Ali, Daud, *Courtly Culture and Political Life in Early Medieval India*, Cambridge: Cambridge University Press, 2004.

Ali, M. Athar, *Mughal India: Studies in Polity, Ideas, Society and Culture*, New Delhi: Oxford University Press, 2003.

Allsen, Thomas T., *The Royal Hunt in Eurasian History*, Philadelphia, PA: University of Pennsylvania Press, 2006.

Alvi, M.A. and A. Rahman, *Jahangir the Naturalist*, New Delhi: Indian National Science Academy, 1968.

Alvi, Sajida S., 'Religion and State during the Reign of Mughal Emperor Jahangir (1605–27): Nonjuristical Perspectives', *Studia Islamica*, Vol. 69 (1989), pp. 95–119.

Andaya, Barbara Watson, 'Women and the Performance of Power in Early Modern Southeast Asia', *Servants of the Dynasty: Palace Women in World History*, Anne Walthall (ed.), Berkeley, CA: University of California Press, 2008, pp. 22–44.

Anooshahr, Ali, *The Ghazi Sultans and the Frontiers of Islam*, London and New York: Routledge, 2009.

Anwar, M. Siraj, 'Malik Ambar and the Mughals, 1601–26', *Proceedings of the Indian History Congress*, Vol. 55 (1994), pp. 355–367.

Anwar, M. Siraj, 'The Safavids and Mughal Relations with the Deccani States', *Proceedings of the Indian History Congress*, Vol. 52 (1991), pp. 255–262.

Asher, Catherine B., 'Architecture', *The Magnificent Mughals*, Zeenut Ziad (ed.), Oxford, UK: Oxford University Press, 2002, pp. 183–228.

Asher, Catherine B., 'Sub-Imperial Palaces: Power and Authority in Mughal India', *Ars Orientalis*, Vol. 23, Pre-Modern Islamic Palaces, 1993, pp. 281–302.

Aziz, Abd al-Sh., *The Imperial Library of the Mughals*, Delhi: Idarah-i Adabiyat-i Delli, 1974.

Aziz, Ahmad, *Studies in Islamic Culture in the Indian Environment*, New Delhi: Oxford University Press, 1964; reprint 2002.

Babayan, Kathryn, 'The 'Aqa'id al-Nisa': A Glimpse of Safavid Women in Local Isfahani Culture', *Women in the Medieval Islamic World*, Gaven Hambly (ed.), New York: St. Martin's Press, 1998, pp. 349–382.

Balabanlilar, Lisa, *Imperial Identity in Mughal India*, London and New York: I.B. Tauris, 2012.

Balabanlilar, Lisa, 'Begims of the Mystic Feast', *The Journal of Asian Studies*, Vol. 69, No. 1 (February 2010), pp. 123–147.

Balabanlilar, Lisa, 'The Emperor Jahangir and the Pursuit of Pleasure', *Journal of the Royal Asiatic Society*, Series 3, Vol. 19, No. 2 (2009), pp. 1–14.

Barbour, Richmond, *Before Orientalism: London's Theatre of the East 1576–1626*, Cambridge and New York: Cambridge University Press, 2003.

Barnett, Richard B., 'Embattled Begims: Women as Power Brokers in Early Modern India', *Women in the Medieval Islamic World*, Gaven Hambly (ed.), New York: St. Martin's Press, 1998, pp. 521–536.

Beach, Milo C., 'Jahangir's Jahangir-Nama', *Powers of Art*, Barbara Stoler Miller (ed.), Delhi: Oxford University Press, 1992, pp. 224–234.

Beach, Milo C., 'The Mughal Painter Abu'l Hasan and Some English Sources for His Style', *The Journal of the Walters Art Gallery*, Vol. 38 (1980), pp. 6–33.

Beach, Milo C. and Ebba Koch, *King of the World: The Padshahnama*, New York: Azimuth Editions Limited and Smithsonian Institution, 1997.

Begley, Wayne E., 'Four Mughal Caravanserais Built during the Reigns of Jahangir and Shah Jahan', *Muqarnas*, Vol. I (1983), pp. 167–179.

Beveridge, Henry, review of Beni Prasad's *History of Jahangir*, London: Oxford University Press, 1922, published in the *Journal of the Royal Asiatic Society*, Vol. 55, No. 3 (July 1923), pp. 483–484.

Blake, Stephen, 'Contributors to the Urban Landscape: Women Builders in Safavid Isfahan and Mughal Shahjahanabad', *Women in the Medieval Islamic World*, Gavin R.G. Hambly (ed.), New York: St. Martin's Press, 1998, pp. 407–428.

Blake, Stephen, *Shahjahanabad: The Sovereign City in Mughal India, 1639–1739*, Cambridge: Cambridge University Press, 1991.

Blake, Stephen, 'The Patrimonial-Bureaucratic Empire of the Mughals', *Journal of Asian Studies*, Vol. 39, No. 1 (1979), pp. 77–94.

Broadbridge, Anne F., *Kingship and Ideology in the Islamic and Mongol Worlds*, New York: Cambridge University Press, 2008.

Buehler, Arthur F., *Sufi Heirs of the Prophet: The Indian Naqshbandiyya and the Rise of the Mediating Sufi Saint*, Columbia: University of South Carolina Press, 1998.

Canby, Sheila (ed.), *Humayun's Garden Party: Princes of the House of Timur*, Bombay: Marg Publications, 1994.

Chandra, Satish, *Parties and Politics at the Mughal Court, 1707–1740*, New Delhi: Oxford University Press, 2002–2003.

Charpentier, Jarl, 'A Note from the Memoirs of Jahangir', *Journal of the Royal Asiatic Society of Great Britain and Ireland*, No. 3 (1 July 1924), pp. 440–442.

Chatterjee, Prasun, 'The Lives of Alcohol in Pre-Colonial India', *The Medieval History Journal*, Vol. 8, No. 1 (2005), pp. 189–225.

Conan, Michel (ed.), *Middle East Garden Traditions: Unity and Diversity*, Washington, DC: Dumbarton Oaks, 2007.

Dale, Stephen F., 'Autobiography and Biography: The Turco-Mongol Case: Babur, Haydar Mirza, Gulbadan Begim and Jahangir', *The Rhetoric of Biography: Narrating Lives in Persianate Societies*, L. Marlow (ed.), Cambridge, London: Ilex Foundation, 2011, pp. 89–105.

Dale, Stephen F., *The Garden of the Eight Paradises: Babur and the Culture of Empire in Central Asia, Afghanistan and India (1483–1530)*, Leiden: Brill, 2004.

Dale, Stephen F., 'Legacy of the Timurids', *Journal of the Royal Asiatic Society*, Third Series, Vol. 8, No. 1 (April 1998), pp. 43–58.

Dale, Stephen F., 'The Poetry and Autobiography of the Baburnama', *The Journal of Asian Studies*, Vol. 55, No. 3 (1996), pp. 635–664.

Dale, Stephen F., 'Steppe Humanism and the Autobiographical Writings of Zahir al-Din Muhammad Babur, 1483–1530', *International Journal of Middle Eastern Studies*, Vol. 22 (1990), pp. 37–58.

Damrel, David W., 'The "Naqshbandi Reaction" Reconsidered', *Beyond Turk and Hindu: Rethinking Religious Identities in Islamicate South Asia*, David Guilmartin and Bruce B. Lawrence (eds.), Gainsville, Florida: University Press of Florida, 2000, pp. 55–73.

Darling, Linda T., '"Do Justice, for That Is Paradise!": Middle Eastern Advice for Indian Muslim Rulers', *Comparative Studies of South Asia, Africa, and the Middle East* XXII, Vols. 1&2 (2002), pp. 3–19.

Dickie, James, 'The Mughal Garden: Gateway to Paradise', *Muqarnas*, Vol. 3 (1985), pp. 128–137.

Dye, Joseph M., III, 'Imperial Mughal Painting', *The Magnificent Mughals*, Zeenat Ziad (ed.), Oxford University Press, 2002, pp. 143–182.

Eaton, Richard M. *A Social History of the Deccan, 1300–1761, Eight Indian Lives*, Cambridge, UK: Cambridge University Press, 2005.

Eaton, Richard M. (ed.), *India's Islamic Traditions, 711–1750*, New Delhi: Oxford University Press, 2003.

Eck, Diana L., *Darsan: Seeing the Divine Image in India*, New York: Columbia University Press, 2nd ed., 1996.

Faruqui, Munis, *The Princes of the Mughal Empire*, New York: Cambridge University Press, 2012.

Fenech, Louise E., 'Martyrdom and the Execution of Guru Arjan in Early Sikh Sources', *Journal of the American Oriental Society*, Vol. 121, No. 1 (January–March 2001), pp. 20–31.

Fisher, Michael, *The Mughal Empire*, London and New York: I.B. Tauris, 2016.

Flores, Jorge, *The Mughal Padshah: A Jesuit Treatise on Emperor Jahangir's Court and Household*, Leiden: Brill, 2016.

Flores, Jorge, 'The Sea and the World of the Mutasaddi: A Profile of Port Officials from Mughal Gujarat (c. 1600–1650)', *Journal of the Royal Asiatic Society*, Vol. 21, No. 1 (2011).

Friedmann, Johanan, *Shaykh Ahmad Sirhindi, an Outline of His Thought and a Study of His Image in the Eyes of Posterity*, Montreal and London: McGill University Press, 1971.

Friedmann, Johanan, 'Nizami, Naqshbandi Influence on Mughal Rulers and Politics', *Islamic Culture*, Vol. XXXIX (1965), pp. 40–43.

Foltz, Richard C., 'Two Seventeenth-Century Central Asian Travelers to Mughal India', *Journal of the Royal Asiatic Society*, Third Series, Vol. 6, No. 3 (November 1996), pp. 367–377.

Forster, E.M., 'The Emperor Babur', *Abinger Harvest*, Boston, MA: Houghton Mifflin, 1950.

Gaborieau, Marc, Alexandre Popovic and Thierry Zarcone (eds.), *Naqshbandis: Cheminements et situation actuelle d'un ordre mystique musulman*, Actes de la table Ronde de Sèvres Istanbul and Paris: Isis Press, 1985/1990.

Gallop, Annabel Teh, 'The Genealogical Seal of the Mughal Emperors of India', *Journal of the Royal Asiatic Society*, series 3, Vol. 9, No. 1 (April 1999), pp. 77–140.

Gharipour, Mohammad, 'Transferring and Transforming the Boundaries of Pleasure: Multifunctionality of Gardens in Medieval Persia', *History*, Vol. 39, No. 2 (Winter 2011), pp. 249–262.

Ghosh, Amitav, 'The Man behind the Mosque', *The Little Magazine*, Vol. 1, No. 2 (2000).

Gommens, Jos J.L., *Mughal Warfare: Indian Frontiers and High Roads to Empire, 1500–1700*, New York: Routledge, 2002.

Gonda, J., *Ancient Indian Kingship from the Religious Point of View*, Leiden: E. J. Brill, 1969.

Gronke, Monika, 'The Persian Court between Palace and Tent: From Timur to 'Abbas I', *Timurid Art and Culture: Iran and Central Asia in the Fifteenth Century*, Lisa Golombek and Maria Subtelney (eds.), Leiden: E. J. Brill, 1992, pp. 18–22.

Gross, JoAnn, 'The Naqshbandiyya Connection: From Central Asia to India and Back (16th–19th Centuries)', *India and Central Asia: Commerce and Culture, 1500–1800*, Scott Levi (ed.), New Delhi: Oxford University Press, 2007.

Gross, JoAnn, 'Naqshbandi Appeals to the Herat Court: A Preliminary Study of Trade and Property Issues', *Studies on Central Asian History, in Honor of Yuri Bregel*. Devin DeWeese (ed.), Bloomington, IN: Indiana University Research Institute for Inner Asian Studies, 2001, pp. 113–128.

Gross, JoAnn, 'Multiple Roles and Perceptions of a Sufi Shaikh: Symbolic Statements of Political Power and Religious Authority', *Naqshbandis: Cheminements et Situation Actuelle d'un Ordre Mystique Musulman, Actes de la Table Ronde de Sevres*. Historical Development and Present Situation of a Muslim Mystical Order: Proceedings of the Sevre Round Table, 2–4 May 1985/Varia Turcica 18, Marc Gaborieau, Alexandre Popvic and Thierry Zarcone (eds.), Paris, 1990, pp. 109–121.

Gross, JoAnn, 'Khoja Ahrar: A Study in Perceptions of Power and Prestige in the Late Timurid Period', unpublished PhD dissertation, New York University, 1982.

Habib, Irfan (ed.), *Akbar and His Age*, New Delhi: Oxford University Press, 1997.

Hambly, Gavin R.G., 'Armed Women Retainers in the Zenanas of Indo-Muslim Rulers: The Case of Bibi Fatima', *Women in the Medieval Islamic World*, Gavin R.G. Hambly (ed.), New York: St. Martin's Press, 1998, pp. 429–468.

Hambly, Gavin R.G. (ed.), *Women in the Medieval Islamic World*, New York: St. Martin's Press, 1998.

Hasan, K.N. and Mansura Haidar, 'Letters of Aziz Koka to Ibrahim Adil Shah II', *Proceedings of the Indian History Congress*, Vol. 27 (1965), pp. 161–167.

Hasan, S. Nurul, 'The Theory of the Nur Jahan "Junta" – a Critical Examination', *Proceedings of the Indian History Congress*, Vol. 21 (1958), pp. 324–335.

Henderson, Paula, '"Elysian Fields such as the Poets Dreamed of": The Mughal Garden in the Early Stuart Mind', *The British Art Journal*, Vol. 10, No. 3 (Winter/Spring 2009/2010), pp. 35–45.

Hodivala, Shahpurshah Hormasji, *Studies in Indo-Muslim History: A Critical Commentary on Elliot and Dowson's History of India as Told by Its Own Historians*, Lahore: Islamic Book Service, 1st ed., 1939; Pakistan reprint 1979.

Husain, Afzal, 'Afghan Nobility under Akbar and Jahangir – the Family of Daulat Khan Lodi', *Proceedings of the Indian History Congress*, Vol. 48 (1987), pp. 187–196.

Inden, Ronald, 'Ritual, Authority and Cyclic Time in Hindu Kingship', *Kingship and Authority in South Asia*, J.F. Richards (ed.), Madison: University of Wisconsin, 1978, pp. 28–73.

Islam, Riazul, *A Calendar of Documents on Indo-Persian Relations*, Tehran: Iranian Culture Foundation; Karachi: Institute of Central and West Asian Studies, 1979–1982.

Islam, Riazul, *Indo-Persian Relations: A Study of the Political and Diplomatic Relations between the Mughal Empire and Iran*, Tehran: Iranian Culture Foundation, 1970.

Jackson, Peter and Lawrence Lockhart (eds.), *Cambridge History of Iran VI [The Timurid and Safavid Periods]*, Cambridge: Cambridge University Press, 1986.

Khan, Iqtidar Alam, 'Akbar's Personality Traits and World Outlook: A Critical Reappraisal', *Akbar and His Age*, Irfan Habib (ed.), New Delhi: Oxford University Press, 1997 and *Social Scientist*, Vol. 20, Nos. 232–233, New Delhi, September–October 1992, pp. 16–30.

Khan, Iqtidar Alam, *The Political Biography of a Mughal Noble*, New Delhi: Munshiram Manoharlal Publishers, 1973.

Khosla, Ram Prasad, *Mughal Kingship and Nobility*, New Delhi: Idarah-i Adabiyat-i Delli, 1976.

Koch, Ebba, 'Jahangir as Francis Bacon's Ideal of the King as an Observer and Investigator of Nature', *Journal of the Royal Asiatic Society*, Third Series, Vol. 19, No. 3 (July 2009), pp. 293-338.

Koch, Ebba, 'My Garden Is Hindustan: The Mughal Padshah's Realization of a Political Metaphor', *Middle East Garden Traditions: Unity and Diversity*, Michel Conan (ed.), Washington, DC: Dumbarton Oaks, 2007, pp. 159-175.

Koch, Ebba, *The Complete Taj Mahal and the Riverfront Gardens of Agra*, London: Thames and Hudson, Ltd., 2006.

Koch, Ebba, 'Mughal Palace Gardens from Babur to Shah Jahan (1526-1648)', *Muqarnas*, Vol. 14 (1997), pp.143-165.

Koch, Ebba, 'The Mughal Waterfront Garden', *Gardens in the Time of the Great Muslim Empires*, Attilio Petruccioli (ed.), Leiden: Brill, 1997, pp. 140-160.

Koch, Ebba, *Mughal Architecture: An Outline of Its History and Development (1526-1858)*, Munich: Prestel-Verlag, 1991.

Kozlowski, Gregory C., 'Private Lives and Public Piety: Women and the Practice of Islam in Mughal India', *Women in the Islamic World*, Gavin Hambly (ed.), New York: St. Martin's Press (1998), pp. 469-488.

Lal, Ruby, *Empress: The Astonishing Reign of Nur Jahan*, New York and London: W. W. Norton, 2018.

Lal, Ruby, *Domesticity and Power in the Early Mughal World*, Cambridge: Cambridge University Press, 2005.

Lal, Ruby, 'Settled, Sacred and All-Powerful: Making of New Genealogies and Traditions of Empire under Akbar', *Economic and Political Weekly*, Vol. 36, No. 11 (17-23 March 2001), pp. 941-958.

Lefèvre, Corinne, *Pouvoir impérial et élites dans l'Inde moghole de Jahāngīr (1605-1627)*, Paris: Les Indes savants, 2018.

Lefèvre, Corinne, 'Messianism, Rationalism and Inter-Asian Connections: The *Majalis-i Jahangiri* (1608-11) and the Socio-Intellectual History of the Mughal Ulama', *The Indian Economic and Social History Review*, Vol. 54, No. 3 (2017), pp. 1-22.

Lefèvre, Corinne, 'Curiosité et pouvoir : les collections de l'empereur moghol Jahāngīr (r. 1605-1627)', Études Épistémè, Vol. 26 (2014), pp. 2-10.

Lefèvre, Corinne, 'Pouvoir et noblesse dans l'empire moghol: Perspectives du règne de Jahāngīr (1605-1627)', *Annales. Histoire, Sciences Sociales*, 62e Année, No. 6 (November-December 2007), pp. 1287-1312.

Lefèvre, Corinne, 'Recovering a Missing Voice from Mughal India: The Imperial Discourse of Jahāngīr (r. 1605-1627) in His Memoirs', *Journal of the Economic and Social History of the Orient*, Vol. 50, No. 4 (2007), pp. 452-489.

Lentz, Thomas W., 'Memory and Ideology in the Timurid Garden', *Mughal Gardens: Sources, Places, Representations and Prospects*, James L. Westcoat, Jr. and Joachim Wolschke-Bulmahn (eds.), Washington, DC: Dumbarton Oaks, 1996, pp. 31-57.

Lentz, Thomas W., 'Dynastic Imagery in Early Timurid Wall Painting', *Muqarnas*, Vol. 10 (1993), pp. 253-265.

Lentz, Thomas W. and Glenn D. Lowry, *Timur and the Princely Vision: Persian Art and Culture in the Fifteenth Century*, Los Angeles and Washington, DC: Los Angeles County Museum of Art and the Arther Sackler Gallery, Smithsonian Institution, 1989.

Maglagan, Sir Edward, *The Jesuits and the Great Mogul*, London: Bruns, Oates and Washburn, Ltd., 1931.

Manz, Beatrice Forbes, 'Women in Timurid Dynastic Politics', *Women in Iran from the Rise of Islam to 1800*, Guity Nashat and Lois Beck (eds.), Champagne-Urbana, IL: University of Illinois Press, 2003, pp. 121-139.

Marshall, D.N., *Mughals in India: A Bibliographical Survey*, New York: Asia Publishing House, 1967.

Matthee, Rudolph P., *The Pursuit of Pleasure: Drugs and Stimulants in Iranian History, 1500-1900*, Princeton, NJ: Princeton University Press, 2005.

Meisami, Julie Scott, *Medieval Persian Court Poetry*, Princeton, NJ: Princeton University Press, 1987.

Metcalf, Barbara (ed.), *Islam in South Asia in Practice*, Princeton, NJ: Princeton University Press, 2009.

Metcalf, Barbara, 'Narrating Lives: A Mughal Empress, A French Nabob, A Nationalist Muslim Intellectual', book review, *The Journal of Asian Studies*, Vol. 54, No. 2 (May 1995), pp. 474-480.

Miller, Barbara Stoler (ed.), *Powers of Art*, Delhi: Oxford University Press, 1992.

Mitchell, Colin Paul, *Sir Thomas Roe and the Mughal Empire*, Karachi, Pakistan: Oxford University Press, 2000.

Moin, Ahmed Azfar, *The Millenial Sovereign: Sacred Kingship and Sainthood in Islam*, New York: Columbia University Press, 2012.

Moosvi, Shireen, 'The Conversations of Jahangir 1608-11: Table Talk on Religion', *Proceedings of the India History Congress*, Vol. 68, No. 1 (2007), pp. 326-331.

Moosvi, Shireen, 'The Mughal Encounter with Vedanta: Recovering the Biography of Jadrup', *Social Scientist*, Vol. 30, No. 7/8 (July-August 2002), pp. 13-23.

Moosvi, Shireen, *Episodes in the Life of Akbar; Contemporary Records and Reminiscences*, New Delhi: National Book Trust, 1994.

Morgan, David O., 'The "Great 'yasa' of Chingiz Khan" and Mongol Law in the Ilkhanate', *Bulletin of Oriental and African Studies, in Honor of Ann Lambton*, Vol. 49, No. 1 (1986), pp. 163-176.

Morinis, E.A., 'Pilgrimage: The Human Quest', *Numen*, Vol. 28, No. 2 (December 1981), pp. 281-285.

Moynihan, Elizabeth B., 'But What a Happiness to Have Known Babur!', *Mughal Gardens*, James Westcoat et al. (eds.), Washington, DC: Dumbarton Oaks, 1996, pp. 95-126.

Moynihan, Elizabeth B., 'The Lotus Garden Palace of Zahir al-Din Muhammad Babur', *Muqarnas*, Vol. 5 (1988), pp. 135-152.

Nashat, Guity and Lois Beck (eds.), *Women in Iran from the Rise of Islam to 1800*, Champagne-Urbana: University of Illinois Press, 2003.

Nayar, Pramod K., 'Marvelous Excesses: English Travel Writing and India, 1608–1727', *Journal of British Studies*, Vol. 44, No. 2 (April 2005), pp. 213–238.

Necipoğlu, Gülru, 'Word and Image: The Serial Portraits of Ottoman Sultans in Comparative Perspective', *The Sultan's Portrait*, Selim Kangal (Ed.), Istanbul: Işbank, 2000.

Nizami, Khaliq Ahmad, *State and Culture in Medieval India*, New Delhi: Adam Publishers and Distributors, 1985.

Nizami, Khaliq Ahmad, 'Naqshbandi Influence on Mughal Rulers and Politics', *Islamic Culture*, Vol. 39 (1965), pp. 41–52.

Parpia, Shaha, 'Reordering Nature: Power Politics in the Mughal *Shikargah*', *International Journal of Islamic Architecture*, Vol. 7, No. 1 (2018), pp. 39–66.

Parpia, Shaha, 'Mughal Hunting Grounds: Landscape Manipulation and "Garden" Association', *Garden History: Journal of the Gardens Trust*, Vol. 44, No. 2 (2016), pp. 171–190.

Paul, Jurgen, *Doctrine and Organization: The Khwajagan/Naqshbandiya in the First Generation after Baha'uddin*, ANOR 1 (1998), pp. 1–79.

Paul, Jurgen, 'Forming a Faction: The Himayat System of Khwaja Ahrar', *International Journal of Middle Eastern Studies*, Vol. 23, No. 4 (1991), pp. 533–548.

Petruccioli, Attilio (ed.), *Gardens in the Time of the Great Muslim Empire: Theory and Design*, Leiden: Brill, 1997.

Pierce, Leslie, *The Imperial Harem: Women and Sovereignty in the Ottoman Imperial Harem*, Oxford University Press, 1993.

Pourafzal, Haleh and Roger Montgomery, *The Spiritual Wisdom of Hafiz*, Rochester, VT: The Spiritual Traditions, 1998.

Prasad, Beni, *History of Jahangir*, London: Oxford University Press, 1922.

Quinn, Sholeh, *Historical Writing during the Reign of Shah Abbas, Ideology, Imitation and Legitimacy in Safavid Chronicles*, Salt Lake City, Utah: University of Utah Press, 2000.

Rehman, Abd al-, 'Garden Types in Mughal Lahore', *Gardens in the Time of the Great Muslim Empires*, Attilio Petruccioli (Ed.), Leiden: Brill, 1997, pp. 161–172.

Richards, John, 'The Formulation of Imperial Authority under Akbar and Jahangir', *The Mughal State, 1526–1750*, Muzaffar Alam and Sanjay Subrahmanyam (Eds.), New Delhi: Oxford University Press, 1998, pp. 126–167.

Richards, John, 'The Historiography of Mughal Gardens', *Mughal Gardens: Sources, Places, Representations, and Prospects*, James L. Westcoat and Joachim Wolschke-Bulmahn (Eds.), Washington, DC: Dumbarton Oaks, 1996, pp. 259–266.

Richards, John, *The New Cambridge History of India: The Mughal Empire*, Cambridge University Press, 1993; repr. 1995.

Richards, John (ed.), *Kingship and Authority in South Asia*, Madison: University of Wisconsin, 1978.

Rizvi, S.A.A., 'Sixteenth Century Naqshbandi Leadership in India', *Naqshbandis*, Marc Gaborieau, Alexandre Popovic, Thierry Zarcone (Eds.), Istanbul: Isis Press, 1985/1990, pp. 153–165.

Roemer, H.R., 'The Safavids', *Cambridge History of Iran*, Vol. 6: The Timurid and Safavid Periods, Peter Jackson and Lawrence Lockhart (eds.), Cambridge: Cambridge University Press, 1986, pp. 189–350.

Rogers, J.M., *Mughal Painting*, London: British Museum Press, 1993.

Ruggles, D. Fairchild, 'Humayun's Tomb and Garden: Typologies and Visual Order', *Gardens*, Petrucciolo (ed.), Leiden: Brill, 1997, pp. 173–186.

Samarqandi, Mutribi al-Assam, *Conversations with Emperor Jahangir*, Richard Foltz, tr. Costa Mesa, CA: Mazda Publishers, 1998, p. 62.

Sax, William S., 'Conquering the Quarters: Religion and Politics in Hinduism', *International Journal of Hindu Studies*, Vol. 4, No. 1 (April 2000), pp. 39–60.

Sax, William S. 'The Ramnagar Ramlila: Text, Performance, Pilgrimage', *History of Religions*, Vol. 30, No. 2 (November 1990), pp. 129–153.

Schimmel, Annemarie, *The Empire of the Great Mughals*, London: Reakton Books, LTD, 2004.

Seyller, John, *Workshop and Patron in Mughal India*, Zurich: Artibus Asiae Publishers in association with the Freer Gallery of Art, Smithsonian Institution, 1999.

Sharma, Parvati, *Jahangir: An Intimate Portrait of a Great Mughal*, New Delhi: Juggernaut Books, 2018.

Sharma, Sunil, *Mughal Arcadia*, Cambridge, MA: Harvard University Press, 2017.

Shivram, Balkrishan, 'Court Dress and Robing Ceremony in Mughal India', *Proceedings of the Indian History Congress*, Vol. 66 (2005–06), pp. 404–422.

Singh, Ram Charitra Prasad, *Kingship in Northern India (c. 600–1200 AD)*, Delhi/Varanasi/Patna: Motilal Banarsidass, 1968.

Smart, Ellen, 'The Death of Inayat Khan by the Mughal Artist Balchand', *Artibus Asiae*, Vol. 58, No. 3/4 (1999), pp. 273–279.

Soucek, Priscilla, 'Interpreting the Ghazals of Hafiz', *RES: Anthropology and Aesthetics*, No. 43, Islamic Arts (Spring 2003), pp. 146–163.

Soucek, Priscilla, 'Timurid Women: A Cultural Perspective', *Women in the Medieval Islamic World*, Gavin Hambly (ed.), New York: St. Martin's Press, 1998, pp. 199–226.

Soudavar, Abolala, 'The Early Safavids and Their Cultural Interactions with Surrounding States', *Iran and the Surrounding World*, Nickie Keddie and Rudi Matthee (eds.), Seattle and London: University of Washington Press, 2002, pp. 89–120.

Steingass, F., *Persian-English Dictionary*, New Delhi: Munshiram Manoharlal Publishers, Pvt., 2000.

Stronge, Susan, 'By the Light of the Sun of Jahangir', *God Is the Light of the Heavens and the Earth: Light in Islamic Art and Culture*, Jonathan Bloom and Sheila Blair (eds.), New Haven, CT: Yale University Press, 2015, pp. 256–281.

Stronge, Susan, *Painting for the Mughal Emperor: The Art of the Book, 1560–1660*, London: Victoria & Albert Museum, 2002, p. 133.

Subtelny, Maria Eva, 'Mirak-i Sayyid Ghiyas and the Timurid Tradition of Landscape Architecture', *Studia Iranica*, Vol. 24 (1995), pp. 19–38.

Szuppe, Maria, 'A Glorious Past and an Outstanding Present: Writing a Collection of Biographies in Late Persianate Central Asia', *The Rhetoric of Biography: Narrating Lives in Persianate Societies*, L. Marlow (ed.), Cambridge, London: Ilex Foundation, 2011, pp. 41–88.

Szuppe, Maria (ed.), 'Women in Sixteenth Century Safavid Iran', *Women in Iran*, Guity Nashat and Lois Beck (eds.), Champagne-Urbana: University of Illinois Press, 2003, pp. 140–169.

Szuppe, Maria, *L'Heritage Timouride, Iran-Asie Central-Inde, XVe-XViiie Siecles, Le Cahiers d'Asie Centrale*, Tachkent-Aix-en-Provence, 1997.

Tandon, Shivangini, 'Negotiating Political Spaces and Contested Identities: Representation of Nur Jahan and Her Family in Mughal *Tazkiras*', *The Delhi University Journal of the Humanities and Social Sciences*, Vol. 2 (2015), pp. 41–50.

Thapar, Romila, *The Past as Present: Forging Contemporary Identities through History*, New Delhi: Aleph Book Company, 2014.

Tod, James, *Annals and Antiquities of Rajasthan or the Central and Western Rajput States of India*, 3 vols., London and New York: H. Milford, Oxford University Press, 1920.

Tripathi, Ram Prasad, 'The Turko-Mongol Theory of Kingship', *The Mughal State, 1526–1750*, Alam and Subrahmanyam (eds.), New Delhi: Oxford University Press, 1998, pp. 115–125.

Truschke, Audrey, 'Cosmopolitan Encounters: Sanskrit and Persian at the Mughal Court', unpublished PhD dissertation, Columbia University, 2012.

Welch, Anthony, 'Gardens That Babur Did Not Like: Landscape, Water and Architecture for the Sultans of Delhi', *Mughal Gardens*, J.L. Westcoat and J. Wolschke-Bulman (eds.), Washington, DC: Dumbarton Oaks, 1993.

Westcoat, Jr., James L., 'Gardens, Urbanization, and Urbanism in Mughal Lahore', *Mughal Gardens: Sources, Places, Representations, and Prospects*, James L. Westcoat and Joachim Wolschke-Bulmahn (eds.), Washington, DC: Dumbarton Oaks, 1996, pp. 139–170.

Westcoat, Jr., James L. and Joachim Wolschke-Bulmahn (eds.), *Mughal Gardens*, Washington, DC: Dumbarton Oaks, 1996.

Wright, Elaine Julia and Susan Stronge (eds.), *Muraqqa: Imperial Mughal Albums from the Chester Beatty Library, Dublin*, Alexandria, VA: Art Services International, 2008.

Zaidi, Inayat Ali, 'The Political Role of Kachawaha Nobles during Jahangir's Reign', *Proceedings of the Indian History Congress*, Vol. 36 (1975), pp. 180–197.

Zaman, Taymiya R., 'Instructive Memory: An Analysis of Auto/Biographical Writings', *Journal of the Economic and Social History of the Orient*, Vol. 54, No. 5 (2011), pp. 677–700.

Zarcone, Thierry, 'Central Asian Influence on the Early Development of the Chishtiyya Sufi Order in India', *The Making of Indo-Persian Culture*, Muzaffar Alam, Francoise 'Nalini' Delvoye and Marc Gaborieau (eds.), New Delhi: Manohar, 2000, pp. 99–116.

Index

Abbas, Shah 69–70, 88, 91, 92, 95; Safavid relations with Jahangir 105–11; Deccan 114–15, 173; seizure of Qandahar 183–86, 192
Abdur Rahim Khankhanan 4, 2, 26, 28, 29, 36, 77; in the Deccan: 113–16, 180, 187, 189; endnotes 208, 225, 237
Abdus Sattar 10–11; assemblies 84–89, 152, 156, 201; endnotes 220, 221, 232
Abu'l Fazl Allami 4, 19, 20, 21, 24, 26, 28, 29; death 33, 34, 35, 36, 45, 72, 75, 83–84, 89, 90, 93, 113; Akbar's harem 120–21; mobile court 131–32, 143
Abu'l Hasan 8, 9, 32; allegorical paintings 90–93; endnotes 221
Adil Shah (of Bijapur) 70, 91, 114–15, 173, 182, 193
Ahmad Sirhindi, Shaykh 157; endnote 237
Ahmadabad 62, 132, 137, 141; dislike of 147–48, 151, 166
Ahmednagar 112–14; Khurram 181–82, 193
Ajmer 20, 21, 24, 29, 72, 89, 95, 97, 101, 102, 120; Jahangir visits 127–30, 135, 139, 141, 147, 155, 166, 184; Khurram 189–90, 198, 200; endnotes 214, 236
Akbar, Jalaluddin Muhammad 4, 9, 18; Salim Chishti 19–20; raising princes 21–24; royal court 25–26; Salim's rebellion 27, 29–37; death 37, 43; as model 44–45; religious policies 46–47, 48, 53, 54, 65, 68; khilat 72; weighing 73; darshan 74, 79; divine kingship 83–86, 90, 94–95; Jesuits 97–98, 103; Safavids 109–110, 111, 113; marriages 119–21, 122, 123; Mewar 127–28, 130, 133, 135–36, 140; hunting 143–45, 152; Sikandra 156, 158, 159; Fatehpur Sikri 166–67; poetry 170–71; 202–03; endnotes 208, 209–10, 211, 212, 220, 230
alcohol 3, 10; princes 28; Allahabad 33, 36, 42, 48, 58; Takt-i Shah 59–61, 66; Hafez 67; Roe 68; Safavid 69, 75; court and family 75–78; majalis 87; Hawkins 100, 137, 139, 140; couplet 148, 149; Inayat Khan 153–54; buza 169; verses 172, 174; Nur Jahan's parties 176, 179, 184, 193–94, 195–96, 196–97; reputation 199–200; endnotes 219, 223, 233
Ali Quli Istajlu 123
Allahabad 28; princely court 30–35, 36, 37, 41, 42, 84, 86, 90, 153
Amar Singh, Rana of Mewar 127; Mughal victory 128–30, 135, 160
Amber 19–20, 23, 26, 77, 120
Aqa Reza Herati 32
Arjumand Banu Begim (Mumtaz Mahal) 175
Asaf Khan 8, 102, 114, 135, 175, 180, 192; Mahabat Khan's revolt 194–95, 197; endnotes 237, 238

Babur, Zahir al-Din Muhammad (see also *Vaqa'i-i Baburi*) 4–8, 17, 19, 20; Kabul 58–60, 69, 71, 85, 97, 103, 104; relations with Shah Ismail 106–07; marriages 118–19; gardens 134–35; fruit 136–37, 156, 157, 171, 191, 202, 203; endnotes 207–08, 225, 228, 233, 236
Vaqa'i-i Baburi 4–8, 17, 31, 38, 59–61, 149, 152, 201; endnotes 206, 223
Bahat (Jhelum) River 168, 193, 195, 196; endnotes 250
Basawan 94
Bengal 18, 29, 31, 86, 111–12, 123, 137, 168, 177, 183; Khurram's rebellion 192–94; endnotes 211, 235
Bhagwant Das, Raja 36, 120
Bichitr 90, 92

Bijapur 70; Mughal war 112–16; Khurram 181–82, 192–93
Bir Singh Deo (Bundela) 33, 42
Bishan Das 32, 91
Burhanpur 77, 114, 181, 189, 194

Coryat, Thomas 47; endnotes 214, 218

Danyal (Prince): birth 21, 24, 28, 29, 34; death 36, 95, 110; endnotes 208, 212

Fatehpur Sikri 8; Shaykh Salim 19–21, 25, 26, 98, 143, 155; Jahangir visits 166–67, 178, 187, 189
Finch, William 94, 99, 114, 122, 166

gardens 17, 44, 58; in Kabul 59–61, 78–79; palaces 94, 130; history 133–34; Jahangir uses 135–36; fruit producing 136–37, 144; couplet 148; parable 149, 151, 152; funerary 156, 167, 170; Anvari 172, 173; Nur Serai 176, 179, 195; endnotes 227–28, 230
    specific gardens of note: Bustan Sara 167; Chashma Nur 130 and 135; Dilamez Bagh 58; Jahan Ara 59; Mahtab Bagh 59; Nur Afza 94 and 137 and endnotes 228; Orta Bagh 59; Shahr Ara visit 59–61 and 195; Nur (Gul) Afshan 135 and 170, 173, 176 and endnotes 234; Nur Mahal 167; Nur Manzil Bagh 135 and 167; Surat Khana 59
Golconda 113, 114, 116, 181, 182
Gulbadan Begim 4, 18, 118; endnotes 207, 225, 226
Gujarat 22, 28, 65, 70, 78, 84, 97, 101, 102, 113, 132, 137, 139; visit 147–48, 150, 156, 160, 165, 183; Khurram 184–85, 189, 200; endnotes 218
Guru Arjun Singh 56; endnote 216

Hamida Banu Begim (Maryam Makani) 34–35, 59, 209; endnotes 212
Hawkins, William 75; at Jahangir's court 99–100, 133; endnotes 215, 221–22
Hira Kunwar Sahiba Harkha Bai (Maryamuzzamani)19, 167
Humayun, Nasiruddin Muhammad 4, 17–18, 35, 54, 77, 93, 95, 104; at Safavid court 107–09, 118, 152, 156, 168, 203; endnotes 208, 211, 212, 216, 220, 236
hunting 3; Akbar 20–21, 22, 28, 29, 45; Kabul 61, 68, 78; failed lion hunt 80–81; hunting vow 86; Solomon 92, 127; with Karan 120; hunting parks 133–35 and 141; *sair u shikar* 141; traditions of hunting 141–47; lions 147, 154, 170, 173, 185, 186, 187, 189, 190, 193, 195; Bahramgala 197, 200
    Qamargha (circle hunt) 61, 142–43, 144, 146, 170, 183

Imam Quli Khan 104, 191, 192
Inayat Khan 153–54
I'timaduddawla, Ghiyas Beg 8, 61, 68, 72, 87, 102, 122–23, 127, 166, 168; death 174, 175, 180

Jadrup Gosain in Ujjain 159, 160; in Mathura 168; endnotes 232
Jahangir, Nur al-Din Muhammad (Salim, Prince): birth 19–21; Shayku Baba 20; education 21–22; counter-court 30–37, 41, 42, 84, 86, 90, 153; knowledge of Turkish 61, 99; endnotes 216, 223; Anarkali 122; marriages (see also *Nur Jahan*) 23–24, 119, 123–34, 124, 175; endnotes 209, 210; conversations with dervishes/ascetics (see also *Jadrup Gosain*) 148, 158; Gosain 159; Gujarat 160; criticism 161; Gosain 168; endnotes 230, 232; Regulations 3, 66; hunting vow 73, 145; health and illness 3, 28, 36, 50, 124, 145, 148, 173, 175, 181, 182, 186, 187, 197, 200; endnotes 236; death 197
Jahangirnama 2, 3, 5, 7–11, 19, 43, 45, 58, 59, 68, 70, 76, 80–81, 87, 89, 90, 124, 136, 143, 144, 145, 147, 149, 150–51, 153, 172; Mu'tamid Khan 186–87; Muhammad Hadi 190–91, 197, 200, 201, 202; endnotes 206, 208
Jains 43, 84, 158–59
Jesuits 10, 11; mission to Mughal court 25, 27, 28, 32, 43, 46, 47, 51, 70, 83,

84, 87, 94, 97–98, 99, 100, 102, 121, 201; endnotes 213, 215, 218, 223, 230, 236, 238–39
justice 3, 24, 44; chain of justice 48–51; darshan 75, 80; majalis 85, 89; Gujarat 148; Ranthambhor 149, 155; endnotes Akbar 209, 215; princes 218, 228

Kabul 8, 17, 24, 30, 48, Jahangir's visit 57–61, 78, 107, 108, 127; fruits 136–37, 139–40, 166, 168, 183, 194, 196; endnotes 208, 209, 223, 225
Kangra 112; conquest of 165–66; visit 174–75
Karan (of Mewar) 128–30, 135, 176
Kashmir 23, 95, 135, 137, 145, 150; visit 153– 54, 161; visit 167–69, 178, 183, 190; visit 193–94, 196, 200, 203
Khan Azam, Mirza Aziz Koka 22; support for Khusraw 36–37, 42, 56, 65; punished and forgiven 79–80, 85, 87, 188; endnotes 236
Khan Jahan Lodi (Pir Khan) 42, 77, 194
Khurram (Shah Jahan) 1, 3, 8, 10–11, birth 23, 29, 43, 50, 57, 61, 66, 72, 73; alcohol 77–78, 102, 116; Mewar 128–30, 149; Kangra 165–66; new title 166, 167, 172, 175, 176; Deccan 180–83; death of Khusraw 182; rebellion 183–85 and 187–96; enthroned 197–98, 203; endnotes 218, 233, 237
Khusraw (Prince): birth 23, 29; revolt 36–37 and 41–43; open rebellion 53–55; aftermath 56–57; blinded 59; sedition 61, 79, 110, 128, 168, 181; death 182, 184; endnotes 212, 216, 236
Khwaja Abdur Rahim 192

Ladli Begim 123, 175, 197
Lahore 36, 43, 47, 53, 55, 57, 58, 61, 78, 94, 104, 122, 134, 137, 143, 156, 158, 168, 170, 178, 181, 183, 185, 186, 187, 193, 194, 196; Shahdara 197, 200; endnotes 228, 232, 237

Mahabat Khan 67, 114, 183, 184, 187, 189, 191, 192, 193; rebellion 194–97; endnotes 237, 238
Malik Ambar 92; wars with Mughals 112–16, 181, 188; conflict and death 192–93

Malwa 28, 29, 132, 147, 185
Man Singh, Raja 26, 29, 36, 42, 54, 56, 65, 120, 173, endnotes 212
Mandu 101, 132, 139, 141, 148, 181, 183, 187, 189, 200; endnotes 214
Manohar 94
Mansur 9, 153, 231
Mewar 9, 29, 34, 42, 79, 104, 112, 123; Mughal campaign 127–30, 135, 160, 176; endnotes 236
Mihrunnisa see *Nur Jahan*
Mirza Nathan 86, 88, 176; endnotes 220, 224
Moinuddin Chishti, shrine 19, 20, 120
Monserrate, Fr. Antonio 27, 121, 135
Muhammad Hadi 3, 30, 190–91, 192, 195, 197, 198; endnotes 202
Muhammad Sharif Khan 30, 42
Muqarrab Khan 70, 78–79, 91, 94, 99; endnotes 218
Murad (Prince): birth 20, 24; death 28, 29, 30, 32, 34, 36, 95
Mu'tamid Khan 3, 10–11, 123, 159, 175, 184; *Jahangirnama* 186–87, 190, 196, 199, 200; endnotes 216, 219, 226, 236, 238
Mutribi al-Assam 79, 91, 157–58, 172

Nazr Muhammad 104, 192
Nizamuddin Chishti, shrine 19, 20, 54, 156, 168
Nur Jahan (Mihrunnisa) 1–2, 11, 12, 61, 66, 73, 102, 117; marriages 122–24, 129, 140; hunting 145–46, 158, 166; Jahangir's health 173–74; power 175–80, 183, 184, 187, 189, 191, 192, 194; hostage 195–96; Jahangir's death 197; reputation 199–201; endnotes 211, 221, 226, 234, 235–36, 238

opium 18, Khusraw's mother 37, 55, 76, 77, 88, 107, 148, 153, 196; endnotes 235
Ottomans 43, 46, 90, 91, 97; relations 103–04; Safavids 107–09, 117; endnotes 216, 223, 225, 238

painting 2; Akbar 4; illustration 8–9; princely court 32, 50, 68; *Jahangirnama* 70; allegorical paintings and portraits 89–95, 115, 151; natural history 153–54; Abdur Rahim 187; endnotes 211, 232

Parvez (Prince) 8; birth 23, 29, 42, 77, 114, 128, 181, 182, 184, 185, 189, 190, 192, 193, 194; death 196; endnotes 219, 238

Qandahar 18, 48; Safavids 104–05; Humayun 108; Akbar 109; Jahangir 110–11, 115, 122; Abbas seizes 183–86, 188, 191, 192; endnotes 237
Rao Suraj Mal 165–66
Roe, Sir Thomas 47, 50–51, 68, 69; Jahangir's court 75–76; alcohol 77–78, 88, 94, 95; at Jahangir's court 100–03, 113, 135; court progress 140–41, 146, 199, 200; endnotes 214, 218, 220, 223, 227, 232

Safavids (see also *Abbas*) 4, 18, 46; gifts 67, 69, 71, 77, 88; painting 90–92, 95, 103; relations with Mughals 104–11; Deccan 114–15, 119, 122, 123, 156–57; invasion of Qandahar 183–86; Uzbeks 191–92; endnotes 212, 224, 237
Salim (Prince) see *Jahangir*
Salim Chishti 19–21, 32, 43, 112, 166–67; endnotes 209
Shah Jahan see *Khurram*
Shahdara 197
Shahryar (Prince) 23; marriage 175, 183, 184, 185, 194; death 197
Sultan Salima Begim 34, 119, 120

Talib Amuli 170, 172
Terry, Edward 47, 85, 124, 132, 133, 141; endnotes 231

Uzbeks 17, 47; Babur 57–60, 69, 91, 103–04, 106, 109, 172, 188; diplomacy 191–92; endnotes 237

Xavier, Fr. Jerome 25, 32, 98

www.ingramcontent.com/pod-product-compliance
Ingram Content Group UK Ltd.
Pitfield, Milton Keynes, MK11 3LW, UK
UKHW021906220326